YUKON

by JACK HOPE
photographs by
PAUL VON BAICH

PRENTICE-HALL, INC., ENGLEWOOD CLIFFS, N.J.

Yukon-by Jack Hope, Photographs by Paul von Baich

Copyright © 1976 by Jack Hope
Photographs copyright © 1976 by Paul von Baich

All photos by Paul von Baich unless otherwise credited

Book Design: Linda Huber
Art Direction: Hal Siegel

Printed in the United States of America

Prentice-Hall International, Inc., London
Prentice-Hall of Australia, Pty. Ltd., Sydney
Prentice-Hall of Canada, Ltd., Toronto
Prentice-Hall of India Private Ltd., New Delhi
Prentice-Hall of Japan, Inc., Tokyo
Prentice-Hall of Southeast Asia Pte. Ltd., Singapore

10 9 8 7 6 5 4 3 2 1

Library of Congress Cataloging in Publication Data

Hope, Jack.
  Yukon.

  1. Yukon Territory—Description and travel.
I. Von Baich, Paul.   II. Title.
F1091.H66   917.19'1'043   76-16207
ISBN 0-13-982595-9

CONTENTS

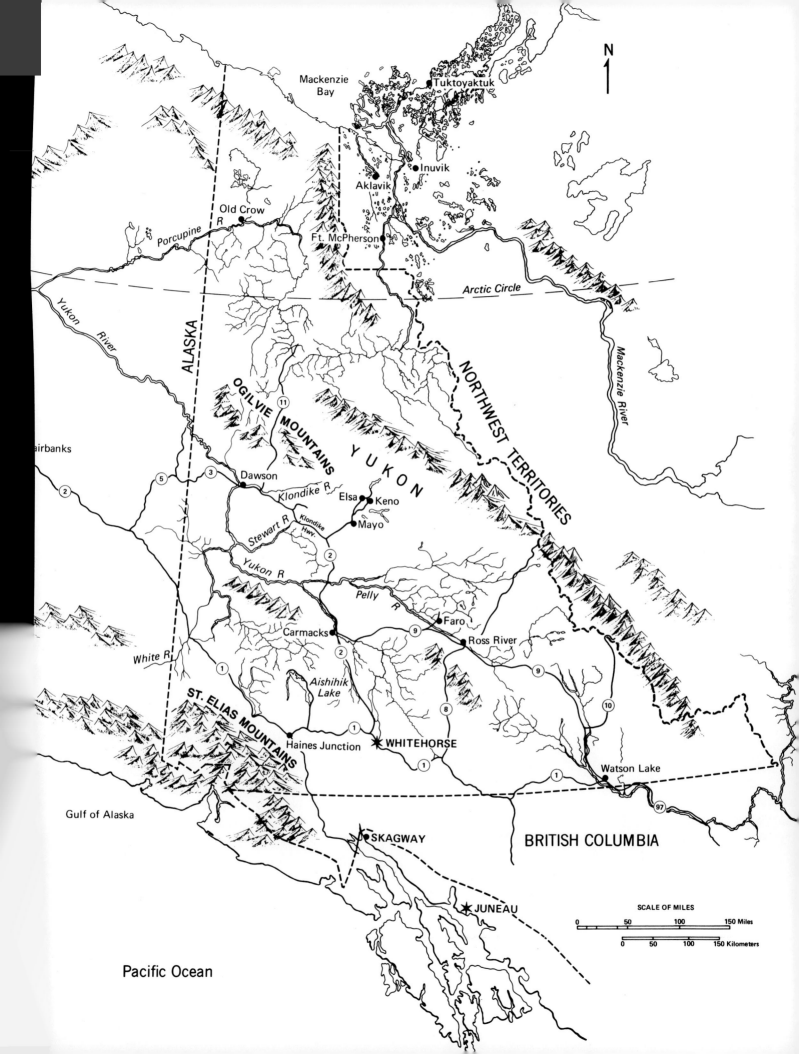

FRONTIER

YUKONERS ARE ALTERNATELY amused and annoyed by the widely held belief that the Yukon is part of Alaska. It isn't. It is a large and wedge-shaped territory of Canada, bounded on the east by the Northwest Territories, on the west by Alaska, on the south by British Columbia, and on the north by the Beaufort Sea, part of the Arctic Ocean. It has a land area of 207,000 square miles and a population of only 23,000. It is a raw, mountainous, and beautiful country of short summers and long, dark winters with temperatures often dropping to 60° or 65° below zero. And unlike most of North America, it is a frontier environment, where human activity is dominated by the power of the natural surroundings and civilization is confined to the fringes of a vast and sprawling wilderness.

The persisting image of the Yukon seems to be that of a lawless land, frozen in time at the turn of the century, with an economy based on claim-jumping and prostitution and a population of tough, bearded sourdoughs, sled dogs, dance-hall girls, mounties, and the occasional Indian scout. This image does not fit very well today. But it is easy to see why the image was born and why it has persisted.

Prior to 1898, the Yukon was a loosely defined portion of the Northwest Territories, inhabited only by its native Indian population and by a handful of white fur traders, gold prospectors, and missionaries. In August 1896 three prospectors—two Indians and one white—made a major gold find in the gravel of Rabbit Creek (immediately renamed Bonanza Creek) in the Klondike River drainage, near the present site of Dawson. When word of the find finally trickled to the outside, one year later, the Yukon was catapulted to world attention. Within weeks, thousands of prospectors, would-be prospectors, con men, entrepreneurs, and soldiers of fortune—mostly Americans—were on their way to the Klondike, participating in one of the strangest human adventures in North American history.

Some reached Dawson by fall of 1897; most got there the following summer. The "stampeders" staked claims, set up tents, cabins, and businesses, built dance halls, saloons, theaters, and gambling parlors, and dug up the Klondike landscape. The ratio of males to females was lopsided, and enterprising women such as Klondike Kate and Diamond Tooth Gertie capitalized upon the discrepancy. By summer of 1898 Dawson had grown to roughly 30,000 (estimates vary) and was known as the largest city in North America west of Winnipeg and north of San Francisco. The town and its people were a bizarre addition to the wilderness landscape and to the trading, hunting, and fishing economy of the Yukon natives. The Yukon was granted territorial status by the federal government.

The rush of '98 is sometimes viewed as a buoyant and optimistic phenomenon. But for most people involved, the times were dirty, drab, painful, sometimes tragic.

Even before reaching the Klondike, the searchers underwent a long and difficult journey, traveling 1,000 miles or more by ocean steamer up the west coast to the Alaska panhandle towns of Dyea and Skagway, climbing 30 miles over the rugged Coast Mountains to the navigable headwaters of the Yukon River at Lake Bennett and Lake Linderman in British Columbia, then building boats and rafts and floating another 560 miles downriver to Dawson. To prevent starvation within the Yukon, the Canadian Northwest Mounted Police required that every stampeder entering Canada come equipped with 1,150 pounds of grub. This, plus whatever shovels, gold pans, tents, cooking utensils, rope, clothing, nails, hammers, axes, ammunition, and other equipment a man needed, weighed roughly one ton. Sourdoughs lugged this gear through the Coast Mountains, over the Chilkoot Pass, often carrying 100 pounds at a time to shorten the project and making at least twenty round trips—1.200 miles or more —to get their gear from the Pacific coast to the Yukon River headwaters. Several thousand stampeders spent the winter of 1897–98 huddled around the frozen shores of lakes Bennett and Linderman, without medical attention, without newspapers or hot water or privacy, eating flour and lard, awaiting spring breakup and the time they could proceed to Dawson. In mid-May they put into the water with their strange array of homemade craft. Most made it, but dozens of boats were destroyed, or their provisions lost, at the Whitehorse rapids. Throughout, stampeders were beset by disease and malnutrition, by shysters and natural disasters, and by their own lack of knowledge of how to survive the frozen sunless winters of the subarctic. Some were suffocated in avalanches. Some froze. Some died in outbreaks of spinal meningitis. Some were robbed or were duped out of their grubstakes. A few were murdered by companions. Some put revolvers to their own heads after realizing the futility of their own endeavors. Most were unequipped—physically or psychologically—to cope with the conditions of Yukon gold mining. Whatever romance existed, existed against a backdrop of mud and bitter cold, bad food and inadequate sanitation, and an unstable, predatory set of social conditions.

Fewer than a dozen of the 30,000 or so who flooded over the Chilkoot Pass in fall and winter of 1897–98 made money from gold. The last significant gold find—the kind that made a man wealthy—was made in October 1897, a half year before most stampeders arrived in Dawson. Months before word of gold reached the men who made the gold rush, it had reached prospectors who were already at work in northern Canada and Alaska; these men, and the first few arrivals from outside, had already staked and claimed every inch of the Klondike's major gold creeks. With poor prospects, most 1898 stampeders deserted Dawson within months of their arrival. The town's population had halved by August 1899. By 1910, with gold fever gone, the Yukon's people numbered 8,500. By 1940 only 5,000 people remained in the territory. The population has grown slowly in postwar years but has never regained its gold rush level. New small towns have appeared, but the former boomtown of Dawson today has only 800 residents. Its old bleached wooden buildings —some restored, some falling—stand empty along the muddy streets of town, interspersed with new silver house trailers, a few motels, and low-cost government housing.

Despite the territory's persisting gold rush image, nothing of equal drama, equal world-grabbing attention, has occurred there since 1898. What has happened in recent years—more roads, more homes, more businesses, more people—has happened everywhere. Most of what the world, south of the 60th parallel, has heard of the Yukon has filtered down to us via the short stories of Jack London, the more fanciful poems of Robert Service, and the adventures of Sergeant Preston and his great dog King, all of which harken back to the romance—real or imagined—of the gold rush era.

While this image of the Yukon strikes its most ambitious citizens as antiquated, inappropriate, an almost intentional misunderstanding of today's Yukon by the outside world, there must nevertheless be a secret pleasure in being misunderstood; for whenever the territory searches for an image of itself—for its license plates, its road maps, its tourist literature—it comes up with a bearded sourdough holding a battered gold pan.

Whitehorse

But any confusion over the Yukon's image, on the part of either residents or "outsiders," is a very understandable confusion. The region is still young enough, at least in terms of its take-over by white culture, that it lacks any theme, any orientation or set of characteristics that can be identified as distinctly Yukonese. In the Yukon's few populated areas, newness predominates. Newness in institutions, technology, population, and architecture, with few visible links to the past. Whitehorse, which is the territory's capital and its only sizable town, with 13,500 people, is almost indistinguishable from any new and similar-sized town in southern Ontario or southern California. It has a small commercial airport, paved streets and sidewalks, drab government office buildings, a trailer park or two, asphalted shopping centers, rows of ranch-style homes with green fiber-glass carports and small, sprinkled lawns, take-out hamburger stands, color television, cautious civil servants, courses in transcendental meditation, disposable beer cans, and most other artifacts of postwar industrial culture. A few old cabins, a beached Yukon River steamboat, and the log White Pass Railroad station are the only visible reminders of a former time.

The fifteen or so remaining settlements are considerably smaller than Whitehorse. All but one have populations of less than 1,000 and most have populations of under 500. Many are of World War II vintage or newer, and like the American frontier one century ago, most have largely white populations heavily weighted by newcomers. Aside from the territory's 2,500 native Indian residents, few of today's Yukoners were Yukoners prior to 1945, and few have lived in the territory their entire lives.

There is a simple reason for the newness. Before World War II the Yukon had no highway connection with the rest of the continent. But within an eight-month period in 1942, the United States military, guided by local Indian people and white bushmen, quickly cut a 1,500-mile dirt and gravel highway from Dawson Creek, British Columbia, to Fairbanks, Alaska, across the southwestern corner of the Yukon. In postwar years, this road—called the Alaska Highway—was straightened, widened, and smoothed, and placed under civilian control. Most of the Yukon's current population, most of its economic change, and most of its present identity have come in postwar years, over this highway.

Whitehorse, because of its location on the route of the highway, evolved from a prewar outpost to its present character and dimensions within a period of thirty years. Dawson, which was far from the road, retained some of its gold rush character but continued to lose population, and in 1953 it was replaced by Whitehorse as the capital city. With a highway link to the outside world, the federal government began a program of road construction within the Yukon, primarily to facilitate mineral exploitation, and company mining towns such as Faro and Clinton Creek sprang up along these roads. The highways also displaced the Yukon River system as the territory's primary transportation network, and the last of the elegant old steamboats used to transport passengers and goods between Whitehorse and Dawson since gold rush days was retired in the mid-1950s. Riverside wilderness dwellers moved out of the bush and into towns.

5

lumbering is notoriously slow. Similarly, commercial agriculture is essentially nonexistent. The territory is a deficit-producing region, and must import most of its food, fuel, and building materials—at enormous expense—from southern Canada and the United States. In the short run, the Yukon's few mines—which are largely foreign-owned—will remain its primary source of income, though the economic health of even this industry is largely dependent upon federal subsidies in the form of tax credits and facility construction. Further in the future, tourism and the outside sale of hydropower from the territory's several large rivers seem the most likely areas for economic growth.

But, as during gold rush days, the primary realities of the Yukon remain the physical ones, the natural ones, of space and cold, mountains and rivers, forests, wildlife, and tundra. The Yukon landscape is diverse, ranging from bleak, almost treeless tundra in the north to a series of rolling, spruce-covered mountain ranges in its middle reaches to the towering glacier-bound St. Elias Mountains in the territory's southwest, all this cut by several major rivers. The most impressive aspect of the territory's geography is not a certain set of peaks or stretch of river or view from a specific promontory, but the sheer bulk and volume of its landscape: mountain after mountain, mile after mile of forest or tundra or big, silt-laden river, with a power not unlike the power of our oceans. Most of this country has at one time or another been traveled on foot or by canoe or kayak, but it is still easily possible to hike or paddle (or, for that matter, drive) distances of a hundred miles without encountering another human being.

The territory's climate is sufficiently formidable, its transportation and communication networks sufficiently limited, and its opportunities for livelihood sufficiently few that the human population is confined to less than 1 percent of the rugged landscape. With a land area twice the size of Colorado and a population that could be seated within a very modest-sized football stadium, the Yukon's population density turns out to be only .1 person per square mile, less than one-fifth that of neighboring Alaska.

Relatively few Yukoners live full-time in "the bush." Most of the people who do so hunt, fish, and trap, clear land and plant a small garden, build a cabin or restore one that has been abandoned, and generally maintain a life-style that is marginal, confining, and, despite twentieth-century technology,

The Yukon today has little to do with gold, except for a few people in the Dawson area. The territory's primary sources of employment are civil service, mining (for zinc, lead, silver, copper, and asbestos), and one or another form of tourist accommodation, such as operating saloons or motels and guiding big-game hunters. And these are about the only sources of employment. Despite the fact that the territory's wages—which typically include the equivalent of an outpost allowance—are the highest in Canada, the economy is not sizable or broad-based enough to provide a variety of work opportunity. The Yukon's timber, which at first glance would seem an important potential source of wealth and employment, is little exploited; due to the extreme and persistent cold, relatively few trees reach marketable size, and regrowth after not unlike that of the United States frontier a century or more ago. By today's standards, this sort of an existence is dangerous. There is always the possibility of cutting your foot with an ax, getting severely frostbitten, setting fire to the cabin, or even running into a female grizzly with her cub. These mishaps are relatively rare, but even a minor accident can become an emergency if you live fifty miles from the nearest neighbor, one hundred miles from the nearest town, and two hundred miles from the nearest hospital.

Many Yukoners lead a sort of semibush existence, living in a cabin without electricity or water or phone, far enough from civilization to see an occasional moose or wolf or bear, but still close enough to get to town twice a week for mail and groceries and to talk with friends. Most Yukoners, 95 percent or more, reside year round in towns and work as government clerks or miners or highway laborers, and typically venture into the bush only long enough to supplement the winter meat supply with the annual moose or caribou.

But even for these people, the natural environment is not a romanticized concept but a real and

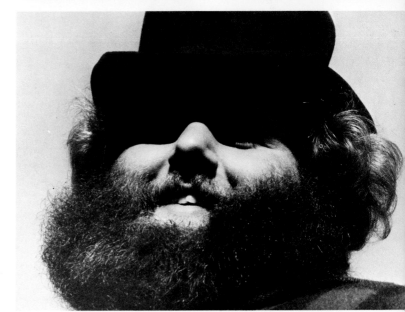

omnipresent force to be dealt with every day of the year, whether this means starting a pickup at 60° below, adjusting to the strange extremes in day length, or simply accepting the fact of isolation from most of North American society. Even an auto trip in the Yukon is a different sort of a thing from what it is in most other places. It is one hundred miles between the small towns, with little but wilderness in between. Cars pass infrequently. A breakdown in summer means a long wait. A breakdown in winter is dangerous, and motorists have frozen while waiting for assistance.

The necessarily intimate contact with overpowering natural surroundings in the Yukon gives rise to attitudes and behaviors toward the environment which include elements of adventure, fear, respect, challenge, and conquest. These attitudes exist elsewhere, even in those places on the North American continent where surroundings are most completely altered from the natural. But lacking the physical reality of a dominant wilderness environment, they are dulled, rationalized, adorned, modified almost out of existence. In the Yukon they are visible and straightforward.

The notion that the territory's wilderness environment is infinite and that it somehow constitutes either a loss or a threat to society is evident both in individuals' interaction with their surroundings and in the aggressive governmental programs designed to open up or conquer the frontier. It is more than coincidence that the Yukon has no effective environmental movements such as those in southern Canada and the United States.

For most North Americans, there is a tendency to romanticize the fact of frontier existence. But even a brief familiarity with the Yukon reveals much that is not romantic. The Yukon, for example, has Canada's highest rate of alcohol consumption (33.33 gallons of beer, wine, and liquor per capita in 1973), its highest and second highest rates of syphilis and gonorrhea, respectively, and one of its highest rates of suicide. It also has a divorce rate almost twice the Canadian average and a birth rate of illegitimate children (one in every four) almost three times the national average.

It is tempting to speculate that there is a direct cause-and-effect relationship between frontier life and these symptoms of social instability, that living in or around the wilds somehow does strange things to one's head and to one's social behavior. There is perhaps some basis for such direct speculation—the reality of "cabin fever," for example—but for the most part, this is not the case. There is after all no established causal link between the number of spruce trees and the number of divorces, or even between the hours of darkness and the number of illegitimate children.

At the same time, it is safe to say that the Yukon's population does have a number of interacting characteristics that contribute to a climate of social instability, and that these characteristics are in one way or another traceable to the fact that the Yukon is a frontier environment. A sociologist would probably point out that part of what is going on is some sort of preselective or screening process: Whatever social characteristics the territory has are largely imported, and have become concentrated in the Yukon as a function of the people who choose to come there.

The highly transient nature of the Yukon's population is not conducive to social stability. The territory's frontier economy is based on construction and resource exploitive occupations, such as mining and mineral exploration, road and dam building. These occupations offer extremely high wages to attract men to the remote, outpost locations, but they do not encourage roots.

(Jack Hope)

At left above, Boundary Creek;
below and at right, the Ogilvies.

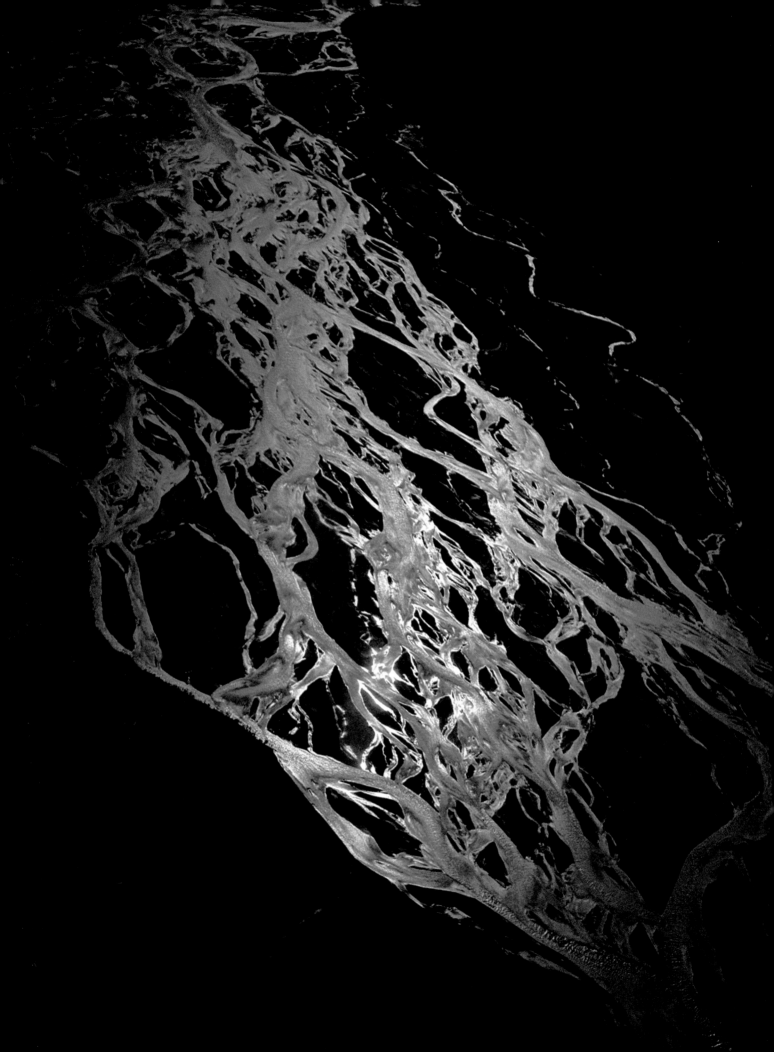

Above, the Yukon River in winter and summer. At left, the aurora borealis. On following pages: the Yukon River near Dawson; an aerial view of the White River; early autumn in the Ogilvie Mountains.

In the St. Elias Mountains

The Territory's human population
occupies less than one percent of its
total land area. The essence of the
Yukon is wilderness.

Teslin Lake

determine. The fact that the majority of Yukoners seem to feel most comfortable in a completely sub-urban existence, with very little time spent in the bush, would seem to indicate that this passion for the land is not an everlasting and omnipresent phenomenon.

For some, though, the land is enough. The country has a bleak magnificence about it, and can provide an independent, outdoor life. Those who can adapt to that life stay, often living within the wilderness or as close to it as their capacities and resources permit.

Curiously, most bush dwellers are not the stereotypical mountain men—strong, uncompli-cated, born with a double-bitted ax in their grasp—but are sophisticated, often well-educated former urbanites, from Detroit, Stockholm, Montreal, or Brooklyn. Statistically, young bush dwellers—in their twenties or thirties—outnumber their older counterparts, though it is also true that older bush dwellers, who are apparently steadier and more

realistic about an existence in the wilderness, are more successful at sticking out the ruggedness and loneliness of bush life. Of the nine or ten young bush couples with whom Paul von Baich and I became fairly well acquainted during 1974 and 1975, three have by now—one year later—split with one another, and five have split with the Yukon, gone south for economic reasons, for medical attention, for easier weather.

Leave or not, most wilderness residents who have gone as far as to renovate or build a cabin and move in generally seem to have an honest attraction to the land. And if their stay is only a year, or a season, they have at least experimented with a life-style that most of us have never known and will never know.

Other dreams and expectations mentioned to me by Yukoners range all the way from proving oneself against the elements to getting away from the bustle of the urbanized south to spending a winter in con-templation to finding a wilderness home that will be safe against the tidal wave that their guru said was coming. In some cases one wonders whether people were drawn to the Yukon by one of its positive attractions or whether their presence is in part an escape from something or someone "outside." The escape element, in fact, seems to operate strongly for a relatively large number of newcomers, from miners to schoolteachers. Often the object of escape is a very real one—communist oppression in East-ern Europe, the United States Selective Service, a broken marriage, an impending jail term. But often the trouble, or its roots, accompany the individual to the Yukon.

Whatever people's reasons for coming, some no-tion of "frontier"—of space, of freedom, of alone-ness, of new beginnings—is important to them. And as a result, the Yukon, within its tiny population of 23,000, contains a wonderfully eclectic collection of religious seekers, poets, pioneers, bird watchers, revolutionaries, explorers, recluses, even the occa-sional sourdough who, somewhere in the back of his head, has the vision of panning one-ounce nuggets from a secret gold stream.

The Yukon is distinct from other frontiers in other times simply because it is a phenomenon of the late twentieth century. A time spent there does not give you the chance to live out the fantasy of going back to a former, simpler time, but rather of living on a frontier that is of our society's own mak-

The men who come to work in the Yukon's mines are from southern Canada, the United States, and overseas. Most are young and most do not intend to stay very long in the remote, essentially womanless company towns. The typical plan is to remain a year or eighteen months, work hard, save five to ten thousand dollars, and depart for a six-month vacation in Europe or Africa or South America. The plan seldom works. Most men seem able to take only a few months of the isolated mining camps, and most drink up a far larger proportion of their income than they intended. The world tour gets shortened to a month's binge in Toronto, or maybe even as nearby as Whitehorse, and then it is back to the mines. A somewhat similar pattern occurs in the Yukon's remote highway construction camps, in the oil and mineral exploration camps, and in the territory's one hydropower construction camp.

There is another transient segment of the Yukon's population made up of people who appear each spring, often as semitourists, and decide to stay on for a year or so to see what the frontier is all about. This group is sufficiently diverse that it is hard to generalize about them except to say that most are young and most do not stay very long. Some try to live in the bush, some take jobs as bartenders, laborers, or cocktail waitresses in Whitehorse or Dawson or Faro, and most go back south at about the time the weather turns cold and the days get short. Some are back the next June with a zealous Yukon patriotism and a fierce determination to stick out the next winter. A few do. Most don't.

Another destabilizing aspect of Yukon society is the collision between the territory's white and Indian cultures. Yukon Indians were not as forcibly dominated as were those in the United States and parts of southern Canada, but their seminomadic hunting and fishing economy nevertheless conflicted with white industrial culture and was overwhelmed by it. And due to the Yukon's physical isolation and the consequently recent influx of white men, this overwhelming occurred very recently, relative to the rest of North America. The first white advance into the Yukon subsided quickly, after the gold rush fizzled. It was thus not until World War II that Yukon Indian culture experienced the steadily growing pressure of a society that would inevitably destroy it. The usual things happened. Traditional Indian skills were largely unmarketable within the white economy; at the same time exposure to new industrial goods and to white standards of living created new wants in the Indian people, which they could not fulfill. Indian bush settlements were relocated to sites along the highway. Indian children were separated from their families to attend white schools far from their home communities. The result is the predictable erosion of family stability and growth of alcoholism, dependence upon government assistance, and confused self-identity of the dominated culture. These problems are further exacerbated by the white culture's typical intolerance for a people who could not make a smooth and instant transition from a relatively primitive society to a modern industrial one.

It remains to be seen how the awarding of land and/or money to the Yukon Indians—as a result of their land claims against the Canadian government—will affect their future. It may restore some self-esteem, but it cannot restore the integrity or existence of the former Indian culture. Even a partially successful linking of Indian and white societies will take many generations and, compared with most other North American locations, the Yukon has just begun.

The Yukon is sufficiently different from more settled parts of this continent to raise the question of what kind of dreams and motivations its people have inside them when they come there, and what happens—there on the frontier—to cause them to remain or to retreat. We know little of everyday life on the planet's few remaining frontiers, and we will have fewer chances to learn as these places are absorbed by the larger, industrial, world society. This is a reason for my own initial interest in the Yukon and is, in part, a purpose of this book.

In some cases, Yukon motivations seem relatively straightforward. Among the transient or semi-transient workers, for example, a primary reason for coming to the territory is, simply, money. And the reason for leaving, similarly, is the end of the job or the end of the worker's capacity to tolerate life in the outpost camps. Money and its concomitant, power, are also motivations for ambitious souls in more elegant fields, such as politics, business, real estate, public relations, even civil service. Physically the Yukon is mammoth, but in population it is a small town; with a minimum of human competition, the possibility of making a name for oneself is a very real one.

An attraction to the land is among the most commonly stated reasons for a stay, or a lifetime, in the Yukon. The validity of this claim is hard to

9

ing. Whoever goes there can still live in that snow-covered cabin, but he nevertheless lives with a perspective that includes a knowledge of McDonald's hamburger stands, atomic warfare, gay liberation, the third world, vitamin E, jet travel, and the finite supply of world energy. And aside from whatever else this pool of information may do to his head, it gives a Yukon frontier resident an orientation to his life and surroundings that is far broader, far more aware of alternatives and the range of human possibility than was possible for frontiersmen of a former era.

No corner of the planet remains unchanged. In the Yukon, the most likely avenues for future change are the various large-scale construction and development projects of government and industry, such as roads and mines. Such projects hold the potential for completely altering the territory's human and natural complexion in a very short time, by increasing human numbers and by shrinking distances. The Yukon's ongoing Dempster Highway, for example, when finished will immediately halve

the dimensions of the territory's still unbroken northern half, will bring millions of auto tourists into a land hitherto traveled only by migrating caribou herds and a few hundred nomadic hunters, and will provide the rationale—some would say, the rationalization—for future linking highways that will again halve and quarter the region.

In a somewhat romantic frame of mind, even in a socially functional frame of mind, it would be nice to believe that the architects of the Yukon's future will make the choices necessary to retain its natural and human diversity, its unmatched opportunities for human experience, while healing some of its social wounds. Certainly, in terms of cultural evolution, the Yukon is a special place and a final opportunity, and as such its human and environmental importance far outshines its value as an economic entity measured in tourist dollars or barrels of oil or tons of zinc. There is little historical reason to believe that the ideal future choices will be made. But the Yukon is one of only four or five places on the face of the earth where this choice is even available.

11

Salmon (below) travel to their
spawning grounds at the headwaters
of the Porcupine River on the Arctic Circle.

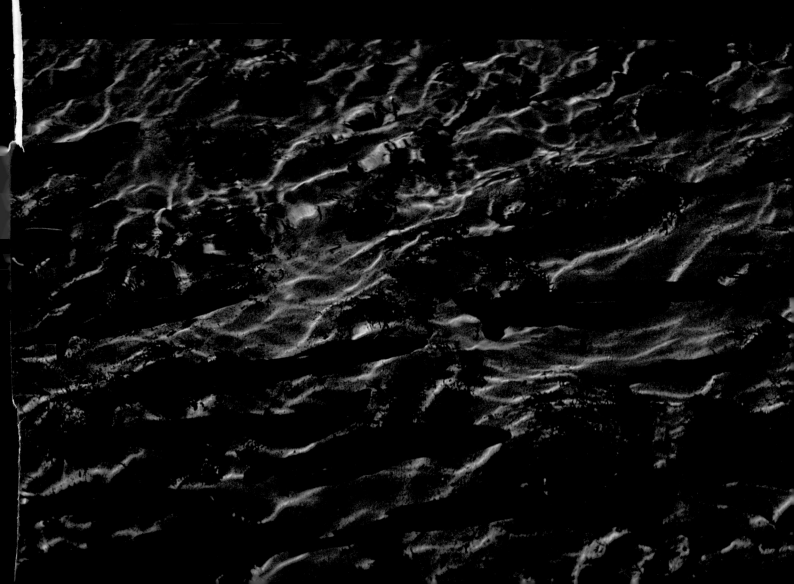

GOLD

AT 7:00 A.M. the sun is already high above the horizon. Light glints from muddy road puddles as I drive east from Dawson. The little pickup rumbles across the Ogilvie Bridge, past Black Mike's Inn, past the muddy lower reaches of Bonanza Creek. Four hundred yards to my left, rocky slopes drop steeply into the west-flowing Klondike River. A half mile to the right, spruce-covered hills rise from the level valley floor. Small streams flow from these hills, cross the valley from south to north, empty into the Klondike and thence into the north-flowing Yukon River five miles behind me, at Dawson.

This is the Klondike, the gold-rich region bounded by the Klondike and Indian rivers on north and south, the Yukon River on the west, and extending forty miles east of Dawson to the headwaters of the Indian. Since the rush of '98, this eight-hundred-square-mile area has been the focus of the Yukon's search for gold, a business that has been given new vitality in recent years by rises in the international price of gold as a speculative metal.

Evidence of this search is abundant along the road I now travel. On both sides of the highway, the valley floor has been overturned by giant dredges, house-sized machines that ground their way along the region's river and creek beds, sucking up earth and gravel, removing its gold, dropping the remains in long, twenty-foot-high piles. Today, the rock piles remain as they were deposited several decades ago, covering the valley bottom for ten miles or so east of Dawson. Here and there a hopeful poplar has taken root in the barren gravel piles. Here and there a hopeful Dawson merchant has perched a small billboard atop them: THE FLORA DORA CAFE; KLONDIKE MOTORS; THE MIDNIGHT SUN.

Eleven miles east of Dawson I make a right turn onto a smaller gravel road which parallels Hunker Creek, one of the small streams flowing from the hills to the south. This creek too has been uprooted by the dredges, and as I go farther into the hills, I see one of these machines two hundred yards to my right, down in the creek bottom, where it ground itself to a halt in the gravel and was abandoned by its owners. On the valley's far wall there is a broad white fan of exposed and eroding soil, where miners at one time turned a stream of water against the hillside to wash out its gold. Along the road I pass various artifacts of the mining process—piles of pipe, the body of a red truck, rusted bulldozer parts, pieces of a sluice box, chunks of an old water boiler.

13

Gold dredge
(*Yukon Government Photo*)

Some of these items—the pipe for instance—are being used by miners now working Hunker Creek. The others are from past operators and remain more or less where they broke down.

In the past Klondike gold mining outfits varied from the individual with a gold pan and shovel to large syndicates or wealthy individuals who owned the big dredges. Today, the typical outfit consists of two or three people operating one or two bulldozers and a metal sluice box to sort the precious metal from sand and gravel. Many of the Klondike's miners reside in the region only from May through September, living in house trailers or bunkhouses. They return home—to Seattle or Vancouver or Toronto—once the weather forces a shutdown of their operations. It is now June. The miners are three to four weeks into their summer's work, and the Klondike's creeks are churned into their seasonal muddy brown by the bulldozers.

I begin to wonder now what kind of person I will find in Marion Schmidt, the gold miner I am going to visit. Like most of the Yukon's rural homes, the Schmidt residence has no phone, and I have thus not been able to call Mrs. Schmidt or to get a sense of what she is like before coming out here. I know only that she owns Ballerat Mines, an operation that—a few years ago, prior to her husband's death—was one of the territory's biggest producers. I have also been told by one well-meaning soul that the woman carries a shotgun, is rougher than any man, and does not take kindly to strangers. This description I tend

to discount as Dawsonese exaggeration. But who knows? Marion Schmidt may have a pet grizzly, a .303 trained on the road, and a musty root cellar filled with the bones of errant passersby.

The day is sunny and pleasant, but this road is lonesome. I meet no cars and see no people. Fourteen miles in the road climbs the headwall of the valley, and at mile 17 I cross "the summit," the four-thousand-foot ridge that separates the headwaters of Hunker and Dominion creeks and divides the drainage systems of the Klondike and Indian rivers. The road forks here, beside a rotting pile of lumber that apparently was once a barn or roadhouse, with the right fork going to Quartz Creek, the left fork —as the sign tells me—leading to "Granville, via Dominion." Granville was once a town. Dominion is just a place. I go left, dropping sharply downhill, paralleling Dominion Creek. The valley here is broad and spruce-covered, with deep mounds of snow remaining in sheltered locations. It is not as dug up as the valley I've just left. Less dredging, apparently.

At mile 24 a narrow dirt track leads diagonally downhill to a group of bleached gray bunkhouses and equipment sheds one hundred yards below the road. There is no Ballerat sign, but the place fits the description given me by the Dawson claims office. I drive down among the buildings, past the remains of a half-dozen trucks and a bulldozer or two, and stop alongside a bunkhouse where a blue Mazda pickup is parked.

14

I sit there a few minutes before getting out. The sun is high now. It is quiet. The wind blows up a little puff of dust down near the equipment shed. Barn swallows fill the air, darting up under the eaves of the bunkhouse where someone has nailed up several open-ended tin cans to serve as foundations for the birds' mud nests.

A tail-wagging, long-haired dog comes trotting up the hill, but still no sign of a person. I get out and pet the dog, looking in the direction it came from.

"Her name is Lobelia."

I look up suddenly to see a small, slim, and attractive woman—about five feet two, probably about forty-five years old—standing at the head of the bunkhouse stairs. I did not hear her come out, and although she speaks softly, her voice startles me. She is dressed in a pink blouse, beige skirt, and loafers. No six-gun. No pet grizzly. She seems shy, feminine—especially for the Yukon—and in general impresses me as something of an anomaly in the bleak Klondike environment of mud and bulldozers. Can this be Marion Schmidt?

It is. I introduce myself, explain my presence, ask if we can talk. She hesitates for a moment, seems to be considering some far-off topic, then smiles and invites me in for tea.

Inside, I find that the front room of the bunkhouse is partitioned into living quarters. One end of the big room is a kitchen, with kerosene stove, cabinets, table, and sink. Like most rural Yukon places, it has part-time electricity generated by a gasoline engine. Unlike most of them, it has running water, led to the house through a rubber hose leading from a nearby snow-filled creek. The rest of the room is a sort of living room/library, with an upright piano and three full walls of books. I glance at them and see Keats, Shelley, Browning, Shakespeare, Marx, Jung, Disraeli, Stuart Little, and Adelle Davis, as well as several books on mysticism, mind control, religious philosophy. On a round table there are recent copies of *Time*, *Western Miner*, and *Scientific American*. This volume and variety of reading matter also seems anomalous in a backwoods miner's residence.

"I was just getting ready to go to town," Mrs. Schmidt says as she puts a tea kettle on the stove, "but something must have made me stay. I guess I was supposed to meet you."

I ask how often she goes to town and she says about every two weeks, to get groceries, mail, fuel, other supplies.

"I try to spend just as little time in town as I can," she says. "Probably you've discovered already that this is a great place for gossip. And the more people get to know you . . ." She shrugs. "Besides, this is my home, out here."

"Don't you get lonesome?"

Her face brightens. "Oh no! How could I possibly get lonesome? It's friendly out here. Do you know, I went to the door just before you came—the wind had blown it open—and as I closed it I said, 'Hello, Wind.' And the wind blew the door open again. He wanted to come inside for a visit."

Mrs. Schmidt seems to have quickly lost her initial shyness; she talks on without pause.

"And I have the swallows. They were just holding a conference when you drove up. You can sit in our bathroom and look up and see them conferring right under the eaves. They sit there with their little white chins sticking out of their nests, talking away. We have a flicker too. I call her 'Weechum' because that's the noise she makes, 'Weechum, Weechum!' She's built a nest in the outside wall, right there behind the bookcase. She's feeding her babies now. She taps on the wall every once in a while with her beak. It's a very regular tap, the kind of human being would understand. I think she does it to tell us something in here."

"What is she saying?"

"I don't know. I don't speak the language. All I know is that sometimes she does it too loudly. Then I go to the wall and tap lightly back, like this." She goes to the bookcase and taps three times. "And then she stops. But she has to be reminded."

This is a gold miner?

I smile to myself. I decide that anyone who communicates with birds and wind, and who is open enough to tell about it, must be a very human sort.

I look more carefully about the room and notice an open Bible, a small blackboard, a few open grade-school textbooks, and a Snellen eye chart tacked to the bookcase. I ask who else lives here, if she has a family.

"Well, you probably heard in town that my husband is no longer with us. I have five kids scattered hither and yon. Two girls are at our home in Vancouver. I have a married daughter in California. Craig is finishing up the semester at vocational school in Whitehorse; he wants to be a miner and I'm glad of it. Stewart and his wife Judy and their baby were somewhere down south, living in a teepee. I can't get in touch with them. But I've been mentally concentrating on Stewart real hard, to try to get him up here. He brought us good luck the three years he worked with me. I think he'll be up here before long. And we have Ben Strand working here with us. He's out working on the claims. We'll go down there later. Then I have Ben's two children here with me now, but they're gone to a friend's for the day, in town. Their mother's dead, and I felt it would be best to have the girls up here with their father, so they could see their dad working at his profession. School isn't out yet, so I'm teaching them here at home."

Barely pausing for a breath, she gestures toward the open textbooks and continues: "See? We use the Calvert Reader and *A Child's History of the World*, and we use the Bible too. I was led to teach them all of Proverbs, and from that we learned many important words—*recompense, penury, preserve, prudent, deceit, abomination, slothful, reproach, abhor, transgression, perish.* . . . And yesterday we were learning about the Medes and the Persians and Nebuchadnezzar and the fall of Babylon—you know, 'Mene, mene, tekel, upharsin.' "

The tea kettle starts to boil and Marion hurries over to it. She laughs to herself. "My, I'm certainly running off at the mouth this morning. Well, you don't see many people to talk to out here. It's just Ben and me, and once in a while we see Gus and Nellie Burgelman, four miles up the road."

As she places our teacups on the table she again becomes serious: "So, you want to learn something about gold mining? Well, we're not really a mine here anymore. We're a family. And that's what I'm working at. I keep the books and I decide where we'll work and I help with the sluicing and I drive the Cat—I suppose you heard that in town too? —but that's secondary to being a family and interacting with other people. Some of the kids tell me these days that they want to learn more about life by becoming a hermit. But I think we are tested by being in society and by proving our philosophies against the pressures of everyday life and against the ideas of others. And if I can help just one other person to do that, then I feel fulfilled."

I don't quite get all these connections, but I somehow feel that these remarks have more personal significance for Marion than I am aware of. I ask how she got started in mining.

"I wasn't a miner by birth," she says. "I got started by marrying Harold in 1941. I came up to Alaska and we worked together on John Wade

Creek. Then we came here. When I met him he owed a hundred thousand dollars on his outfit. That's strange," she reflects quietly, "because that's just the amount we owed when he died. He left in just the same shape as he started."

I want to ask Marion about this, but she is off on another topic before I can frame the question.

"Anyway, my husband was a mining engineer, you know. He did things scientifically. He made these diagrams that I want to show you, if I can find them." She gets up and searches in the bookcase. "Now every miner does it differently. But we made money while a lot of others failed, so naturally I think our way is best. It's funny, but he revealed to me all his secrets of mining before he died. He spoke just as if he knew one day I would be doing it alone. And we continue to use the diagrams he made to guide our operation today. Here they are."

She spreads several large sheets of paper on the kitchen table. "I suppose the best way to acquaint you with our operation is to go over these. Then we can go down to the cut and I can show you what I'm demonstrating on paper. But maybe we ought to have a little lunch too. Are you hungry?"

For the next forty-five minutes, Marion and I eat ham sandwiches, look over her husband's drawings, and discuss her mining techniques. The drawings are neat, cross-sectional diagrams of the Schmidt claims on Dominion Creek. The gold, she explains, is found mainly in gravel and sand, below the soil layer and above bedrock. Here, the soil layer —including its two feet of moss—is about twenty-five feet thick, and the underlying gravel layer is seven to eleven feet thick. The basic technique of extraction is to bulldoze away the soil and to then dig up and rinse the gravel and sand in a sluice box, leaving only gold. Panning is performed throughout most of the process as a sampling technique, to determine the location and concentration of gold within the gravel layer. While certain amounts of gold can be found in many locations, the costs of removing the soil overburden are often prohibitive, except along valley bottoms where natural erosion has exposed the gravel. Unlike most placer miners, Harold Schmidt made slurry drillings along both sides of his creek to calculate the richness and depth of the gold deposits. He then compared the estimated value of the gold to the estimated costs of extraction and pinpointed the locations worth mining.

Marion also gives me some other facts about

herself and her operation, though she is careful to avoid any information that would tell me just how much money she makes. She tells me that she is fifty-two years old, that she was raised in Seattle but is now a Canadian citizen, that she owns a small farm in California as well as her home in Vancouver. Her Yukon operation, she says, includes the three bunkhouses, which are largely unused; two pickup trucks; six bulldozers, five of which are in running condition; a sluice box; three water pumps; and a loading conveyor. She controls roughly one hundred placer or surface claims, some on Dominion Creek, some on Quartz Creek. She owns forty-eight of these outright and leases the remainder from other operators, paying a royalty of 10 percent of the gold extracted. The Schmidts' best year, she says, was in 1968, when they produced 1,759 troy ounces of gold; their yield these days is "a lot smaller."

Finally, she tells me that she does not peddle her gold on the open market, at least not this year, but gets a better price for it by selling it to Walter Knott, owner of the well-known California tourist attraction Knott's Berry Farm. Knott apparently sells panning lessons to tourists, using Marion's Yukon gold to salt the claims and simulate the conditions that prevailed in California in 1849, during the gold rush.

After lunch, Marion changes into jeans, a work shirt, and a pair of muddy rubber boots, and we drive up the road in her Mazda to visit the Dominion Creek claims. Lobelia leaps in the back of the pickup, balancing on a big wooden toolbox while we bounce along the road.

I now ask Marion about the $100,000 indebtedness she mentioned earlier, and which I cannot resolve with the fact that Ballerat Mines has been one of the territory's top producers.

"Oh, I got that paid off," Marion says. "But I had to sell part of our ranch to do it."

"But how did you get that far in debt in the first place, if your operation was so successful?"

Marion hesitates. "You see," she says slowly, "my husband was very scientific. All our gold here is very finely divided. It's not nuggets, it's flour gold. So he had this dream that a process could be perfected to collect even finer gold, colloidal gold, the stuff that slips through our operation now. No one has ever been able to do that, but he subsidized this inventor who assured him he could develop the process. He mortgaged our ranch to do it. But it never worked out. And the inventor never repaid the money."

"And that's how you lost the hundred thousand?"

Marion nods. "My husband was very disillusioned with the failure of that experiment," she says. "He wrote the inventor and asked for a return of the money, or for some of it. The man wrote back and said that he considered the money my husband lent him as a salary for working on the process and had no intention of paying it back."

"Did he make any more attempts to get the money?"

"No," Marion says. "He died of a heart attack right after he received the letter. May 14, 1969. We found him up here near this little stream. He looked at peace with the world. We scattered his ashes on Solomon's Dome, up near the summit."

I do not ask any more questions on the way to the claims.

Two miles along the road, Marion turns left and we jounce downhill toward Dominion Creek on one of her bulldozer roads. When we get within three hundred yards of the creek, Marion breaks the silence.

"We won't be getting any gold till later in the summer," she says. "But Ben is doing some stripping and you can see that, and you can watch us sample for gold with a pan."

"Anything you show me will be new."

"Well," she says, "one thing you should know is that all these creeks around here have been worked over before. They say in town that the Schmidts are just walking on gold out there, but that's not true. We do all right, but it's only through hard work. A dredge went through here thirty or forty years ago. It's still stuck up there at the end of the valley. But they got the pay streak. All we get is the side pay. And there were three or four thousand other miners in here before the dredges, way back when. In all the years we've been here, I have yet to find my nugget! We have to work hard for what we get. That's why I've been concentrating hard to get Stewart back here. Ben is a wonderful worker, but it's too much for him and me alone. Stewart is a real miner at heart, and I sure wish he'd get back here to bring us some luck."

I ask Marion how it is possible to get any gold out of areas that were mined previously. She says that much of the more finely divided gold is too small to have been picked up by the dredges and that some of these claims can be successfully reworked. If the area was previously worked by hand techniques, close to the turn of the century, it is often not profitable to rework it. She always samples such areas with the gold pan to get a notion of their current gold content before proceeding.

Eighty yards from the creek Marion stops the truck and we get out. The valley bottom here is three hundred yards wide and is crisscrossed with bulldozer roads, piled high with mounds of earth and gravel, with stagnant puddles among the mounds. On our side of Dominion Creek the bank—or what remains of it—slopes gradually down to the muddy water, and retains a few small poplars and willows. On the far side of the ten-foot-wide creek, the bank rises abruptly for thirty feet and then continues steeply uphill, with patches of white spruce dotting its slope. At one time the stream flowed two hundred yards or so behind us; we see the black mucky remains of its path. Now Marion's operation has rerouted the creek to flow against the base of the opposite bank, to help cave it in so that its gravel and gold can be reached.

Marion explains the stripping operation. She points to the far creek bank, which is frozen into a large block of earth and ice. The moss-covered ground here is always frozen, permafrosted. But by removing the moss and upper soil with a bulldozer, the lower soil is exposed to sun and water and loses its frost. The process is repeated again and again, a few inches at a time, and the ground is thus thawed and removed down to the gold and gravel. This, she says, is the most time-consuming part of the mining process.

Later in summer this gravel is bladed into a sluice box—a rectangular steel box twenty feet long, three feet wide, and eighteen inches deep, with open ends and with steplike graduations in its bottom. The box is set up at streamside, tipped at an angle, and water is pumped into its upper end, washing over the gravel, rinsing soil, sand, and small gravel back into the creek—"clean up." The small but heavy particles of gold collect in the angles of the steps.

Turn-of-the-century miners, without bulldozer-era technology, usually sunk well-like shafts down into the frozen soil, digging with hand shovels and picks and thawing the soil a bit at a time with wood fires, sometimes with heated water. Ten, twenty, or thirty feet down, at the gravel layer, they

Marion Schmidt, sluicing.

"drifted," dug sideways into the layer, hoisting the gold-bearing gravel up to the surface with a windlass, accumulating a pile of material, then washing it in wooden, handmade sluice boxes.

A short distance up the creek Ben Strand is working with the bulldozer, stripping away the soil from a streamside area roughly sixty by seven hundred feet. We walk up there. He shuts down the bulldozer and stands alongside it, smoking a rolled cigarette, waiting for us to approach. He is a tall man, probably fifty-five or so, with thick, muscular hands and a suntanned face. He wears greasy coveralls, rubber boots, and a narrow-brimmed black hat. Like Marion, he seems serious and warm. Unlike her, he speaks little. Marion introduces us.

"Ben is just the best worker in the Klondike," she says. "I don't know what I'd do without him. Everybody offers him work, but he feels sorry for me and stays here."

Ben smiles broadly. "Oh no," he says with a thick Norwegian accent. "Dat's not true."

"Ben," Marion continues, "I thought we might do some panning. We should do it anyway, to test this cut, and I know Jack would like to see it. Could we do that?"

"Ya," Ben says. He grins good-naturedly, in a way that makes me believe that the panning is not at all necessary, though he will be glad to accommodate us. It occurs to me that he has spent all day alone out here in the cut, and is probably glad to have people around. He strides back to the truck and returns with a shovel and a battered gold pan, about eighteen inches across and four inches deep. He smiles. "Vere do ve go?"

"Gee, I don't know," Marion says, wrinkling her brow. "How about down there . . . oh no, we can't do that, you've covered it up. Well, how about over that way then?"

Ben nods. He waits for Marion to lead the way. She sets off across the muck and gravel, hopping from rock to rock, talking as she goes, with Ben following and taking one step to her two. Lobelia trots happily ahead, runs up the side of a gravel bank, and then jumps into a chest-deep mud puddle, stands there looking back.

The four of us scramble across the piles of earth and gravel looking for a suitable spot to pan, a spot where bedrock and its overlying gravel have been exposed. To me, everything looks the same, undifferentiated mounds of overturned soil and rock. Apparently, though, Marion and Ben can make some order out of this mess, perhaps in the same way that an Eskimo can distinguish a dozen different kinds of snow.

We search for five minutes. Finally Marion points. "How about there, Ben?"

Ben nods. "Ya."

We walk down to the bottom of a small depression.

"Do you see that bedrock?" Marion asks me.

"No. Where?"

"Don't you see that green? That's bedrock. It's always green around here."

I look again, but don't see any rock. Ben strikes his shovel blade against the bank of the depression, exposing a small lens of broken and greenish-colored stone—maybe five inches wide by three feet long —that was previously camouflaged from me by the mud that has flowed down over its surface. He sets the pan on the ground and digs into this lens and just above it, taking out bladefuls of rock and mud and mounding the pan high with probably thirty pounds of this material. Even though I look hard, I cannot distinguish between the splintered bedrock and the overlying gravel. They look identical. I had somehow expected the bedrock to be black and smooth, the gravel to resemble the gray regular chunks that are used on highways.

"Look at the panful Ben takes," Marion says. "I couldn't handle half that amount."

Ben grins, begins the panning, submerging the pan beneath the water in a nearby pool, swirling it gently for perhaps ten seconds, with a semicircular movement, then raising it out of the water, tipping it slightly, rinsing off most of the mud, and leaving the rock fragments. He picks the two-inch chunks out by hand, tosses them aside, submerges the pan again, swirls and jostles it for another twenty seconds, and tips it once more, permitting the circular movement of water in the pan to wash some of the gravel up its four-inch edge, and out. At this stage any large, nugget-sized gold would be visible among the stone. Any fine gold particles, due to their weight and small size, would be sifted down close to the bottom of the three-inch layer of sand and gravel still in the pan.

The process is repeated several times, taking seven or eight minutes in all. Near the end, all that remains in the pan is a fraction of an inch of fine black sand. Ben swirls more gently, tips the pan cautiously and frequently, spilling out only a teaspoon or so of sand with each tip. Twenty or thirty mosquitoes swarm about Ben's hands, and another hundred or so alight on his back, attempting to drive their prods through the coveralls.

Ben now points a thick brown finger into the pan. In one edge of the bottom there are five or six flecks of pure gold. "Colors," Marion says. Another swirl, another tip, and only the gold remains. Ben picks out the flakes and holds them up in his hand. They stand out sharply against his dark palm. The largest piece is three-sixteenths of an inch across. The others are one-eighth inch or less. None is thicker than a matchbook cover. Two or three dollars' worth, Marion tells me.

I am excited, and Ben and Marion laugh at my excitement. It somehow seems incredible that some peculiar combination of geologic events in past eons has sprinkled the gravel beneath this muddy flat with the world's most precious metal, and that we should now be standing here witnessing the subtle outcome of events that took place thousands or millions of years before.

I mention this to Marion, and she nods and looks off in the distance. "Yes," she says. "And how did anything get here?"

Ben digs into the bank and fills another panful, smaller than the other, begins to pan again.

"Jack, did I show you that mastodon tooth and the tusk in the living room?" Marion asks. "Well, this is where we found them, just a little way down the creek. Now you tell me how they got here? Was the climate different, and why? Was there a sudden shift in our poles? You know, some of those tropical mammals were found in this century in northern Russia, frozen stiff, with grass still in their mouths."

I nod. "Yes, I've heard that. I just don't know."

"You see, Ben," Marion says, now addressing her remarks to him, "that was Velikovsky's theory. That there was a great tidal wave, which may have created conditions very much like the flood we read about in the Bible. Or some other natural cataclysm."

"Ya," Ben says, concentrating on the pan. He reaches up with a big hand to brush away a mosquito from his neck.

When Ben gets the second pan half done, he hands it to me. I squat down near the water and try it for a while. It is not as difficult as I thought, though I alternate between spilling too much from the pan and not spilling enough. The mosquitoes are maddening. In my stationary position, they alight on my back and arms and face. After two or three minutes I back away, cursing.

Marion and Ben laugh. "You'll never make a miner, Jack," Marion says. She takes the pan and finishes quickly, finding another few flakes of gold.

We walk back toward the truck, occasionally sinking in muck above our ankles. I am again reminded of the upheaval caused by the search for gold, and ask Marion how she can reconcile her operation with her affection for the natural world.

"I don't try to reconcile them," she says. "I don't like this mess any more than you do. But I'll point out to you that we don't do nearly the damage that dredges do. And we don't add any chemical junk to the ore like they do in some kinds of mining. We don't poison the water and soil."

"Have you ever considered quitting and going into something else?"

"No," she says. "There wouldn't be much sense in that. I have all this money invested in equipment. Anyway, I like mining. Maybe I was a miner in a former life or something. But I do think miners have a responsibility to put some heart into it." She waves her hand at the bulldozed valley. "We do intend to clean all this up and level it off when we're through . . . and you have to put things in perspective. In the Yukon, you know, it's always been this way. Mining is our only industry. And it's such a big place that I suppose nobody ever worried about damage. But if the government would sponsor some sort of cleanup program, we'd be glad to follow it. Well, maybe I'll do it on my own, anyway."

It is late afternoon. We all get in the truck to go back to the house.

"I knew you wouldn't like what we do to the land," Marion says pensively. "Stewart's wife didn't like it either. She's well versed in ecology because she was studying to be a biologist, and she was sure that we were ruining everything. She was adamant about it. She didn't think we ought to be mining at all, even though Stewart was mining himself."

I recall Marion's earlier comment on the family nature of her operation. I wonder if that is wishful thinking?

"But you know," she says, "I told her that all we were doing really was hastening the processes of nature. You see that little flower over there? Well, 's spreading its roots. And what is it spreading m in? Soil. And what happens when miners dig up the rocks and break them? It makes soil. And soil provides a medium for plants. And animals eat plants, and we eat animals." She pauses. "We're not really ruining the land, we're actually freeing the rock to advance to a higher state."

"A higher state?"

"Yes. Right. The rock is actually more content when it is brought up from the ground for some purpose and used. And it is relieved to be free and in motion, instead of underground and inert."

"Do you really believe that?"

"I'm sure you know of these recent experiments that show that plants have feelings and that they respond sympathetically to human emotions? Well, I suspect that in years to come we will find a similar phenomenon with regard to rocks and other inert objects. It was always my thought that the earth was in a more peaceful state when it was serving a human function, and I was very pleased recently to find a confirmation of that thought—or a parallel thought—in two different sources. One is Dr. Rudolf Steiner, a scientist and philosopher. He founded the Waldorf Schools in Germany. And the other was Max Heindel, a Rosicrucian. He wrote the *Cosmo-Conception.* Do you know that book?"

"I think I saw it on your shelf."

"Well, I'll show it to you when we get back to the house."

We drive back. At the house Marion fixes us a supper of chicken and dumplings and homemade bread. Ben retires early—about eight o'clock—but Marion and I continue talking.

She takes down the Heindel book—the *Rosicrucian Cosmo-Conception*—published by a London firm, and quotes the mystic author's words on mining:

> It might be supposed that mining operations would be very painful to the earth, but the reverse is the case. Every disintegration of the hard crust causes a sensation of relief and every solidification is a source of pain. Where a mountain torrent washes away the soil and carries it toward the plains, the earth feels freer. Where the disintegrated matter is again deposited, as in a bar outside the mouth of a great river, there is a corresponding sense of uneasiness.

"So you see . . ." Marion says.

I realize that I do not really understand what makes Marion tick. My primary impression is, simply, that she is an unusually intelligent and compassionate person. At the same time, I do not know how these mystical notions fit into her personality. The best I can do is to attribute such things to the Yukon air. I say something of the sort to her.

Marion laughs, but then wrinkles her brow and becomes serious. "Well," she says, "that's what worries me. I don't want to come out sounding like some kind of nut. It's better, around here, to just keep your business and your thoughts to yourself. I don't need any more strange looks in town than I've already got. You probably know that a lot of the miners here spend all their spare time in the saloons. Some of them stay there until they fall off the stool. But if I want to spend my time talking to the wind or something, then I'm different and weird. It's like they said about an old miner over here when he died. They said: 'You know, he was sort of strange. He read books.'"

We both laugh. "If it's any consolation," I say, "you're no weirder than a lot of the people I've met around here."

Marion smiles pensively. "I know what you mean," she says. "I guess we really are a little weird, aren't we? The thing I can never decide is whether we're weird when we come here, or whether we get that way once we're here awhile." She thinks a moment, then shrugs. "Probably both."

It is early August before I see Marion again. On the way out to her place I stop for a few minutes along the road and watch one of the miners down on Hunker Creek using his sluice box, bulldozing rock and soil into its upper end. Another man is alongside the box, removing some of the larger rocks that are pushed into it. A large hose hooked to an engine-powered pump sprays water over the material in the box, washing a stream of mud into the creek. These particles of stone and earth, I think to myself, will remain in a positive state of mind until they reach the delta at the mouth of the Yukon River, off the Alaskan coast, whence they will again become unhappy as they settle to the floor of the Pacific.

I go on up the road. It is overcast today, warmer than during my June visit, with a gray still sky overhead. The snow is gone and the alder and poplar leaves are green. In another month, there will be new snow. In two or three places adjacent to the creek, large segments of the twelve-foot road width

are washed away. The road crew has put small red flags on both sides of these holes, and I slow down and pass far to the side. At the summit, I see a fresh set of truck tracks leading from the direction of Dominion toward Quartz Creek. There is little enough traffic on this road, so these tracks could well be Marion and crew, headed to their other claims. I hope not.

It is 10:00 A.M. when I arrive at Ballerat Mines. Marion is there, dressed in sneakers, jeans, and a blue-and-white-checked blouse. It is good to see her. We have our cup of tea and chat about things that have happened since June, about the people I've visited, about the frost on July first, about the two-week washout of the Alaska Highway—which Marion says occurred when Venus squared the sun. Marion tells me that her sons Stewart and Craig are here, as well as Stewart's wife, Judy, and Ben's children, Josephine and Diane.

I ask if the operation has fared well so far.

"Oh yes. Things have been happening around here this summer," she says. "Stewart has brought us good luck, just as I thought he would."

"You've been doing well then?"

"Not terribly well, but well enough. You should see those boys lifting the rocks out of that sluice box. I never could have done that. They've been a big help."

"Has Stewart's wife been helping too? Is she still opposed to the mining?"

"Yes, she has been helping some," Marion says. "I haven't talked to her about her thoughts on mining these days, but I guess they need the money, so they're willing to do it. But I don't know if Stewart wants to continue mining. I guess probably he doesn't know either. Craig wants to continue though. It's good to have one in the family who wants to go on."

"And how's Ben?"

"He's fine," Marion says a little hesitantly. "This may be his last year with us though."

"That's too bad. How come?"

"Oh, he has lots of opportunities to work elsewhere, you know." She looks out the window. "He's out working on the truck now. Everybody else is asleep. The boys went out moose hunting last night and they didn't come in until eight o'clock this morning. So I don't know if they'll be doing any work today. But I've got a lot of work to do here. You can help me with that. And later I'll show you what we've done at the cut."

We finish our tea, then go out back of the house where Marion is working alone on the final series of processes involved in gold collection. I had thought that sluicing was the end process—or almost the end process—and I mention this to Marion.

She laughs. "Not for me. Of course not every miner goes through all I do. The mint will take it with quite a bit of sand mixed in and not dock you for it. But as a woman I feel I have to do a little better than that. My gold is clean. The gold broker said it's the cleanest he's ever seen. He says he doesn't even bother to check its purity; he just rebags it and sends it on to Walter Knott."

In the back, Marion shows me a sort of miniature sluice-box arrangement—a wooden trough about eight feet long, one foot wide, and four inches deep, set up at a 45° angle. The bottom of the trough is lined with an old household carpet and has a diamond-shaped wire mesh over the carpet. The mesh is coarser near the lower end of the trough than near the top and serves the same function as the steps in the full-sized sluice box—capturing the gold flakes, while letting the lighter gravel and sand particles wash over it and out the bottom. A length of old fire hose is attached at the top of the trough to wash over the material.

Around this contraption are a dozen or so water pails of fine gravel and sand that have been collected from the sluice box. Marion has already run several of these pailfuls through the wooden trough this summer and runs some more through while I watch. Looking in the pails, I cannot see any gold. But when Marion dumps one of them into the trough's upper end and turns on the water, a profusion of gold flakes sparkles in the water, washes down the trough, and settles on the faded green carpet, catching behind the rusted iron mesh.

It seems peculiar to me that the planet's most precious metal is being collected by this crude gadget in Marion Schmidt's backyard. I had anticipated, I think, that the final stages of gold collection would involve some sort of sophisticated machinery—or in Marion's case, maybe some sort of mystical process.

When a quantity of gold has collected, Marion lifts the mesh, scrapes the gold and remaining sand off the carpet with a tablespoon, deposits it in a gold pan, and carries it into a back room of the house. There are several of these pans here, each containing a mixture of fine black sand and gold. Now Marion pours an inch or two of water into the pan and begins a modified panning process. She gently swirls the pan, spilling out the lighter black sand over the edge and into a waste container. She continues this for several minutes, then, with the pan tipped, takes the metal lid from a Kraft mayonnaise jar, sticks a small magnet to its bottom side, and moves this device rapidly over the mixture of gold and sand. The black sand has a high iron content and clings to the magnetized mayonnaise lid in long black strands. Periodically, Marion pulls the magnet from the lid, letting the sand drop into the waste container.

"I don't know what that stuff is," Marion says. "I guess it must be magnetite or something like that."

With most of the sand removed, the remaining gold-sand mixture is spread out in the pan and left to dry in the warm room. Several other pans of this mixture are already dry, and Marion takes one of them into the kitchen, where she deposits its contents in a cylindrical, five-tiered brass sieve, about ten inches high and eight inches in diameter. She then works the material through the sieve, occasionally passing the magnet over each tier. The Formica kitchen table on which she works has a gold-fleck design, and before beginning the sifting process she spreads white sheets of paper over the table, so that any escaped gold will be visible. She removes the larger pieces of gold that remain in the upper tier and puts them in a small plastic bottle. These pieces are too large for Knott's Berry Farm. She will sell them to jewelers or to other individual buyers.

After she has gone over each layer of the sieve with the magnet, she empties their contents—one to two tablespoons at a time—into a shallow copper pan that is about ten inches long and tapers in width from eight inches to four inches. The pan has a one-inch lip surrounding its three longest sides; the four-inch side is open. Marion spreads the gold-sand out in the pan, then holds the pan up to her mouth and blows gently into it, blowing the black sand out the open end, while the heavy gold remains in the pan. She puffs for a minute or two, inspects the remaining mixture with a ten-power magnifying glass, goes over it with a magnet, blows again. It is a tedious operation. But it's gold.

We hear a car on the road. Marion puts the pan down quickly and hurries to the window. The car goes by.

"I don't like to have visitors when I do this," she says.

It now occurs to me that any time after mid-August, every Yukon gold miner probably has several thousand dollars in gold—either pure or mixed with sand—sitting around his camp. I ask Marion if she has ever had any trouble with thieves. She hasn't. I ask her then how she gets her gold from Dawson down to her broker in the south, whether she sends it through a bank, mails it, ships it by plane or truck, or maybe even drives it down herself.

"Well," Marion says hesitantly, "we can't very well mail it because only a hundred dollars' worth can go by insured mail at any one time. You can use the bank. That's the safest. But of course they always take their cut. . . . Let's just say we use whatever way suits us best. I'd rather leave it at that."

Marion continues with her gold-blowing for forty-five minutes or so: puff, puff, poke with a finger, examine with the glass, go over with a mag-

net, puff again. Periodically, she puts the beautiful separated gold in a plastic bag and puts this in a white cotton sack.

As I watch, it occurs to me that an inordinate amount of sweat goes into every ounce of gold. It occurs to me too that there is a certain human craziness associated with this precious metal. Gold, as metal, does have a number of practical uses. But its value to man does not come so much from its utility as from its scarcity and beauty, and most of its historic uses derive from that. Some is used for jewelry, for adornment. Marion's gets scattered around the premises of Knott's Berry Farm. Most of the planet's gold is cast into bars and is stored in a vault somewhere. It is bought and sold by speculators who may never see it, never touch it, and whose only real use for the metal is to have a valuable substance to speculate upon. It is used by nations as a backing for the currency they issue and for the international debts they owe, and thus serves only as an IOU, a function that could be performed equally well by a slip of paper. Humanity has faith in gold, but that faith seems almost a mystical one.

Marion's face is red from her blowing. She stops for a rest.

"See, Jack, I do this for hours and days on end until I'm weak in the head."

Ben's two children now get up and come into the kitchen. They are pretty kids, half Indian and half Norwegian. Marion puts some lunch on the stove for them. They go over and look at the pile of gold and sand.

"When the poplar leaves are all golden in the autumn, they fall on the black earth and they look like that," Marion says to them. "Don't play with it, dear," she adds as Diane pokes her finger into the pile.

I ask how much gold they have collected thus far this summer. Marion says that there will be more, soon, since they have been sluicing only about one week, but at this point, they have twenty troy ounces.

"That doesn't sound like much to me."

"No it isn't," Marion says, sighing. "It's only a tiny little bit. It's pitiful almost."

It is now past one. We have some lunch and check to see if Marion's sons plan to work on the creek today.

Stewart and Judy stay in a little cottage near the

equipment shed, and we go down there. They are an attractive couple, both dark, looking a little like American Indians or gypsies. Stewart wears a sheepskin vest and a green turbanlike cloth over his hair. Judy has a colorful Indian headband. But their most noticeable characteristic—today—is their coolness to both Marion and me. They are polite but distant, and anxious to see us leave. No work today.

We then find Craig in the equipment shed. Marion attempts to introduce us, but Craig does not introduce readily. He turns his head as we come in and stands facing the wall as Marion tries to persuade him to turn around. She gives up after a minute or so, and we walk back uphill. She laughs uneasily. "Well, what can I say? That's my boy."

"Did I make him do that?"

"No," Marion says. "He's that way sometimes."

"I guess I don't understand."

"I don't either," Marion says. "Lately it's like walking on eggshells around here. But I guess that's my karma."

We drive the two miles over to the cut. Lobelia and a visiting Siberian husky hop in the truck and balance on the toolbox. On the way, Marion tells me of a day, earlier in the summer, when she, Ben, and Craig were plagued with mechanical breakdowns—a leaking gas line, broken radiator hose, a loss of power in one vehicle—while trying to transport the sluice box and water pumps from Quartz Creek.

"I think it might've had something to do with road gnomes," she says.

At the cut things look much as they did before, except that more earth has been removed and more machinery is now collected here—two water pumps, three bulldozers, hoses, the sluice box. It seems strange to see this collection of machinery with no one working it. I ask Marion if it is unusual for placer miners to miss a day of work during their short summer season.

"We used to work seven days a week," she says. "But now I'm trying to take it easier. The Bible says to rest one day out of seven, and I don't really care which day that is."

We walk alongside the creek. Marion points out the pile of large rocks alongside the sluice box and again says that she could not have managed the operation without the boys. She also shows me a hillock in the middle of the cut that has not been bulldozed. "There's an old miner's shaft in there," she says. "We didn't know it was there when you were here. Once we discovered it, we didn't even bother to strip it. My husband never did drillings right here. But if he had he would have found muck right on top of bedrock. Those old miners got out every bit of the gravel."

She sighs. "We've had a bad year, Jack. The only place I can make any money is where man hasn't been," she says. "And where hasn't he been? Look over here." She laughs. "See this wall of dirt? Craig had it pushed right against the bank, and it was keeping the creek from eating away at the bank. That's no good, because there's still money in there and we want to get at it. Ben and he fought over it. But Ben was right. Finally Stewart took the Cat and pushed it back out here again, where it should be. But that took a lot of time and fuel."

"Is there much friction on the job?"

"Well, Craig and Ben can't seem to get along. But that's only natural, 'cause Ben is a Cancer and Craig is a Pisces. I try not to interfere too much," she adds, "because I don't want to absorb anybody else's karma."

I laugh. "Marion, you have a mystical explanation for everything."

She laughs too. "Well, why not? Things behave according to some set of laws, and if it explains the situation, why not?"

We walk away from the cut and back toward the truck. The profession of gold mining seems far less romantic to me now than it did at the time of my first visit. It is primarily hard work coupled with considerable economic risk and complicated by the difficulty of maintaining some sort of productive interaction among a small group of human personalities thrown together for the summer. It would be devastating for most people, I decide, to spend even a month on a Yukon placer mine, with the same few faces, the same mud and rock and lonesome wind. I am reminded now of the several times I have overheard gold mine owners on repeat visits to Dawson saloons in an attempt to recruit a new cook or Cat operator to replace someone who has wandered off the job.

I am reminded too that people exposed to the peculiar life of a Klondike placer miner can be expected to evolve peculiar adaptations to it. I decide that while Marion has avoided the most common

25

and destructive adaptation—excessive drinking—she has nevertheless evolved her own coping mechanism: a mystical interpretation of life's experiences—especially problems, frictions—that enables her to keep their reality at a distance. This, I decide, is probably the source of her happy rock hypothesis and road gnomes and her ready acceptance of karmic destiny. I tentatively mention some of these thoughts to her.

She smiles quietly. "So you think I'm some sort of harmless kook?"

"No. Not at all. I just think I would be inclined to accept more straightforward explanations for things. Not ones based on mystical philosophies. Or the stars."

Marion is not annoyed, but seems saddened by my comment. "Well," she says, "I just wish you could spend a summer out here looking for gold and see if you changed your mind any."

"On the contrary," I say somewhat smugly, "I think that might help confirm my point. I think I

would probably develop my own peculiarities. They might not be mystical, but they'd be something."

While we stand there chatting near the creek, we hear two people talking, somewhere between us and the main road. We listen for a minute, then continue talking, hearing the voices come closer, with the people still out of sight behind one of the big gravel piles 150 yards uphill.

"I wonder who that is," Marion says.

"Stewart and Judy?"

Marion shakes her head. "That's not their voices. And we would have seen them approach on the road." She points uphill. She's right. The little-traveled main road, 350 yards away, is visible; we would have seen and heard a car approaching from either direction. And the bulldozer road that leads downhill to where we stand is also visible, save for its middle stretches.

I pay closer attention to the voices now. I can catch an occasional laugh or word or phrase—an "I think" or a "Let's see"—but cannot make out what the conversation is about. The dogs hear them too. They prick up their ears and the four of us stand staring at a spot, about a hundred yards away, waiting for the people to appear. We wait for two or three minutes, while the distant conversation continues, now fading out, now coming back, sounding something like an automobile radio.

"It must be somebody on foot," I say. "They're right there behind that gravel pile."

"I think maybe it's the voices of the stream," Marion says thoughtfully.

I laugh. "Good God, Marion. What's that?"

She shrugs. "Just the voices of the stream. If you want to know about them, ask Gus and Nellie Burgelman. They hear them a lot."

"You mean like ghosts?"

"Well, don't forget," Marion says, "there were a lot of people living in this valley seventy years ago. Miners. Mounties. Two brothels. The works."

"And now they're spooking around? Baloney. That's no ghost we hear. It's two people."

"Okay, it's people. Do you want to take a look up there?"

We get in the truck and quickly ride the distance to the sound, following the bulldozer road and keeping our eyes on the big gravel pile. But there is no one behind the pile. The voices have ceased now.

"Let's look around all the piles," I suggest.

"Probably it's somebody hiking along and they heard us coming and got scared they were going to be thrown off."

"I've never seen anybody on foot out here," Marion says.

We drive among the mounds of gravel, covering every location that we could not see from our former position. Twice I get out of the truck and climb atop high rock piles. Anyone attempting to hide, or walking away, would be easily visible. This is weird. We look for ten to fifteen minutes and even drive back to the creek.

Finally we give up and ride uphill to the main road. Alongside the road there is a falling, abandoned telephone pole, one from the old Dominion line. Two broken wires hang from its single crossarm, and I wonder if a passing radio wave could have somehow been picked up by these wires and transmitted to us for a period of five or six minutes. But at the same time, I remember that no radio reception reaches this valley; my car radio loses the signal from Dawson—the closest transmission point—two miles out of town, thirty-four miles from here. And the voices did not come from here anyway; they were 200 yards closer to the creek. With no wind, we couldn't have mistaken their location.

"How many cars a day go by on this road?" I ask.

"Oh, three or four," Marion says calmly.

"Then somebody could have parked here, walked downhill, got out for a few minutes, talked, and walked back, right?"

Marion smiles. "Weren't we looking at the road?"

"Yeah. You're right. . . . What was it then?"

"Well, I don't want to tell you what you heard. You said it was people. That's probably what it was."

"But where did they go? This place is wide open. We would've seen them."

"That's right."

"Well then, how do you explain it?"

"I already told you."

This is insane.

"Okay," I say. "Let's forget about it. What was it we were talking about?"

Marion laughs. "Gold mining, I suppose. But I don't know what else to say about it, except that I have to get back to the house to make supper for some miners, if any of them come to eat. You're invited, if you want."

"No. I'd better get back to Dawson. I think maybe I've been here too long already."

Marion laughs again. She drives me back to my vehicle at the house. We hug each other and I set off on the road toward town, taking the curves slowly, thinking about the oddities of gold miners, and keeping an eye out for road gnomes.

KASKAWULSH

IN THE COLD sunlight of late afternoon, the mountains look raw and lifeless. In another three weeks, the patches of spring snow will be gone from their peaks and their brown lower slopes will bloom with wild flowers. But now, in mid-June, the eastern rim of the St. Elias Range holds neither the sterile bright beauty of winter nor the friendly color of the Yukon's brief summer.

One mile ahead, the silty Slims River emerges from the range, crosses under the Alaska Highway, and empties east into Kluane Lake. A west wind, from the mountains, blows gray clouds of dust down the river's mud flats and across the highway. We turn left off the road and drive back into the foothills, following the original—now abandoned—route of the Alaska Highway. The narrow dirt track winds upward among the willows. Beside it are discarded fuel drums, the remains of road construction cabins, and the rusted bodies, chassis, and engine blocks of trucks abandoned by the U.S. Army Corps of Engineers as they hurriedly slashed this road across the Yukon wilderness in 1942 as a supply route to American troops stationed in Alaska.

The St. Elias Range, in the Yukon's southwest corner and overlapping into Alaska, is a young one as mountains go, less than twenty million years old, and contains some of the highest peaks in North America, notably 19,850-foot Mt. Logan, seventy miles within the range. The range is also the site of relatively recent volcanic activity: About fifteen hundred years ago, geologists say, one or more of its peaks erupted, spreading volcanic ash several hundred miles from its cone. This gray ash can still be seen, and I have seen it, just beneath the surface layer of soil within the road cut along the highway between Whitehorse and Dawson. The mountains' eastern edge, where we are now, is sparsely vegetated with spruce, poplar, willows, and alder. But its central core is forever locked in ice. The high mountain peaks intercept most of the precipitation moving inland from the Pacific coast; the interior Yukon remains dry, almost arid in places, while the St. Elias Mountains form glaciers. Its glacial fields are exceeded only by those at the two polar ice caps. Nothing lives there, save for a dozen or so glaciologists who are flown in for several weeks each summer by the Arctic Institute to a research station on Mt. Logan.

Our hike, for the next few days, will take Paul and me to the snout, the nearest edge, of the Kaskawulsh Glacier, the source of the Slims River, about

29

fifteen river miles within the mountains. The trip has no specific aim. But I feel drawn by the trip, by the glacier at the far end of the Slims River valley, as if that ice mass held some secret, some knowledge, some frozen mystery wrapped in snow clouds. I have never seen a glacier. I do not know what that secret is, but I know it is something we can find only by going there.

Andy Williams, director of the Arctic Institute, drives Paul and me to the end of the overgrown road and drops us one mile uphill from the Slims. We put on our packs and continue southwest, angling slowly toward the river, walking toward the place where its valley narrows and funnels back into the mountains. It is strangely quiet. We see no birds or ground squirrels, not even a grasshopper. A cold, brown, 6,500-foot peak rises to our left. Its lower slope is dotted with white spruce. To our right and below us, the two-mile width of the Slims delta stretches across the valley floor and rises into terraced and treeless brown foothills on the opposite shore. Here, the tortuous, sluggish river occupies only a small fraction of the valley's total width. In its lifetime, the Slims has deposited so much material that it must now wander about its mud flats, seeking out new paths as the old ones are blocked by its own silt and sand.

We pass through a quarter mile of eight-foot-high balsam poplars and stop at the near edge of a talus slope strewn with boulders and rocks from the peak to our left. The boulder field is a half mile wide and extends four to five hundred yards up the mountain slope. Nothing grows on its gray surface. Just above us, a half-dozen thirty-foot spruce trees lie broken by the falling rock. We sit on one of the boulders and plan our route. We finish some cookies baked by Paul's wife, Marie, two days before and three thousand miles to the southeast.

Since the Kaskawulsh Glacier is the source of the Slims, all we need do to reach it is remain within the valley, somewhere between the rows of 7,500-foot peaks that line both sides of the river. But there are no trails here, and it is not clear whether we should angle down to the river and follow its bed or parallel it from our present position, three quarters of a mile up the valley's southeast slope.

Through the glasses, the mud flats seem to offer the easiest walking, though it also appears that we will have to pick a winding course among the braids of the river, which unpredictably appear and then disappear back into the mud, across the full width of the valley. The uphill route offers the most direct path, but we will have to travel through the evergreens and will have to climb and descend the many ridges that run down the mountain slopes to river level. In either case, it appears that the fifteen-mile direct-route hike could easily extend to twenty or twenty-five. We finally opt for the river route simply because it offers the easiest going—downhill—for the next half hour or so. We angle down across the boulder field, stepping carefully and heading toward the tip of a finger of spruce that protrudes out into the mud flats. Above us, an unseen boulder breaks loose and briefly rattles down the slope. The silent dust clouds move along the river valley. The open end of a metal tent pole protruding from my pack makes a low moaning sound as the wind blows across it.

Now, about halfway across the boulder field, I wonder what brought these rocks here to rest. Water and gravity, obviously. But where is the water now? We have not come upon any stream, and

30

looking up at the peak above, I cannot detect any water falling from it. Perhaps, like the Slims River, the water has deposited so much material that it has crowded itself out of its own bed and now flows, unseen by us, on the far side of the fan. At the same time, I fantasize that this raw landscape may not yet be completed. Perhaps these mountains, these lumps of rock, have only recently been flung down upon the earth and await the finishing touches—birds, mammals, fertile soil, water—which will be added during later days of creation.

But I am quickly proven wrong, at least about the water. Without first hearing its sound, we suddenly come upon a cold, fast, and silty stream, twenty feet wide and a foot deep. It is sunk down ten feet into the rock it has deposited; the noise of its water, apparently, is muffled within this channel. We take off our boots and wade.

At the bottom of the slope, we round the spruce point and go out onto the mud flats. At the edge of the flats, where the mountain slope meets the valley bottom, there are hundreds of standing, dead black spruce, their trunks buried two feet in the firm brown mud. I wonder about this. Has this mud been deposited by a slide from above? Or has this two-foot thickness been deposited throughout the valley, during the short lifetime of these trees? If the latter, we must be standing atop an incredibly thick layer of mud, washed down from the mountains and accumulated in the valley since this river was born. The St. Elias Range is a young one, but because of the steepness of its peaks and the lack of stabilizing vegetation in this cold Yukon environment, it is wearing away at a rapid rate, washing into Kluane Lake, the Yukon River, and the Pacific.

Paul now calls my attention to another aspect of the mud—a footprint. Rather, a set of footprints, probably a half day old, along the spruce-covered shoreline. The hind foot is longer than my hiking boot. The forefoot is rounded, five to six inches across, with the marks of long curved claws extending another two inches beyond the foot. We quickly change our route, move away from the shoreline, and continue our walk two hundred yards out on the mud flats. There is animal life here after all.

On our hurried walk toward the center of the valley, Paul has suggestions: "Iff he approaches, ve chust talking quietly, and not run avay." And a few strides farther: "Ve lie faze down. Even iff he turns you over, ve continue to play dead."

By eight o'clock the valley is in shadow. The wind has reversed and now blows dust clouds upriver, back into the mountains. The cream-colored sun rests upon the jagged horizon across the river. It will disappear only a few hours tonight. We could travel all night if we wished; there will be enough light. But we are tired from the walk and from the long bus ride from Whitehorse this morning, and begin to look for a camping spot. We round a mile-long bend in the river and head toward a patch of willows on the shoreline. There is water there, a five-foot-wide stream coming out of the spruces, bubbling through the gravel and winding through the mud until it reaches the Slims, half a mile out in the valley.

As we approach the willows, I sing "The Teddy Bears' Picnic" as loudly as I can, to warn any grizzlies of our approach. We throw down our packs and set up camp. Paul finds enough standing dead spruce to build a fire; I set up the tent in the only place I can find that is dry enough to sleep in, yet soft enough to take the pegs, back in the organic edge of the spruce forest. We hang the food items in a ten-foot spruce a safe bear distance from the tent.

We drink tea and eat bannock fried in lard. It is warm and tastes good. The mountains across the river are black now, silhouetted by the glow behind them. The flame of our fire is warm and comforting. I walk to the little stream, fifty feet away, and refill the pot with silty water for more tea. The pot's bottom is already coated with black gummy pitch from the spruce. Over our second cup, we discuss our plans for tomorrow. We look at the map. We now notice that the broad mud flats in this portion of the river have changed location since the map was made several decades ago. So have the tributary streams. The map shows the first stream we crossed emptying into the Slims a half mile northeast of where it now joins. There's nothing reliable about this country.

At eleven, we take a few pictures of the still-light horizon. The moon is up. From this position, for the first time, we can see our destination, the three black mountains at the end of the valley, near the terminus of the glacier, still a dozen or more miles away. The moon casts a strange blue light upon these mountains, upon the white cloud around their peaks, and upon the white snow that streams down their flanks. Whatever waits for us up there waits in that eerie whiteness.

I awake at five. It is chilly, probably around 40°, and I go to the stream for some tea water.

But the stream is gone. Its gray silty bed is there and damp, but not a drop of water flows where, six hours before, there was a brook five feet across and six inches deep. Perhaps, somewhere up the mountainside, a rockslide or a fallen tree has blocked the stream and altered its course. Or perhaps I was right in my original supposition that this primitive landscape is not yet complete. Things are still being worked out. I walk a hundred yards downriver and find the trickle of another small brook and fill our teapot.

But we have bigger worries than disappearing streams. The day is a gray one. Clouds enclose the tops of the mountains on both sides of the river, and rain feels close. I now remember hearing at the Arctic Institute that yesterday's sunny weather was unusual. I urge Paul out of his sleeping bag. Over a hurried breakfast, we sort out our gear to lighten each of our packs by seven or eight pounds; we cache two pots, a pair of sneakers, some sugar and flour and lard, and a can of halvah in a nylon sack and hang it in a nearby spruce tree. In an hour and a half we are under way, with more bannock in our bellies. The clouds sink lower in the valley. The air is heavy and wet.

The Slims River valley narrows from two miles to one in its middle reaches. Instead of following the shoreline, we follow a straight-line course across the mud flats, aiming from the spruce point on which our camp was located to the tip of the next point that protrudes out into the valley, three miles upriver. We move along rapidly. But after an hour of travel, a braid of the river—which we did not see from camp—loops in our path, and we are forced to choose between wading through two feet of water and heading back in toward the shoreline. The thought of wet trousers—which would never dry on a day like this—is less appealing than the loss of time involved in changing our route, and we go toward shore, heading toward a low rocky cliff four hundred yards away.

But at shore, we encounter a hundred-yard-wide marsh between us and the cliff. Slim stalks of marsh grass and bog cotton grow up through a foot of water. From the middle of the valley, this looked like dry grassy ground; we have worked ourselves onto a neck of land from which we must retreat, or wade a hundred yards through water and mud. We retreat, going back downriver a quarter of a mile, to a point where we can walk from the mud flats onto the shore and then to higher ground.

We now stay a quarter mile up the mountain slope, crossing a broad alluvial fan, passing through a two-hundred-yard-wide patch of white spruce, then climbing the east side of a long, fingerlike ridge running from a fogged-in peak on our left down to river level. Once, on the climb, a piece of sod gives way beneath my boot; I fall on my left side and slide ten feet down the slope. I kick at the mountain. Near the crest of the ridge, we stop briefly to rest and to look at the map. But with the country socked in by fog, we cannot correlate the map with any landmarks. We know only that we are two to three miles upriver from our last night's camp, wherever that was.

A light rain begins. We put away the map and cross the ridge. On its west side, it falls away steeply into a large marsh. And the marsh indents deeply into the base of the mountain. To skirt it, we will have to detour three quarters of a mile to the left. Either that, or go back down the ridge a quarter mile to the river and out on the mud flats again. We head for the flats—taking long slippery downhill strides through the grass, pushing through the now wet spruce—and at valley's edge discover that we are perched upon the same fifty-foot rock ledge we tried to reach forty-five minutes ago. We now have the choice of descending the ledge and wading through the hundred-yard marsh or following the ledge a half mile upstream, in the hope that it will make a dry connection with the mud flats. This seems unlikely, but we naturally choose this route, holding on to the hope that we will not have to slog through the water. We walk along the ledge top. The rain increases. My glasses fog over. The landscape that yesterday looked open and promising today looks sodden and inhospitable.

I remember now, from the map, that none of the mountain peaks or other landmarks here are named. In another frame of mind I would applaud the freedom, the lack of human presence and control, implied by this fact. But at the moment, it occurs to me only that if I am unfortunate enough to perish here, my obituary will be imprecise. What will it read? "The intrepid mountaineer met death within the muddy gulley beneath the brown peak, next to the rotten log near the small patch of soapberry"?

The cliff offers no dry connection with the mud

flats. We walk to its end, but cannot make it down the sheer, fifty-foot face of the rock. We walk back a hundred yards to a place where folds and chinks in the rock create a ten-inch-wide discontinuous ledge that we can safely descend. Belly against the rock and holding on with both hands stretched over our heads, we go down this shelf to river level. There, we step off onto a heavy clay soil topped with a foot of stagnant, oily-surfaced water. Our boots sink in and make hungry sucking sounds with each step. I detour around a ten-foot-wide patch of rust-colored ooze emitting from a crack in the clay. Briefly, for distraction, I pretend to myself that I am interested in bog cotton—this unusual little green-spiked marsh plant with thumb-sized cotton bolls at its tip—but my act is transparent; right now, I would trade the Yukon's entire crop of bog cotton and a fifty-dollar bill to spend the night in a Howard Johnson's motel.

Back on dry mud, the walking is easy. But now the rain is coming full force. We stop and get out our rubberized ponchos, but after a half hour of walking in these airless garments, we are wet with perspiration. We round a gravelly point and head for a patch of high, level ground on the river's south bank, where some tall spruces provide shelter. Our immediate comfort is irrelevant now; we are soaked through and our boots are filled with clay. Our sleeping bags, tent, and extra clothes are still dry, but they will not stay dry much longer; the water is just beginning to soak through the sides of my waterproof pack. To reach the high ground, we wade a hundred yards through another marsh. It is easy this time, now that we are already drenched.

The place we stop is a grassy level space, thirty feet above river level and maybe sixty feet across, containing thirty or so white spruce trees, facing the marsh and the river and backed by the slope of the mountain. We drop our packs on the ground beneath the spruces and stand for a minute to rest, before starting the series of chores that must be performed to make this place livable, at least for the time being. We spread out the rain fly on the ground and unload the entire contents of both packs upon it, separating the dry items from the wet. We change our wet clothing, dry out our packs with a towel, replace the dry items, and hang the wet ones —including my sleeping bag and both sets of clothing—on a nylon rope stretched between two trees. We then search the ground beneath the spruces for dead and dry wood. We saw up the trunk of a felled, five-inch-thick spruce and find—by counting the annual rings—that it is eighty-eight years old. Things grow slowly here. We also break a few dead limbs from the lower level of live standing trees. Normally, I don't like this. But this is not normal, I tell myself, and I rip away at the limbs with gusto, bringing showers of raindrops down on my head. Like most people, my aesthetic standards, my sympathies for the natural world, seem to crumble as soon as I am confronted with a situation that I can define as a challenge, or an emergency.

I remember now that a portion of this St. Elias region—save for the extensive areas gerrymandered out by local mining interests—is about to become the Yukon's first national park, Kluane Park. I wonder what the place will look like once its visitation has increased from the present dozen or so hikers per summer to several hundred. It occurs to me that the real friends of nature, of wilderness, are not the ones—like us—who get out and muck through it, but the ones who sit at home and read Thoreau.

Building the fire is a joint project. Since its success is so vital to both our futures, neither of us quite trusts the other to do it. I hold the handful of tiny, bent spruce boughs, and Paul puts the match to them. It catches, sizzles, and flames. I thrust the handful of burning twigs down beneath the half-inch sticks that we have leaned against a soggy log lying in the middle of the clearing. There is a moment of worry as the fire transfers from the twigs to the sticks. Then it takes. When the half-inch sticks are burning, we slowly add the other wood we have gathered, even using wet branches that will be dried by the time the flame is ready to ignite them. I scramble down the thirty-foot bank and get water from the marsh. When I get back up to the clearing I notice I have scooped up a hellgrammite in the teapot.

The rain gets harder for a time, nearly puts the fire out, and we shield it with our bodies. Then the rain lets up; we bring our wet possessions from beneath the spruces and drape them upon limbs of the dead log that protrude over the fire. The clothing steams as it heats. Now that we are stationary, mosquitoes cluster about us. We stand close to the smoking fire in the hope that they will be repelled by it; it doesn't seem to have any influence.

We stay here for six hours, waiting, drying, retreating under the spruces with our gear as the rain increases, coming back out when it stops, turning our drying sleeping bags and trousers, shirts, underwear, socks, and boots, swatting at the mosquitoes, adding more wood to the fire, picking up the teapot when it spills and blowing life back into the fire, eating—more out of boredom than out of hunger—watching the clouds move upriver, hoping it will clear. We try to busy ourselves with chores, and do not talk much. The top of one of my heavy wool socks catches fire and I yank it away. My body is sticky and uncomfortable from the dried sweat, but there is no really good place to wash, except in the oily water of the marsh. We stand, squat, and pace. There is no dry place to sit down and nothing dry to lean against. I take a few notes, but soon tire of it from a standing position. There is nothing to do except refill ourselves with tea, bannock, oats, and raisins, and wait.

In a search for more wood, Paul discovers a half-dozen five-inch spruce trunks—fifty feet from our clearing—that were cut by a man, or men, using a blunt inefficient instrument. From the looks of the cut marks it appears that each stroke of the cutting instrument penetrated the wood only a quarter of an inch or so. A Boy Scout could have done better. We examine the cuts carefully. In a warmer environment, where the growth of fungi, lichens, and other decay-promoting organisms is rapid, these trees—by their looks—could have been cut as recently as twenty years ago. But here, the land of two-month summers, we estimate that this work was done several decades ago, perhaps as much as eighty or ninety years ago. Given the apparent age and inefficiency of the cuts, we can only conclude that these trees were cut sometime near the turn of the century by an Indian, perhaps using a stone ax. This leads us to speculate that the little patch of flatland we are on, notched back into the mountain with a good supply of firewood, protection from the rear, and an overlook of the river, has probably been a stopping, camping spot for centuries, used by Indians who came back in here to hunt for moose or caribou or mountain sheep, to trap (not to fish, because the mucky Slims River has few if any fish of catchable size), or maybe simply to travel, as we are now, to search for some ill-defined something at the end of the valley and the beginning of the ice.

By four o'clock the rain has almost stopped, and we begin to see mountain peaks through brief patches in the clouds. We throw our gear together, pack our dried clothes, and slosh off through the marsh and out onto the mud flats. Our spirits lift, now that we are walking, progressing, again. With the objectivity of a changed mood, I wonder about my impatience with the six-hour delay, with the inactivity the country imposed upon us. How might a primitive Yukon hunter have reacted to such a situation? Would he have grown impatient or would he simply have flopped under a spruce and slept it out? For that matter, would he even have had a concept of "wasted time," except as imposed by the needs of his belly? And would the wetness and sweat and dirt and mosquitoes have bothered him as they did us? Our discomfort, after all, only exists by contrast with the hot meal, dry clothes, and warm, wooden shelter we know we would have if we were back at the Alaska Highway and the Arctic Institute. If we were stone age hunters, without access to such luxuries, it might be a different story.

I decide that the next time I am rained on, stung, shut in by weather, I will try to be cool and play it as a savage. I will take considered, reasonable steps to protect against the weather, and will then curl up in my caribou hide and ignore it.

We walk close to the sandy shoreline now. In this stretch of the river, the shore is made of black sand, ground out of the mountains by ice, water, rock against rock. It is mounded in low grass-covered dunes whose beachlike appearance reminds me of the ones along the Atlantic Coast. The clouds continue to hang in the air, about halfway up the mountains on both sides of us. We can see only a few hundred yards ahead. In the sand we see the tracks of two wolves and the track of a moose, sunk far down in the earth.

We walk for two and a half hours before the rain hits again. The clearing was never complete, and the sky has closed up again. We increase our speed, looking for a shelter, but there are no spruces here. The ground behind the beach is gently sloping—too poorly drained for white spruce—and contains only willows and a few clumps of eight-foot poplars. The rain comes harder, and we jog across the beach and back under a larger-than-average poplar whose branches and emerging summer leaves offer some shelter. There is nothing better around, and we quickly set up the tent and its rain fly, tying the ropes to rocks, poplar seedlings, a nearby rotten log. We crawl inside without bothering to gather firewood, trying not to think about the tracks of two grizzlies, one quite fresh, we had spotted on our run from the beach. They had come from an opening in the willows that seemed to mark a path, a trail frequently used by wildlife, less than eighty feet from where we pitch the tent. But our desire to stay dry is more immediate than our fear of a passing bear. We draw our packs in after us and close the mosquito flap. It is seven o'clock now. This will be our place for the night. The water from the wet grass begins to come up through the floor of our tent.

After three quarters of an hour, the rain lets up for a time, and we get some silty water from a nearby stream, gather wet wood, and cook some tea and bannock. The greasy balls of white flour look sodden and gray in the pan, as if they have become part of the landscape. They feel leaden in my stomach. A light, rainlike mist falls as we eat but, accommodatingly, does not turn to rain until we have cleaned our dishes. A hard wind blows from the river. We leave the fire smoldering as we crawl back in the tent.

Despite a hard day, we cannot go to sleep. We lie awake for two hours, talking some, speculating on how far we are from the Kaskawulsh Glacier, squashing mosquitoes that have somehow made it inside our shelter, and, after a corner of the rain fly blows loose, worrying when the first drops of rain will work themselves through the surface of our tent.

We wake early again next morning. Through the orange haze of the tent we cannot tell what the sky is like, but the rain has stopped. While we lie there, we twice hear a faraway rumble—once on our side of the valley, once on the far side—very much like the sound of a distant jet plane. But it is not a jet: The noise does not change location; and while its early stages are a steady, ripping, jetlike sound, this pattern then gives way to a discontinuous series of booms and lighter clicking noises, echoing throughout the valley and lasting as much as forty to fifty seconds each time. The second time the noise occurs, we identify it—a boulder avalanche, heavy at first with many rocks moving, then stopping, with only a few large rocks continuing down the slope in long bounds.

I unzip the mosquito flap and perform the contortions necessary to get out of the little tent without knocking over the front ridgepole or stepping on Paul's head. A little water-filled indentation in the ground next to the tent is covered with a skim of ice, and a cold wind comes from the direction of the glacier. But the weather is clear, or at least

clearing. The air has a drying-out, poststorm feeling, and most of the sky is blue. We are in sort of a big bowl here, near the end of the valley where its level floor has widened out into a roughly circular shape surrounded by jagged brown peaks. Looking up at those peaks I see a new white powder; what was rain down here was snow up there.

And the glacier is there, visible, at the head of the valley, the great mass of ice sprawling from the base of the mountains to the southwest. At this hour of the morning the sun has not reached the glacier and it has a gray look, but the snowy peaks of the mountains surrounding it are touched by a strange white light that seems to come from within them.

I am surprised that we are so close to the glacier. I estimate that it is about two miles away, though it could be slightly closer. It is hard to tell: The valley between us and the ice is level and treeless, strewn with rocks and low mounds of earth, nothing that provides a sense of proportion or distance. We must have covered more ground yesterday than I thought. I duck back into the tent, tell Paul, and get the binoculars.

We take our time with breakfast. The glacier is close enough that we can reach it easily, and it is nice to savor this thought, and the sight, at a distance. We gather the needed firewood—for supper, when we get back, as well as for tomorrow's breakfast —and build a neat, efficient fire. Today Paul mixes raisins with the bannock and it tastes good. While we eat, a whisky jack lights on the ground a few feet from our fire and we toss him (or her) pieces of our pancakes.

We do not get started until about ten-thirty. We take only one pack, carrying the glasses, Paul's cameras, a notebook, a length of nylon rope, the teapot and frying pan, enough food for lunch and some hard chocolate for a snack, in case we don't get back before five o'clock. A shallow braid of the river flows near our camp and we walk south, along the curving shoreline, to reach a place where we can leap across, from gravel bar to gravel bar. According to our old map, another river joins the Slims from the southeast, somewhere within this basin. Due to a river's constantly changing paths within this mud flat terrain, we are not sure just where this junction will occur, but we expect to cross the tributary river sometime during this morning's walk. Nor can we tell, from the map, just where the Slims emits from the Kaskawulsh Glacier. Hopefully we will not have to wade it. We set off across the gravelly mud flats, heading for the northwest edge of the glacier's snout.

I look at the rocks we are walking over. Many are brightly colored—red, white, black, green. I pick up a white one that looks like chalk and scratch it across the surface of another; it *is* chalk, or at least has a high chalk content. I pick up another one, smooth and polished by water. It has alternating, colorful layers of pale green, dark green, and black, and is clearly of sedimentary origin. It is strange to think of the material in the peaks that surround us as having once lain on the floor of a sea, then being uplifted into this range, and now, finally, being broken down and carried out to the sea again.

It is chilly, but the sun is in our faces and warms us. Paul stops many times to take pictures of the patches of cloud around the peaks. While he works, I look at the glacier through the glasses. The sun is on it now and its long white body curves in a south-westerly direction back into the mountains and out of sight. The Kaskawulsh Glacier's total length, I remember, is almost forty miles. It's width varies from two to four miles. The farther back it goes, the whiter it is, until, at the base of the farthest visible mountain, it blends with the snow-covered slopes above it. Just now, the glacier is framed within a ring of clouds. That frame is the dividing line between the brown, earth-exposed, seasonal portions of the St. Elias Mountains and the interior regions that are perpetually white and frozen.

The glacier's closest portions are dark, and are apparently topped by many years' accumulation of dust, dirt, and rocks that have either fallen onto it or have been plucked by it from the surrounding mountains or rooted up from the valleys between them and moved down toward the Slims valley by the plastic flow of the big block of ice.

At this distance I cannot tell the precise location of the glacier's snout, but I can see a large black and wet-looking pile of what appears to be rock and earth just this side of the last strip of white, and assume that this is its terminal moraine. Its snout should be just behind. Between us and this pile are several other parallel but discontinuous piles of brown earth and rock which seem to be past terminal moraines, formed as the glacier retreated, in stages, melting and dropping the load of material embedded in the ice.

As we walk along, clouds alternately form and dissipate in the valley. The glacier is temporarily shut off from view. Maybe the rain is not quite done. We stop for a minute to discuss this possibility. If we get another storm, we will not get a decent look at the glacier, even if we walk right up to its face. And Paul will not get any pictures. We decide to go on. Even if it clouds over now, it may clear by the time we reach the ice.

But when will we reach it? It is past noon. Even at our slow, picture-taking pace we must have covered at least two miles, and if our original estimate of the glacier's distance from camp is correct, we should now be there, or almost there. Yet, as far as we can judge, the glacier seems only slightly closer than it did when we left. There is only one possibility: Our original estimate was wrong. Because of the clear air, our lack of experience with Yukon mountain perspective, or some combination of the two, we have grossly miscalculated the distance of the glacier from camp. We revise it upward to five miles.

We walk on across the flats and come to the outer moraines, these loose collections of earth and rock raised fifty feet above the level surface of the valley. The first ones we come to are the oldest, and some of them have begun to sprout vegetation, even a tree or two. At one-thirty we climb upon one of the moraines to eat some lunch and look around. As we poke our heads over its top, my eye catches a movement on a neighboring moraine, a hundred yards away. We stop abruptly and look. A big brown bird, with a windspread of six to seven feet, dives from a branch of a twenty-foot spruce tree, flaps its wings once, and disappears below the horizon of the moraine. The bird is in sight for only two to three seconds, but that is enough to identify it. A golden eagle. Its nest must be over there somewhere. It is tempting to go over and look, but we don't. This is one of the continent's rarest creatures. Not so rare in the Yukon as farther south, but still very scarce. It seems peculiar to me that this majestic bird should make its home on one of these unpretentious little mounds of earth. But what drew it here, I suppose, is the very undesirability of the place, in human eyes.

The moraine we stop on has many ground squirrel burrows, and one of these little brown animals stands erect and looks at us as we build our fire. From the top of the moraine, we discover that the main body of the Slims River is between us and the glacier, running parallel to its forward edge. We have been aiming toward the glacier's northwest corner, now about a mile and a half away, hoping we could get around the water that way, but we now see that we will have to wade if we continue in this direction. We will walk to the river after lunch, see if it is wadable, follow it back to the southeast if it is not. We begin to worry a little whether or not we will reach the ice.

The clouds are gone. We rest in the sun and drink tea and eat oats and raisins and brown sugar. We get our water from a small clear blue pool that has formed in the gravel of the moraine. This is the first clear water source we have encountered on this trip. After lunch we move on without taking time to rinse our few dishes. I realize now that because of our misjudgment of the glacier's distance, we will be returning to camp later than I thought, and I wish we had brought more food. A deceitful country.

We reach the riverbank thirty minutes after leaving the moraine. The Slims here is a light gray-brown color, only sixty yards across, but fast-moving, with two-foot bouncing waves. We discuss the possibility of wading. Because of the lack of vegetation here there are no sticks or poles along the riverbank and we cannot measure its depth. Paul guesses five to six feet; I guess a little less. I pick up a five-inch rock and toss it out into the middle. The heavy rock strikes the surface and is abruptly snatched along by the current before it sinks out of sight. Too fast. We turn left and go upriver, hoping to find a safer spot.

The Slims angles closer to the glacier and leads us back in among a mazelike clustering of moraines. We walk along the loose sides of the moraines and upon the level, cracked plates of hardened mud between them, unable to see the river for more than a hundred yards or so ahead because of the mounds of earth and rock. It is slow walking. Feeder streams enter the Slims from the glacier side. Even though we follow the river back toward its source, it does not seem to get any smaller. I suddenly remember that we did not cross the tributary river in our morning walk, as we expected. Maybe this is it. If so, there is no reason to expect it to get significantly smaller. And if so, we will not get across to the ice.

By four o'clock we have paralleled the width of the glacier's forward edge and are only a half mile from its southeast corner. I am again tempted to wade. We go down to the edge of the river. I stick my hand in to test the temperature and now notice that the fast-flowing brown water is saturated with tiny, quarter-inch fragments of ice. "It vould numb

you in seconds," Paul warns. He's right. We decide to go on through the moraines for another half hour before turning back to camp.

The river angles sharply to the right and goes out of sight behind a hundred-yard moraine. We walk around the other side of the long pile of earth. It takes us only five minutes, and when we reach its opposite end, the river has vanished. Only a twenty-foot stream remains of its original width. We look upstream and see that it leads directly to the southeast corner of the glacier, only a hundred yards away. We jog up the stream, and in ten minutes are alongside the glacier.

It takes us a few minutes to figure out what happened. Apparently the river we have been following is in fact the Slims, not its tributary, and apparently the Slims has quickly veered back under the glacier to its source of melting ice. But what happened to the tributary? Where did it go? Why didn't we have to cross it? We can't explain that. Maybe our map was sloppily made. Maybe we are

reading it wrongly. Or maybe things have changed enough, here at the snout of this powerful, ever-moving block of ice, to render our old map inaccurate.

We sit down, ten feet from the glacier, on the slope of the ridge that rises steeply behind us. Now that we are here, we don't know just what to do. But for the time being, it is enough just to relax and look. The glacier here at its tip rises fifty feet above us and shuts off the sun. We do not know if its bottom is at our level or whether it extends another fifty feet down into the earth. It is overlain by a thick black layer of wet earth and stone, with gray ice showing through only where the glacier's vertical slope has shed this coating. Its appearance—though on a much larger scale—is very much like three-day-old soot-covered snow that gathers along the curbs in Manhattan.

The little stream we followed here roars up out of the ground immediately alongside the glacier, shooting five feet into the air before obeying the laws of gravity and settling down into an earthbound stream. Its force seems to indicate that a far greater volume of water lies compressed under the glacier, seeking escape wherever a block of ice or a chunk of earth gives way. The stream is forty feet wide where it comes out of the ground, but it abruptly splits, and half its water rushes back under the glacier while the other half runs around its edge and out onto the flats. A six-foot-thick and twenty-foot-wide ice bridge arcs up over this stream, joining the ridge behind us with the glacier. Undoubtedly, in winter, the increased weight and volume of accumulated snow and ice at the tip of the glacier completely closes up this little notch between the glacier and the adjacent ridge.

Earlier, I had pictured walking onto the solid ice of the glacier from a mountain slope above it, but now, due to the space between the glacier and the ridge that parallels it, I can see that this is impossible. Besides, it is late, five o'clock. To walk far enough into the mountains to reach a point where we could safely step out onto the glacier would take another two hours. Then another two hours back, and two to three hours more to reach camp. No, too late. Especially if anything happened.

But climbing onto the glacier via its melting snout does not appeal to us either. This is structurally the weakest part of the glacier, undercut by the melting cavity and by the several streams that form the Slims River. How thick is the ice above this

moving water? Forty feet? Ten inches? And are there other crevasses in the glacier's top, camouflaged by a thin layer of ice and mud? We realize that we should have gotten some advice on glacial travel before we set out.

We decide to try it. We tie the fifty-foot nylon rope around our waists. I walk across the ice bridge first, since I am twenty pounds lighter than Paul. Then he comes. A washtub-sized chunk of ice falls—not from the arc of the bridge but from its side—as he crosses. We watch it drop into the stream and go under the glacier. "I don't tsink ziss iss safe," Paul says. But despite that sentiment, he begins to walk up the sloping, mud- and rock-covered nose of the glacier. I follow a few feet behind. Walking in this mud is like walking in thin oatmeal; the stuff goes over my boots and oozes inside. Beneath my feet, the pebbles and mud slip downward on the ice, so that I lose three quarters of the distance I gain with each step. We bend forward to keep our balance and go twenty feet up the snout. Ahead, suddenly, Paul makes a subdued "oh" sound and quickly begins to back down the slope, sliding his boots through the mud. I look up. Above him I see a ten-foot square of the mud and rock—probably loosened from its precarious hold on surrounding mud by the disturbance of Paul's feet—sliding down toward us, ever so slowly. And at the point of Paul's highest ascent, I see some of this oozing muck dropping into a small opening in the ice. I can't tell whether this hole opens down into the depths of the glacier or whether it is simply a broken skin over an air bubble, with fifty feet of solid ice beneath. But it doesn't make any difference. I turn and leap the four downhill strides out of the muck and run across the ice bridge, with Paul right behind me. Our glaciology is done.

Back on the other side of the stream, we elect to climb three hundred feet up the spine of the ridge behind us and get our look at the glacier from there. Even this is a hairy business. The ridge is so sharp that we can keep one foot on its east slope and one foot on its west as we climb up. As we ascend, rocks dislodge from the west slope, rattle down, and drop into the stream alongside the glacier. If you started to roll here you wouldn't stop. But we make it up without mishap, and find a six-foot-square patch of level ground near the top, with small patches of purple vetch and blue lupine growing in it. We flop down and look out over the Kaskawulsh Glacier.

I see now that the first half mile or so of the glacier is covered with the black muck. We have a view probably eight or ten miles back into the mountains. The glacier arcs throughout this length, following the contours of the valley in which it lies, curving among the bases of the mountains, with the dark streaks of the debris it has collected through the decades accenting the curvature. Overall, its form very much resembles an equal volume of water poured into the valley forty miles away: thicker at its rear edge, flowing around the solid obstacles it encounters, gradually thinning as it comes this way, and finally ending in a tapered snout. On its southern edge, we see other, smaller, unnamed rivers of ice—which would probably qualify as individual glaciers in a less ice-filled place—feeding into the Kaskawulsh. It is an enormous thing. Making all sorts of assumptions—length forty miles, average width three miles, average thickness two hundred feet—I try to come up with a weight for this monster. I arrive at the figure of twenty trillion tons.

Maybe my arithmetic is wrong.

We stay on the ridge only a few minutes while Paul takes pictures and I look back along the glacier's length. Somewhere, beneath the calm white surface of the ice, earth and rock are being pulverized, as the Kaskawulsh moves slowly along its path. But from where we sit, the glacier is quiet. It does not reveal its life to our eyes. Ten miles back, a swirl of snow rises up and over a 10,000-foot peak, blown by a silent wind from within the mountains. Nothing else moves.

I feel let down, in a way. I feel we have yet to touch whatever knowledge or secret is held by this collection of ice and rock. To reach it, to get at the heart of it, we would have to go farther, probably somewhere near the point where the Kaskawulsh makes its ponderous arc and curves out of sight behind the base of the farthest mountain.

But we cannot do that today. It is late. We are tired and hungry. We back down the slope and begin the long walk across the mud flats to camp.

FIFTY BELOW

"I COULD SEE these two old Indian people sitting there," Fred says, as he planes down the runners of his dog sled, "right there in the parking lot alongside the saloon in Ross River. It was night. And it was hellish cold, probably fifty or sixty below. I was with a local cabdriver, and I asked him: 'What are those people doing there?'

"And he said: 'Oh, they're just singing. They're singing one of their songs.' He didn't seem too interested. But I thought it was peculiar that they would be sitting outside at fifty below, singing. So I asked him how long they'd been there.

" 'Oh,' he said, 'they've been there quite a while.' It seems that he had been to the saloon two or three times that night, to pick up and deliver passengers, and the two old Indians had been sitting there most of that time, after they'd come out of the saloon. He never went over to investigate."

"Were there other people going in and out of the saloon right along?" I ask.

"Well, I don't know," Fred says. "I was there only a short time. I suppose there must have been."

"Is the cabbie white or Indian?"

"Oh, he's white."

"And the saloon's clientele?"

"Well, you know how it is. The white people live on one side of the road, the Indian people live on the other. It's about fifty-fifty, I'd say. And I guess the saloon's clientele is about the same. Anyway, I told the cabdriver we'd better see if they were okay. We walked over to the two Indians. I could see it was an old man and his wife. And you could tell, for God's sake, that they weren't singing. It wasn't any song! It was just the old man, and he was moaning, moaning, moaning. It was a dirge, if anything. He was grief-stricken. I spoke to the old man but he kept moaning. I spoke to his wife and she didn't move. I felt her face. Then I put my hand inside her coat to feel her heart. She was frozen! Her stomach was as hard as—as plywood!"

"She'd been dead quite awhile then?"

"Sure. Long enough to freeze solid, anyway."

"What about the cabbie? What did he feel, after passing them by two or three times?"

Fred shakes his head, gestures in exasperation, returns to working on his sled. "I don't know. I guess he was sort of shaken up. But it was a little late for that."

41

AN ISLAND

As WE LEAVE the mouth of the Stewart River, our canoe is snatched along by the current of the Yukon and is pressed close to the big river's eastern bank. On our right, the shoreline has been undercut; tipped, forty-foot spruces slant out over the fast-moving gray water. We are cold and wet from the morning's rain and tired from two days' canoe travel. The mile-wide river and its rolling, tree-covered landscape seem monotonous, even hostile.

Now we hear the barking of a dog team, the characteristic sound of riverside settlement; we are getting near the Burians' island. A half mile ahead, on the right, we see a fifty-foot river freight boat and two beached canoes. We dig in with our paddles and a few minutes later slide our own craft in alongside the others, at the foot of a fifteen-foot gravel bank. The Burians, Rudy and Yvonne, are there waiting for us. The dogs have announced our coming. Rudy is a short, wiry, suntanned man, probably in his mid-fifties. He has gray eyes and a thick shock of graying black hair and is wearing a green flannel shirt and black flannel trousers. Yvonne is plump, fair-skinned, dressed in blue slacks and a flowered top. They have met Paul before, and they welcome us warmly.

"The buns are in the oven and the coffee'll be ready in a few minutes," Yvonne announces from the top of the bank, as if she had anticipated our arrival.

"You must've come down the Stewart River," she adds.

"How did you know that?" I ask as we unload the canoe.

"Oh, I would've known it if you'd been on the Yukon," she says confidently. "Did you see signs of anybody else up there?"

"We found a fresh fire pit one night," I say.

This seems to trouble Yvonne. "That's peculiar," she says. "Are you sure it wasn't last year's? I don't know of anybody that's come down the Stewart this spring. You're the first ones."

Again, I am reminded that in the Yukon, one's actions are highly visible, even out here. Yvonne Burian apparently commands an almost complete knowledge of river traffic through her own observation and through information given her by passing boaters.

We scramble up the bank. At the top we can see the extent of the Burians' spread: a blue stuccoed house with red-tiled roof, a half-dozen log cabins,

several storage buildings and wood sheds, a garden and plastic-covered greenhouse, a white clapboard store, a metal Quonset hut, and a dozen or so dog coops—Rudy's team near the river, Yvonne's back of the house—with the occupants lying atop them. The place is neat and trim, set a hundred yards back from the river in a large clearing that is seeded with a close-cut green lawn. Real grass. It impresses me, as it must impress all river travelers, as the Shangri-la of the Yukon bush, an orderly, welcome, and well-kept patch of civilization after days or weeks of river wilderness.

The Burians have been the keepers of this 150-acre island at the junction of the Stewart and Yukon rivers—72 miles upriver from Dawson and 180 miles downriver from Carmacks—for three decades. Yvonne was raised here. Her father was a White Pass agent at a time when the island was a stopping place for commercial river traffic. Rudy came here in 1936 from British Columbia as a wood-cutter for the river steamboats. The island—called Stewart River or, more casually, Stewart City—once held a small RCMP detachment, a post office and government telegraph office, two roadhouses, a Hudson's Bay post, and an essentially transient population of twenty to thirty people. With completion of the Whitehorse-Dawson highway in 1952, river steamboat traffic declined, then ceased. The island was stripped of its economic importance and most of its people moved elsewhere. But the Burians stayed on, purchased existing buildings and raised their five children, worked at trapping and small-scale river freighting—the activities that still provide 90 percent of their income—raised their vegetables, shot their meat, built rental cabins for recreational river users, and continued to carry a few grocery items in the former Bay store.

Today, by bush standards, the Burians' life is a secure one, though that security is sustained by the rigorous life of trapping and freighting and could suddenly be altered by an illness, an accident, even by a drop in the price of fur or a decline in the already small volume of river freight that supports Rudy's summer business. The couple—who have probably spent more time in the bush than any other white couple in the territory—have become something of a tradition in the Yukon, and their insular outpost is an expected stop for almost all of the twelve hundred rafters, canoeists and motorboaters who make the 450-mile river trip from Whitehorse to Dawson each summer. It is an opportunity to see people, to exchange river stories, and to spend some time with this couple who have spent all but one or two months of the last thirty years on an island in the middle reaches of the Yukon River.

We follow Rudy and Yvonne back toward the house. I notice that a barn-sized storage shed near the river is on log runners, and I ask Rudy about it. He explains that this is so it can be pulled back if the river begins to cut away the bank. When he first moved onto the island, he says, Yvonne and he leased ten 50×100-foot lots from the crown. But since then, the ever-shifting Yukon has washed away those lots, taking five of the Burians' cabins as well. In recent years, they have moved their house, the store, and several other buildings back 150 yards or more from the river to their present locations, either by dismantling and reassembling the buildings or by using a bulldozer, cables, and rollers. Rudy speaks casually of this operation, but it occurs to me that it was a monumental undertaking.

I ask Rudy if there is any question about their rights to the land their buildings now rest on—if someone who wanted the land might claim it and be upheld by law.

He smiles. "I'd like to see 'em try to move us out of here," he says. "I'd meet 'em with the thirty-thirty. This is still a free country, you know."

Rudy Burian

While Yvonne goes into the house to look after the coffee, Rudy gives us a brief tour around the property. He has just returned from a four-day freighting job up the river, and it occurs to me that he might rather be relaxing than showing us around. But he seems to have an endless supply of energy and compulsively picks up, sorts, and straightens things as we walk around. He shows us the store, a small log cabin museum of historic river artifacts which the couple maintains free for the interest of passing boaters, a shower they have rigged up by setting four 45-gallon fuel drums on the roof of a tool shed to provide a gravity feed, and a skinning cabin hung with traps, stretching frames, wire snares, and several dried pelts of wolf, lynx, fox, wolverine, and marten. Rudy tells us that he operates a thirty-mile trapline upriver, and in winter spends five of every seven days up there, at a line cabin, tending his three hundred traps. Yvonne runs a line of about fifty traps nearer by, and returns to the house each night to keep the fires going and prevent the place from freezing up.

As Rudy shows us his rental cabins ($2.50 per person per night) he mentions that a while back a couple built their fire ineptly and burned out a wall in one of them.

"You have to watch these city people," he says. "They've never had any experience with stoves, and they'll burn you out if you're not careful."

Last, Rudy shows us the garden. It is large—about half an acre—and lush, one of the few really successful gardens I've seen here. It is planted with lettuce, potatoes, rutabagas, carrots, and beans. In the nearby greenhouse there is a wood stove and about three dozen large tomato and cucumber plants. Most vegetables, he says, are planted directly in the garden as seed, in late May. Tomatoes and cucumbers are started in the house, in winter, then transferred to the greenhouse in April or May. I ask if the garden is often killed by frost.

"No. We just can't let that happen," Rudy says, "or we wouldn't have any vegetables."

I remember now that the nearest grocery is seventy-two river miles away. And that grocery has no fresh vegetables and only a limited selection of wilted ones. The Burians' garden has a more vital function than the ones I have raised, for fun, whenever I had a backyard.

As we head back toward the house, I notice a large number of objects around the property that, back home, would fall into the recreational or part-time or even frivolous categories of human experience, but that are necessary and everyday for the Burians: axes, wedges, saw blades, boat propellors, vises, an anvil, toboggans, snowshoes, dog harnesses, auto and boat batteries, drums of outboard fuel, several huge piles of firewood, Briggs & Stratton engines, a big chain hoist for lifting bear and moose, several hundred pounds of dog feed, several sets of moose antlers, two or three snowmobiles.

From my experience with snowmobiles in the States I have learned to dislike them as wasteful, noisy, and environmentally destructive toys, and I ask Rudy how he feels about them.

He seems surprised at the question. "Well," he says, "the snow toboggans are only good when it's warm. After about forty below, you can't depend on them to start. And the metal on 'em breaks like glass if you bump it with something. One broke down with Robin last winter and he had to walk fifteen miles home. When I want somethin' dependable, I always take the dogs."

A large and whitened grizzly bear skull—probably the most coveted trophy of the North American big-game hunter—rests atop a chopping block near one of the woodsheds. Paul asks who shot the animal.

"I don't remember," Rudy says. "One of us anyway." He pauses to roll a cigarette. "But I don't bother with bears anymore. You can't get anything for 'em. I only shoot 'em if they get in a cabin. But if they don't bother me, I don't bother them." He lights the cigarette. "I don't like to kill anything if there's no need to. I wouldn't kill anything if I didn't have to make a livin'."

Yvonne joins us.

"A couple of years ago," she says, "bears were bringing three hundred dollars apiece. We heard that was because all the hippies wanted fur coats."

We go into the house. On the screened porch are a kerosene refrigerator and a gasoline-powered electric generator. I ask if they use the generator for light in winter. "No," Rudy says. "It's too big. I can't afford the gasoline. We only used it a couple of times and then we went back to kerosene lights. We've got one we use for cuttin' hair and washin' clothes, but that's all we use it for."

Also on the porch are a dozen or so rifles and shotguns, old-model lever-and-bolt actions. The guns, stacked carelessly in one corner, are clearly tools. I ask Rudy what animals they kill, and he says that the family—he and Yvonne and their sons Ivan and Robin, who still live on the island—kills up to eight moose every year, plus an occasional grouse or wolf or bear.

"I don't believe in those big high-powered guns the hunters use," Rudy says. "It costs too much for ammunition. I use a thirty-thirty myself, and if I go through a half box of shells a year, that's a lot." He stops at the woodpile and gets an armload of wood before coming in, stacking the fifteen-inch pieces along his left arm in a pile that reaches over the top of his shoulder and taking one last stick in his free right hand.

Like the rest of the Burians' property, the yellow-painted kitchen is neat and clean. There is a hand pump on the counter next to the sink and an enameled Findlay Condor wood stove. Yvonne opens the oven and removes two pans of cinnamon buns. The smell of the buns and coffee is good, and seems eminently civilized after the diet of bannock and lard that Paul has been fixing for us on the river.

The food is delicious. For a few minutes, we discuss trapping, the kinds of sets to make for different animals. Rudy tells me that last winter he caught forty lynx, ninety-eight marten, twelve foxes, five wolverine, six mink, and two wolves. Yvonne mentions that a wolf will sometimes act tame and friendly when the trapper approaches, thinking, she supposes, that he is about to be set free.

Rudy pounces. "You'd better not put anything like that in your book," he says. "Those damn hypocrites'll read it and the first thing you know they'll be passing a law against trapping." He waves his hand annoyedly. "They got all these city guys in there makin' laws for us," he says. "Most of 'em have never been out of Whitehorse and they got no idea what we need. They push things through even if we don't want 'em. They might better leave the law-making to the old-timers. I heard this spring that now a trapper even needs a permit to build a cabin. Well. You better believe that if I decide to build a cabin I'm not gonna ask those guys about it."

Yvonne questions us again about what and who we saw on our trip down the Stewart, and we mention that we stopped in on Bob and Rosemary Russo.

"They're a hardworking couple," Yvonne says. "They'll make it out here. So will Peter and Mary. But don't give the impression in your book that people can just come out in the bush and live off the land, 'cause they can't! Lately we get all these people coming in here, maybe they've read one of Jack London's stories or some little tourist thing on the Yukon, and they think they're going to become trappers or pan gold or raise millet or some other marvelous thing, and make it big in the bush. Well, comes the first snow, they tuck their tails between their legs and go home to wherever they came from."

"Who *are* most of them? And where do they come from?"

"Most of them are kids," Yvonne says. "They come from all over—Montreal, New York, Edmonton, anyplace down south."

"If any of them think they're gonna make it by trappin', they've got another think comin'," Rudy says. "We've been trappin' for twenty-five years. The last couple of years there's been a rise in the fur price. But you can't depend on it. I made forty-five hundred dollars last year and seven thousand the year before, but before that we barely made enough to buy the dog food. Our trapping income is usually around two or three thousand dollars, and lots of times it's been under a thousand."

He shows me some of his trapping accounts. Lynx are the main money-earning fur, but Rudy points out that the prices he gets for lynx have varied tremendously in the last few years, from a high of $212 down to $44. Last year, the $4,500 year, he sold 40 lynx pelts; but three years back, when he sold 185 lynx pelts, he only grossed $3,300, due to the low price. There are similar variations in the prices for wolf, wolverine, marten, and fox.

I remark that, in general, making money in the bush seems difficult.

"It's not so tough," Rudy says. "If a man is willin' to work, he'll always make out somehow. But a lot of them who are comin' in now aren't willing. They want to scrounge off somebody else. I just don't understand that."

"We got this guy down the road here," Yvonne says. "He was going to be a trapper. Well, all last winter, he caught just one lynx."

"He's too busy sleepin'," Rudy says. "We told him, 'Look, these animals aren't just gonna come in the house to get skinned. You have to go out and get 'em.'" He shakes his head.

I ask about the location of the Burians' neighbors and about the number of young people who have moved into the neighborhood in recent years.

Yvonne tells me that the young neighbors include "Cowboy," forty-five miles up the Yukon River, Peter and Mary Beattie, a few miles farther, Bob and Rosemary, fifty miles up the Stewart, "Custer," nineteen miles downriver, and Roger and Donna Mendelsohn, twenty-five miles or so beyond Custer.

"And they've all come within the last few years," she says. "Then there's John Lammers and the Bradleys, a hundred and ten miles away, up the Pelly, but they've been there a long time."

"Do you feel there are getting to be too many people? Do you think too much of the land is getting taken up?"

"No," Rudy says. "If they want to move out here, that's their business. If they don't bother me, I don't bother them. It's a free country, or supposed to be."

"We don't mind more people out here," Yvonne adds. "Though *some* people in Whitehorse want to keep new people off the river."

"What do you mean, *some?*" I ask.

"Well," she says, "I'm not saying, 'cause you'll know who. But we found out that he had spoken to welfare and put them onto this young couple that used to live out here across the river. Paul, I think you remember that couple. He told 'em that their baby wasn't getting its TB shots and that they should look into it. He didn't really care about the shots. He just thinks nobody should be living on the river except people he approves of. I know that 'cause he once said: 'Don't you think that everybody who lives on the river should be required to register with the mounties?' Anyway, he wanted to get a helicopter in here and fly that couple right out. I was in Dawson and the welfare came to me and asked me if their baby had its TB shot, and I said, 'I don't know. That's not my business. It's a free country. But I do know that I raised *my* five kids out here, and *they* never got any shots.'"

"Did the couple finally move out?" I ask.

"They did," Yvonne says, "but that was because she got a bad toothache. Then they had to go. They got a ride into town on the boat, and they've never come back."

Yvonne pours us more coffee.

"Maybe if we had more people out here," she says, "we'd get our mail service back."

"You had delivery out here? When?"

"When the boats were running we had it all the time," Yvonne says. "And in winter there were enough people that they delivered by dog team twice a month. Then they stopped the dogs and delivered by plane for a while. I used to run the post office. Then they stopped altogether in 1960-something."

She pauses to drink her coffee. "There's all this talk of opening up the Yukon. But they won't do anything for the people who already live here. There's all kinds of people who'd live out here but they don't want them to have land. They want them all to live in the cities."

"There's no telling what those government guys are thinkin'," Rudy says. "They've got to have a say in everything. And they've got to get a few cents on everything that happens. They get fourteen cents on every gallon of gas we buy, and sixteen cents on diesel. They get a little bit on every fur we ship out of the country. What they get doesn't even pay their salaries, but they do it anyway."

"Which government are you talking about? Ottawa or Whitehorse?"

"I don't know," Rudy says annoyedly. "They're all about the same. They don't want to work like regular people. They spend so much time drinkin' coffee that they never get any work done. Now we got three guys down here in forestry and one could do the work. They write reports all winter. They fly a helicopter. Anyplace they have to go, they fly. It's costing a fortune. And what good do they do?"

"There's more fires now than when they came in," Yvonne adds.

"One of these guys from forestry even told me I had to have a permit just to build a brush fire," Rudy continues. "Now I've been burnin' brush for forty years, and this guy wanted me to tell him just when I was gonna burn a pile I had out here. I said maybe I'd build my fire this fall, maybe I'd wait till spring, but I was gonna do it when it suited me. We don't live in Russia, y'know."

I laugh. "You really don't have much use for government, do you?"

Rudy answers angrily, punctuating his remarks with curses that are normally omitted from his conversation. "There's nothin' I want from them!" he says. "Except maybe to help me keep the river from cuttin' my land away here. Otherwise, there's nothin' I give a damn about. We've made out without 'em so far, so I guess we always can. We don't want any favors from anybody, the family and I. I figure the land is for the people, and not to give a lot of soft jobs to those deadbeats. They're a bunch of 'damn leeches, as far as I can see."

I ask Rudy if he doesn't feel that government provides many services that individuals could not provide for themselves—education, health services, communication and transportation networks.

"We educated our kids right here," Yvonne says. "Though it was through correspondence. And one or two of 'em did go outside to high school."

"But that's something I'm not too sure about anyway," Rudy says. "I think we got too many people with education today and they don't want to work with a pick and shovel. Don't get me wrong. I'm not against education. But there aren't enough jobs for the educated ones anyway. I had to go to work when I was twelve, and I was glad to get any job I could. I still am." He pauses, then smiles. "As far as transportation goes, we got our own road right out here." He gestures toward the river. "That's all we use."

"Don't you ever drive to Whitehorse?"

"I only been to Whitehorse three times since I came up here in 1936," Rudy says.

"And what about this Dempster Highway?" Yvonne says. "Why do we need that highway? That's costing a fortune, and it doesn't have any use, does it?"

"How about communications?"

"Well," Yvonne reminds me, "they took our mail service away. All we have now is a radio they gave us."

"And that thing is no good anyway," Rudy says.

"Now wait a minute," Yvonne says. "It's not that bad."

"But how many times could you get through to Whitehorse with that thing last winter?" Rudy says.

"About three times."

"How about something like health care?" I ask. "What happens if you get hurt? Or seriously ill?"

"Knock on wood," Yvonne says. "But nobody in the bush ever seems to get too sick."

"I crushed my fingers once," Rudy volunteers. "I was wearin' floppy gloves and I got 'em caught under the roller when we were movin' the store. It was my own fault."

"And what happened? Were they broken?"

"I don't know," Rudy says. "I never went in. They were cold for a couple of winters, but they're okay now." He rubs one hand with the other.

I start to laugh. I know that if I were to pursue this line of questioning long enough, I would find several ways in which they rely upon government; but at the same time I am impressed by how much one can do for oneself, how much the Burians do for themselves, out here on this wilderness island.

Outside, the dogs begin to bark.

"Somebody's coming," Yvonne announces. She ambles out the door. Paul and I follow her to the riverbank. Rudy seems relieved to get a chance to get outdoors. As we go toward the river, he upends two or three fuel drums near the store and rolls them toward the woodshed. Paul volunteers to help him. "No, no," Rudy says. "You go ahead. I don't need any help."

At the riverbank, we see a red canoe going by a hundred yards offshore. There are three people in it, and the canoe has hoops sticking up from the gunwales, apparently to accommodate some sort of rain tarp. They wave and we wave back, but they do not come ashore.

Yvonne seems truly puzzled. "I wonder why they didn't stop?" she says.

We stand there a minute or two, then turn and walk back toward the house. "I thought it would be that big freighter canoe that Rudy saw yesterday up at Kirkman Creek," she says. "I wonder what happened to them? Maybe they went by already. Or maybe they're just taking it easy."

I remember that while the Burians' guests visit the island in passing, the Burians themselves remain from one season to the next, from one year to the next.

As we walk back, Yvonne comments upon the two horses grazing in the high grass alongside the garden.

"Robin brought them up in the boat two days ago," she says, "but I don't know what he expects to do with them out here. And that mare is eatin' my lilacs! Get out of there!" she yells at the horses, who ignore her. "They've got to be fenced," she says good-naturedly. "But Rudy says he won't build fences."

We are close to the house by this time, and Rudy overhears us.

"I can't stand fences," he agrees. "They always get in your way. If I wanna walk somewhere, I just want to *go* there and not have to worry about climbing over some damn fence."

We have talked so long with the Burians that we decide to stay the night, instead of going on down the river to Dawson. They invite us for supper. We unload our canoe and spend the rest of the afternoon lounging around our cabin. A log raft with four young men—one from British Columbia, two from Illinois, and one from New York—arrives in late afternoon, and Rudy sells them some cigarettes and powdered milk and gives them a tour of the museum before they go on downriver.

It is seven o'clock when we sit down for the supper of moose meat, cooked carrots, dumplings, homemade bread, and a salad from the Burians' garden. It is a more balanced meal than most bush people eat, and we comment on how good it is.

"That's an outside cucumber you're eating there," Yvonne admits.

We talk about cities. Both Rudy and Yvonne express the Yukoner's typical incredulity when I mention that I enjoy living in New York.

"I haven't been in many cities," Rudy says, "but I been in some, and I can't see that any of 'em are worth livin' in. Everything's so busy out there."

"Do you see yourself ever living in a city?" I ask. "Maybe even by necessity?"

"No," Rudy says. "I suppose we might have to move to Dawson someday. But I can't picture myself movin' to Whitehorse. You might as well live outside as live there. There's too many people."

"Everybody's in such a rush," Yvonne adds. "Whitehorse is just about as bad as Vancouver. Nobody knows anybody else. They don't even speak to you. At least in Dawson they'll speak to you on the street, even if they don't know you."

"I wouldn't even go to Dawson," Rudy says. "Except that I have to take a couple loads of fur in every year."

"Don't you ever take a vacation?" I ask.

"I haven't got time for a vacation," Rudy says. "The only time you have is about three weeks around the last of March, after trapping and before you get the gardens and boats ready. Anyway, I don't like to go outside. You can't call that a vacation. We been outside three times since I came here."

"On the other hand," Yvonne interjects, "if somebody offered me a trip around the world, I'd go. The last time we were outside was in '72, and the time before that was back in 1950."

We talk about Rudy's freighting work, and he tells us that his job this week involved hauling several boatloads of rock samples from a mineral exploration camp at Coffee Creek, 45 miles upriver, to

Minto landing, 135 miles upriver, and returning to the camp with helicopter fuel. He made this circuit four times in four days, working from seven in the morning to ten or eleven each night. He mentions that there are a dozen men in the camp, with a helicopter.

"What are they looking for? Copper?"

"I don't know," Rudy says. "I didn't ask. But they're lookin' for somethin' all right." He laughs. "That's one good thing a government did," he says. "The B.C. government put in all those tough mining laws, and it scared all the mining companies into moving up here."

"What's the name of this outfit?"

"Amoco," Rudy says. He pronounces it A-mo-co.

"Is that the American Oil Company? Amoco?"

"I don't know," Rudy says. "Somebody said something like that but I didn't ask. Chuck Frisa is the boss. They seem like a nice outfit."

I suddenly have visions of the Yukon River wilderness giving way to an open pit mine and a new, raw mining town, of the Burians' way of life being wiped out with a swipe of a bulldozer blade.

"You know, if that's the same Amoco, they're one of the biggest corporations in the world. Don't you worry about what a firm that size could do to the country?"

"I never worry about that," Rudy says. " 'Cause that's about all it's good for up here is mining. That's what keeps the country goin'. That's what the Yukon is." He rolls and lights a cigarette. "And the world needs minerals. Of course, I hope they don't export it all. I'd like to see us use some of it ourselves."

It seems strange to hear the independent and hardworking backwoodsman talking like a corporate vice-president. It puzzles me, too, that a man with Rudy's zeal for maintaining the freedom of his lifestyle could have so little concern for the possible existence of a mine near his home.

Yvonne adds a note of reservation. "But on the other hand," she says, "when a mine comes in, the country's done. Just look at those stinking dredge piles around Dawson."

"Yeah," Rudy says. "But in a few years you'll never even see that. It will be just the way it was."

"I don't think so," I say. "Those piles at Dawson have already been there several decades. The land hasn't come back yet. This is pretty fragile country."

"Maybe," Rudy says. "But there's too much land

for it to disappear like it does outside. It might happen someday. But not in our lifetime."

It seems perverse to me for an urbanite to be cautioning an outdoorsman on the extinguishability of the outdoors.

"We've got an ecologist living up the river," Yvonne says. "John Lammers. We've discussed mining some with him. Now I can't agree with his ideas because he doesn't think anything should be done. He's against mining. He doesn't want any trees cut. He doesn't want anything put in the river. He doesn't even want any tourists coming down the river, and he makes his *living* from tourists. He's just too radical."

Rudy nods. "His ideas to me are more or less communistic," he says.

"Communistic?"

"He wants to save everything," Rudy says. "He even believes in suing the government if they do something he doesn't like. He's a nice guy, but he's just too radical in his conservation ideas."

"He wants to have everything his own way," Yvonne volunteers. "He had a little run-in with Occidental Minerals. They were staking his property for mineral claims and he wanted to sue them. He said they were cutting the trees and polluting the river. Well, after all that, a pilot we know flew over there and he told us that John had all his winter's garbage set out on the ice, just before breakup, waiting for it to go into the river! The pilot took pictures of it, he said. And since then we haven't heard any more about John's lawsuit."

"Well," I say, "whether this guy puts his garbage in the river or not, I don't blame him for worrying about having a mine near his place. And I'm surprised that you people aren't worried about the same thing at Coffee Creek. It seems to me that if they made a big mineral find and opened a mine, it would change your whole way of life. You said that you don't even like to go into Whitehorse, because of all the people. Well, a mine would bring in a lot of people. They'd probably build an access road to it, maybe a town. The whole character of this area would change."

"They'd have a tough time building a road along this river," Rudy says. "It would wash out the first spring after it was built."

"There was talk a while back of putting a railroad along here," Yvonne says. "They had some fellows flying over and picking out a route. But we've heard no more of that lately. I don't think they're going to build it."

"If they really wanted a road, they'd find a way to do it. But even if they didn't, just having a mine and a permanent population of four or five hundred men up the river would mean a constant flow of people past here. It would affect your trapping, your hunting, just about everything you do."

"I suppose it might bring in some people we might not like," Rudy says. "But it's a free country. As long as they mind their business, I'll mind mine. And," he adds, "I'd probably get to do the freighting for them."

"Yes," Yvonne says, nodding knowingly, "and then we'd probably get our mail service back. And we might even get electricity."

We talk awhile longer, and go to bed at ten, carrying a pail of water from the Burians' sink and a can of Off to battle mosquitoes in the outdoor toilet.

At eight in the morning we are wakened by the chain-saw-like sound of the power generator and its two-cycle gasoline engine. Yvonne is washing clothes in her electric machine. Rudy is splitting wood. He has already spent two hours in the garden, hoeing potatoes.

We are ready to go. The Burians invite us into their house for coffee and the rest of the cinnamon buns. Rudy tells us that he has made the river trip to Dawson in as little as eight hours but, with our canoe, we will probably take twelve to fourteen hours. They escort us to the riverbank. We all wave as we push off downriver. Paddling is easy in the fast, powerful river. It is a bright sunny day. The silt-and-sand-laden water makes a strange sifting sound as it slides across the canvas-covered hull of the canoe. An eternal sort of sound. We round a broad bend and the Burians' pinpoint of civilization disappears. The shoreline closes in behind us. The big blue-gray river and the soft spruce-covered slopes fill our view, from horizon to horizon.

CABIN FEVER

IT IS LATE, probably about eleven o'clock, when I walk into the Cedar Lounge in Whitehorse. The lounge is part of the Shannon Motel on Jarvis Street, across from the New North Motel and nightclub and three or four blocks from the center of town. There are only two people there when I arrive, a young man seated at the bar and the young waitress perched on a stool behind the bar. They are talking. The place is dimly lit and quiet. At first I wonder if I am interrupting something, but that doesn't seem to be the case; they are talking about the Yukon's high cost of living. I sit down at the bar. From their conversation, I gather that the young man has just come here from southern Canada to work for Whitehorse Copper. He speaks with an Eastern European accent.

The waitress takes my order and fixes me a drink. Then she sits down again, lights a cigarette and continues talking, addressing her remarks now to the two of us. She is an attractive woman, probably about thirty, with dark close-cut hair and angular features. She wears a short, black, sleeveless dress and a gold flake pin.

"When I first came up," she says, "the money was better here. But now they're getting the same wages down south as we are. My friends in Calgary tell me they're making around six hundred a month. And that's at jobs they've been working at for only a couple of years. It's not like they've got a lot of seniority on me. So with prices up here, I figure I can make out better down there now, eh?"

She is probably right, since the cost of living here is about 25 percent higher than in southern Canada.

The young man asks how long she has lived here.

"Six *years!*" she says. She laughs. "I was just going to stay a little while, to earn some money. And here I am, still here." She throws up her arms in a theatrical gesture of exasperation.

"Are you thinking of leaving, then?" I ask.

"Not this year," she says. "But next year, before the snow flies, Shirley will be *gone.*" She makes flapping gestures with her hands near her shoulders.

"What don't you like about it?" the young man says. He asks this, I think, somewhat defensively, perhaps to reassure himself on his recent move to the Yukon.

"There's nothing to do here!" Shirley says. "There's no plays. There's no shows. There's no real events. There's two movies and a library. Big deal!

The one event all winter is the Rendezvous, if you like to stand outside at fifty below and watch sled dogs and backpacking contests. There's really nothing going on. So what are we gonna do this weekend? Go to Faro? To Elsa? To Keno Hill?" She again throws up her arms. "So let's go to Clinton Creek and we can eat with the miners. Wow."

"Do you think most of the other young people up here feel there's not enough to do?" I ask.

"I don't know what they feel. Maybe I've just spent more time here than most of them. Most of them only stay for the summer. Or maybe one winter. But I've been here six years!"

In response to more questions, I learn that Shirley has been married, lived with her husband in Whitehorse, bought property, and is now divorced or separated, living in an apartment. Her divorce, though, does not seem the source of Shirley's cynicism about the Yukon.

"Do you get out in the bush much? Do you like to do things like that?" I ask.

"No. I have horses, and I love to ride them, but I just don't get turned on by the bush, and the cold." She thinks a minute. "You know, I think it's really a man's country up here, eh? We've got a friend here who's a doctor, and he just loves it. He's a real man's man. He's into cross-country skiing and being out in the bush. He's got a four-by-four and he spends the whole weekend driving it around. And you don't have to go very far here, eh? Just a few feet off the road and you're in the bush. But I don't go for that sort of thing. I don't see driving and winching yourself forty miles into the bush just to see more of it!"

"It's beautiful country though," the young man says.

"Sure," Shirley says. "But that flatland down south sure sounds awful good to me, right about now. You know, I can see the same damn mountains in Carmacks as I can see in Whitehorse, or in Ross River, anyplace you want to name up here. It would be different if it weren't *all* mountain. But once you've seen one mountain, you've seen 'em all."

"What can you do in winter?" I ask.

"Not much," she says promptly. "Curling. That's a big thing up here. Or drinking. That's the *really* big thing. You can spend the whole day at it." She shrugs. "But that's about it. I ski some. But up here the snow and the temperature never get together. When it's warm, there's no snow. And when there's snow, it's sixty below. It's too damn uncomfortable. All we have anyway is this little rope tow out beyond town. In Calgary I got used to places like Banff, but there's nothing like that up here."

Some customers come in and sit at one of the tables in the unlighted, rear portion of the lounge. I can hear them but cannot see them. My eyes have become accustomed to the light at the bar. Shirley excuses herself, fills their order, and returns.

"You've heard of cabin fever, eh?" she says, as she puts the change in the register. "Well, that's not just a rumor. It's real. Along about February, the hospital over here is filled with people having mini nervous breakdowns. *Filled.* They stay a few days and go home. It's mostly wives whose husbands are working and they're all alone in the house all day. Don't forget, it's pitch-dark. Maybe they don't have a car or any friends nearby. By February it gets to them and they go off the track." She circles her finger near her temple.

"Did it ever get to you?" I ask.

"I never went bonkers," she says. "But sure, I've seen myself getting bushed. In winter I just want to get out! And every time I go to the airport to see somebody off, I nearly get *hysterical*. You just want to get on that plane and go with them. Well, you can, I suppose. But you can't really, eh? Because you've got a husband, or kids, or a job. You have to stay and stick it out. It's no wonder we have the highest alcohol consumption in Canada, or whatever it is."

"You don't paint a very inviting picture of the place. Why do you suppose most people come up here?"

"I suppose they think it'll be exciting," she says. "I guess that's what we thought." She laughs, remembering. "It was exciting all right. My girl friend and I arrived here with all our things in the car and there wasn't even enough housing to find an apartment. There just *weren't* any. We had to live out of a motel for weeks."

"You said you bought some property up here?"

Shirley nods. "On the Carcross Road," she says. "That was after I got married. We got a hundred and sixty acres. Back in the bush. *Land*. That's another reason people come up here. They hear these stories about homesteading and they come up with all these dreams. Ho-ho. *Let* me tell you about land! When you get here, you find out that it's probably harder to get land here than it is outside. We bought it for five dollars an acre from the government. Okay. That's a good deal, eh? But to get their permission to buy it, we first had to lease it and *improve* it. We spent between twenty-five and thirty thousand on that place! They said we had to clear it. We cleared it, and burned all the brush and trees. It had to have a road to it, just so we could get there. So we got a Cat and built a road. They said we had to build *structures*. We built structures. And a fence, to keep out the moose, or whatever . . ." She gestures in annoyance. "Some bargain! Every year we had it, we went in the hole five thousand dollars."

She pauses and lights a cigarette. "They say that a lot of people come up to see the country, eh? It's this big beautiful landscape and all these friendly people? But I think that's a put-on to get people up here. They really come up for the money. Or because they can't hack it outside."

"Do you think the Yukon attracts a certain kind of person?"

"Losers!" Shirley says. "I think we really get the riffraff of the world up here. Sure, we have some terrific people. But we've got a lot of screwballs too. Divorcees. People running away. People who can't get a job. Most of us are definitely second-rate, in one way or another."

The young man looks hurt.

"With some notable exceptions," Shirley says, smiling at him. "But I mean it. Most of the people here would never make it outside. They're incompetents. They're second-rate. It's hard to find a good mechanic, or an electrician, or whatever. You name it. Nothing works right. Have you ever watched television here? You're lucky if they finish the show! I was watching the other night, and right in the middle of the movie—no explanation—they switch on the news. I thought, okay, they're going to continue it later. But they never did. You let something like that happen outside and you'd be looking for another job. So the very next night I'm watching another movie, and the same thing happens. No explanation. Nobody comes on to say, 'I'm sorry, but due to technical difficulties . . .' So I called up the station and I asked, 'What happened to the second half of that movie? And what happened last night?' And he says, 'Oh, I'm sorry. We never got those tapes from Vancouver.' Can you imagine that happening outside?" She rolls her eyes upward in an exaggerated gesture of contempt.

I start to laugh. I have had my own experiences with Yukon technology.

"And did you ever try to get an operator? I takes ten minutes. You probably came in on the plane," she says to me. "How many dimes did you lose in that phone at the airport before you found out it didn't work?"

I laugh again. I had forgotten that event, a month ago. Apparently it is a tradition. "Three," I tell her.

"And how many of the phones were broken?"

"Just one."

Shirley snorts. "Well they're both broken now. I was up there just the other day."

While we talk of phones, the one on the wall behind the bar rings and Shirley goes to answer it.

The young man asks me where I come from, and I tell him New York.

"Where you don't even know your next-door neighbor," he says sarcastically. I hasten to tell him that I do know most of my neighbors, but he isn't listening. He turns to Shirley, now back from the phone.

"You mean to tell me you'd rather live in a place like *that*, instead of here?"

She cocks her head questioningly. "Where you're anonymous, you mean? I don't know. Right now that sounds pretty good to me. I'd love to live someplace where everybody didn't know me and where I could choose who I want to talk to."

"Is that a problem?" I ask.

She snorts. "A problem? No, it's no problem. If you don't mind living in a goldfish bowl. Everybody knows everything about you. And what they don't know, they make up. And, oh yes. 'Who *was* that you were with last Saturday night?' " She shakes her head. "A couple won't make it up here," she says, "unless they're really together. All these well-meaning friends with nothing to do all winter'll sit around and give you advice, and your relationship is talked all over town. And suppose you don't want to see somebody. Well, you can't avoid them. You run into them on the street or in the drugstore or in the grocery. So you learn how to speak to people you absolutely *detest* and to draw out some little conversation into fifteen minutes. 'Oh. And how are you doing? Some weather, eh? I haven't seen you since Rendezvous. Oh, isn't that nice. . . .' That kind of nonsense."

I observe that, in general, the whole Yukon seems to me like a small town, where everyone knows everyone else.

Shirley nods her head vigorously. "They sure do." She sighs. "It would be nice right about now to be caught in a half-hour traffic jam in downtown Vancouver. It probably sounds silly to you, but I'd just like to see some civilization. Some new people. Some lights. Something. You know, this place—the whole damn Yukon—only has three traffic lights!?"

The young man again rises to the challenge of the city-versus-Yukon issue, says something about urban smog. But Shirley quickly overwhelms him.

"I'm even starting to wonder about that," she says. "They talk about how bad the air is outside, but have you walked on the streets in Whitehorse? In August? Dust? My gosh, you're covered with it. It's all over you, and in your car. And clear water? Beautiful rivers? You turn on your water in the spring and its full of silt. You run a bath and it's gray. There's enough dirt in it to pot a plant! And how about the ice fog? When it gets about forty below, the air in town is full of these little crystals of ice. It's from the cars, and people. It gets in your lungs. And you can't see a damn thing fifteen feet in front of you.

It's pitch-dark. And with that stuff in the air, when I drive to work, I just pray that a pedestrian isn't going to walk out in front of me."

There is a clatter from an adjoining back room. I look up.

"Don't worry," Shirley says. "It's just the ice machine."

I look at the clock. It's late.

"I guess I don't understand why you're still here," I say.

Shirley shrugs and smiles. "I have a couple of things to do yet. And some money to save up. You know how it is. You get attached to people. I'm hoping to be out of here by next fall." She shrugs. "But who knows," she says. "Maybe if you come back in two years, I'll still be here."

MEN

A SMALL BROWN swirl of dust moves ahead of me, spiraling slowly down the road, across the narrow-gauge railroad tracks leading from Elsa shaft, skimming along the ground toward the row of bunk-houses. To my right, swallows dart beneath the eaves of the beer parlor. Their white droppings streak its brown log walls and accumulate on the green wooden bench set in front. Bottle caps, cigarette stubs, small pieces of broken bottles, and the bones from a chicken carcass are embedded in the dry earth alongside the building. It is early afternoon, sunny and quiet. Lunch is over. The night shift is asleep. The day miners are still underground. The store, the coffee shop, beer parlor, mess hall, bank, and pool hall are apparently closed and locked. The place seems deserted, save for an old man, dressed in a T-shirt and brown suit, who sits on the steps of bunkhouse 3, asleep.

One of the ore trucks roars by, heading for the crusher. The driver does not slow down as he approaches. The truck's big wheel passes within two feet of me, covering me and my suitcase with dust.

I go into the camp manager's office in the rear of the cookhouse. The manager is not there, but Horace, the short, fat, moustached assistant chef, fills in for him, gives me two sheets, a pillowcase, and a brown blanket for my cot. He removes the key to room 14, bunkhouse 2, from the pegboard.

"Here's your key to paradise," he says to me.

The company town of Elsa, stuck against the southeast slope of the McQuesten River Valley in the central Yukon, is owned by United Keno Hill Mines, Ltd., in turn owned by Falconbridge Nickel, an international company headquartered in Toronto. Though mining began here early in the century, much of what now exists at Elsa was built in postwar years, after a road, created to service the mine, was built from Whitehorse to Mayo. The mine is Elsa's only reason for being. There are no other businesses or sources of employment. Enterprises such as the food-catering and garbage-removal services, the beer parlor, coffee shop, and grocery store are either owned by the mine or under contract to it and its employees. There is no elected town government; all that happens here is subject to approval, or disapproval, by the mine manager.

United Keno Hill is a lead-zinc-silver mine. Its ore is concentrated in rich, relatively slim underground veins, and several underground shafts have been dug—horizontally and vertically—into sur-

59

rounding hillsides, with secondary curving tunnels branching off to follow specific vein formations. One of these producing shafts—Elsa—opens within the town proper. The other five—Husky, No Cash, Dixie, Keno, and Townsite—are located within a few miles of town.

Of the mine's roughly 300 employees, about 120 are married and live with their families in company houses at the southwest end of town, with the mine manager and other high-level employees generally living farther up the hillside. The 180 or so men who are single, or whose wives are not with them, live in a half-dozen large bunkhouses at the northeast end of town, near the beer parlor, pool hall, coffee shop, and mess hall. Aside from work, and the occasional company softball game, there is little contact between residents at the two ends of town.

Life is drab at Elsa, as it is in all the Yukon's company towns or camps, especially for the "single status" employees. The typical underground worker rises at seven, eats in the mess hall, takes a company bus to his shaft at eight, works till four in the damp, unlit tunnels, showers in the "dry," busses back to town, eats an early dinner, and spends the long evenings ·reading, talking, or, most commonly, drinking in the company beer parlor. A few of the men have cars, but having a car does not give you anyplace to go for a change of atmosphere or social scenery. Whitehorse, the Yukon's one sizable town, is 285 miles to the southwest, too far to drive except for special occasions. Mayo (population 401) and Keno (population 24) are nearby, thirty and ten miles respectively, but going there usually means only another night of drinking, in slightly different surroundings, with other men from the mine. There are no single women in Elsa, except for the occasional nurse, schoolteacher, visitor, or daughter home from college. The drabness and danger of days underground is at least matched by the monotony and frustration of social life aboveground.

The mine, nevertheless, does draw many men, mostly young, mostly from southern Canada, and with a considerable number from Eastern and Western Europe, Australia, New Zealand, and the United States; over twenty languages are spoken here. But most of the men do not stay long, typically less than a year, often less than a month.

Now, beginning my stay in town, I am beginning to wonder if even one week is not too long a time to spend in Elsa.

I carry my gear and blanket to bunkhouse 2, a long low Panabode building, constructed of factory-cut spruce logs. Outside, the building has an attractive, rustic appearance; inside, it is another dormitory, with linoleum floors, a white-tiled community bathroom, and a dim overhead light in the long hallway. From somewhere, a snore. From the bathroom, the sound of a running toilet. Above the fire extinguisher, a strangely worded warning sign from the personnel office:

> Everyone commits mischief who wilfully tampers or renders inoperative any fire or safety device unlawfully, is guilty of an indictable offence, under section 372 of the criminal code of Canada and is liable to imprisonment for five years. United Keno Hill Mines, Ltd.

My room contains a desk, gooseneck lamp, and iron cot. The previous occupant has left a pinup calendar and cartoons—one of a man with his head beneath a woman's skirt, one of a pair of hands reaching up out of a toilet, one of a nude with "start the year with a bang!" printed beneath. Below the pinups, a mimeographed set of "Bunkhouse Rules" threatens that I am responsible for behavior of guests and cleanliness of the room, that I am prohibited from changing rooms, making noise after 11:00, having a firearm, using a hot plate, having a woman in my room, and "harbouring or feeding cats."

The room is hot, about 90°. I throw open the hinged windows and try to shut down the radiator, but its valve handle is missing. I notice now that my predecessor has left a penciled note on the desk: "My last night. July 14. I'm going. I'm never coming back. I been here November 14, 1973. Goodby. Brian Eldridge." The cryptic departure note reminds me of something that might have been left in a cell at Devil's Island. I remain in the room only long enough to throw down my things. Before leaving the bunkhouse, I read a poem inscribed on a toilet door: "Make sure that you stand on the seat, 'cause Elsa crabs can jump six feet."

Outside, there is still no one around. The sleeping old man has vanished. Dust blows across the yard. I walk back to the camp manager's office to report the broken radiator valve. Horace is working in the kitchen.

"They're all broken," he says without looking up from his minestrone. "There's nothing you can do."

"*All* broken? You mean every valve handle in camp is broken?"

No answer.

"You got a pair of pliers then? I can probably get it turned off with them."

"No. No pliers."

"Yeah? How about another room then? It must be ninety in there."

"No more rooms. Nothing you can do."

I stomp away. Horace continues stirring. It does not surprise me, I guess, that he lies easily. What does surprise me, though, is his persistence, when he must know that I know he is lying.

I go back out into the yard. There is nothing to do. I am tempted, almost, to go back in the hot room and sleep, but instead I create a project of walking around to inspect the buildings. I walk across the yard, past a series of gray, numbered buildings with posted No Parking signs—"Authorized parking only," "No parking," "*Positively* no parking"—and back toward the center of town. The town is on stilts: Due to its location on the southeast slope of the valley, the northwest side of most mine buildings, bunkhouses, and homes is supported on concrete or wood pillars. The buildings immediately abut the road, rising up out of the dust. I see few people. I would like to talk to somebody, but there is no excuse I can use. The store, bank, and post office are still closed. I see other signs and mimeographed notices here and there: "Effective immediately, the Elsa Market and the Post Office will be closed every Saturday." "The following Elsa residents are underage and will not be served alcoholic beverages" (a list of names—apparently teen-age children of miners—and birth dates). "Dining Hall to be vacated fifteen minutes after meal hours." "Definitely *no* long distance calls." "Soccer practice tuday, toesday. Meet at coffie shop at 7 PM. Come out and play you lasy bastards!" Near the post office, I overhear a conversation between two young employees:

"How was it outside? Any women?"

"All kinds of fuckin' women. I never saw so many fuckin' women."

"Did you get laid a lot?"

"Oh yeah! I never saw so many fuckin' women. And you know what? The fuckin' barber in Edmonton is a fuckin' fag!"

Edmonton is a big town; what does he mean, *the* barber?

It occurs to me that the beer parlor may now be open for the afternoon. I walk back to the bunkhouse end of town. The beer parlor doesn't open until 7:30. I walk next door, into the lobby of the coffee shop. It doesn't open until 4:30. There is a sign near the door: "Persons who wish to continue the privilege of using this room . . ."

I walk back outside and again debate sleeping the rest of the afternoon. Now, though, I see a young man, long-haired, tall, lanky, sitting on a set of bunkhouse steps. He is alone, not doing anything, so I walk over there and we introduce ourselves. He is Denis Theriault, twenty, from Trois-Rivières, Quebec. He is a loky (locomotive) operator, drives the narrow-gauge underground trains, but has missed today's shift. Denis has sad-looking eyes. He is serious, never smiles, but is talkative, and friendly.

"I came here December twentieth of last year," Denis says. "It was the loneliest bloody Christmas of my life. I quit April sixteenth, and I just came back June eighth."

"How come you came back?"

"I want to work until next summer, and leave here with four or five thousand dollars in my pocket."

"No trouble getting rehired?"

"No. They'll take anybody back. They can't keep people. They'll even pay your plane fare from down south."

"What'll you do once you save up your money?"

"I don't know. I guess I'll go on a trip. Maybe to New Brunswick. Then I'll go home and live with my mother again. I send home money every month. My mom always writes and says, 'Why did you send so much?' But I say 'Look, Ma, go buy a dress. Go out and get drunk. Do something for yourself. You took care of me, now I'll take care of you for a while.' "

I laugh. "That's nice. . . . Did you save up any money from your last time here?"

"From December to April, I earned thirty-six hundred, and I spent twenty-six hundred of it on booze."

"My God! Why so much?"

Denis shrugs. "I don't know. I was lonesome. And that's all there is to do here. There's nothing else to spend money on. But I'm not drinking at all now," he adds.

"Do you like it here at all, or are you just looking forward to the day you leave?"

"I can say I have a pretty full life right now,"

Denis says. "I'm doing what I want. I work and I earn money and I get tired. Sometimes I go crazy. But you get a good night's sleep and it's all better. And it's a beautiful place to get rid of a cold. If I've got a cold, I just go in and ask the shifter [shift boss] to give me something that will make me sweat. You work until you sweat and then you sit down and you're the coldest you've ever been in your life. Then you work again and when you come up you turn on the shower, first the hot and then the cold, and you're all better. You lose it in one day."

"Just what do people do here in their spare time? I mean, I realize that there isn't much to do in a formal or organized sense, but people must have some sort of routine they set for themselves. How about you?"

"Right now, I'm talking to you," Denis says. Then, perhaps feeling that I find this answer too flippant, he says: "You see, if we were outside, sitting on the steps having this discussion, we'd be bored stiff. But here, we're happy to have it. You learn to fill up time. And you have plenty of time to think. Sometimes I like it, but sometimes I go wild. I run around the camp to find somebody to talk to."

I nod, remembering my own earlier desperation to find someone to speak with.

"But you can't talk to everybody," Denis continues. "Like yesterday, I worked with a guy who never talked all day. I finally blurted it out. I said, 'What's the matter with me?! Does my breath smell? Do I stink?' And he just said, 'I don't talk much.' And of course there's a lot of the guys you can't talk to because you don't even speak their language," he adds.

Workers are now returning in buses from the day shift. Denis and I take an ambling walk, back toward the center of town, to kill the time remaining until supper hour. We stroll across the steel tracks leading from the Elsa shaft. On our right two workers, probably in their forties, stand in front of the Elsa dry, the overheated tin building where miners change and shower. One of them picks up a big stone from the ground and throws it at Denis. Not hard, but hard enough to hurt if it hit him. Denis ducks and the stone clangs on the railroad track. The two men laugh and one of them throws another stone, which also misses. I look at Denis.

"What the hell was that for?"

"That's nothing," he says. "They didn't mean it." He seems barely to notice the incident.

"I sometimes try to picture myself with half a million dollars," Denis says. "You know, some of these old miners up here have that much saved up."

"No. Really? It seems to me it would take a lifetime to save that much."

"Well, maybe not a half million. Maybe three hundred thousand. But a good miner can earn a hundred twenty dollars a day. Only the mine manager and the assistant manager make more than that. And there's nothing to spend money on here. So, if you were a miner, it would only take ten or fifteen years to save it, even if you drank up a third of it. By the time you're thirty-five, you could have it. That's what I'd like to work myself into, being a miner, or a miner's helper. They make the real money."

"Is that old for a miner, by the way? Thirty-five?"

"Some of them are in their fifties," Denis says. "But most of them don't last that long. They get that disease in the lungs. Most of them are burned out by the time they're forty-five."

Briefly, I have a vision of Denis, still here at forty or forty-five, working twelve or eighteen months, leaving for three, returning, never really liking it, but trapped in the pattern.

"What do you think you'll do after next summer when your money's gone again?"

"Well, I suppose I might be back."

"Do you really think so?"

Denis doesn't answer.

"Hey," he announces suddenly. "You want to know a little secret? You know where the best drinking water in the place is? Down by the garbage dump. It comes out of a little pipe in the hill. I'll show it to you later, if you want."

"Sure. Okay. . . . You're pretty young to be working here, aren't you?"

"I guess so. But a lot of the guys are just a year or two older than I am."

"How do you like the work? It's dangerous, right?"

Denis nods. "You know Eddie? No? Well, he got buried in a cave-in the other day. It is dangerous all right, but usually not something like that. It's usually that somebody falls off a ladder or gets a rock on their foot when they're standing on the grizzly. But you learn to live with it. I thought I'd die the first time I handled dynamite. But now I do it with a cigarette in my mouth. Do you know Sal the Guinea? Well, I worked with him a little while as a miner's helper, and I used to throw the sticks of dynamite to him when he asked for them. He said, 'My God, Denis, don't do that.' But I just laughed. It's not dangerous. Because when he sets them in the hole, he tamps them anyway."

"Do you ever worry about getting trapped in one of the tunnels?"

"No," Denis says emphatically. "I never let myself think about what would happen if a piece of loose came down on me. It doesn't pay. In fact, I hardly think at all when I'm working. I just sit there on the loky and daydream."

"What do you daydream about?"

"Sometimes about girls. Sometimes about getting stoned. Sometimes about getting out and going home."

Despite his six-foot-four frame, Denis reminds me of a Dickens character, a street urchin somehow displaced from his rightful home and stranded here, within this bizarre world of dangerous underground work and aboveground monotony, his twenty-year-old's spark slowly being extinguished by Elsa's grayness. And as we turn around, head back to the mess hall, and get in line for five o'clock supper —where I have my first chance to see a gathering of Elsa men—I realize that Denis is not unique.

The mess hall is hot and wet, with the moisture rising from the long steam table. It is a large, buff-colored room, pipes overhead, with large, formally framed black-and-white photos of mining operations on the walls and the usual notices stuck here and there ("Effective immediately, use of the river road is restricted to . . . ."). At one end is a sandwich counter, where evening-shift workers are preparing their midnight lunches. Two sticks of butter are set in sauce dishes atop each of the thirty gray Formica tables and are already half melted into a yellow liquid. The young workers, the majority, seem to be seated in one end of the room, four at a table, and the older men—mostly European—have their area, with Hungarian spoken at one table, Polish at another, German, Swedish, and Italian at others. The young men are dressed in jeans, T-shirts, sneakers or work boots. The older men wear dark, wide-legged pants, street shoes, generally more formal, conservative attire, even including a sport coat here and there. There is little laugher or noise in the mess hall. People—even the young men—speak in low voices.

Denis and I heap our trays high. The food is good, plentiful, and free—steak, three vegetables, soup, salad, homemade bread and pie—even though served from a steam table. There is a sign on the milk cooler that, due to the washout of the Alaska Highway, there is no milk this week; the cooler is instead filled with Kool-Aid. We sit at a table and continue our talk.

"You were talking before about getting stoned. Is there much drug use here?"

Denis looks at me and smiles. "Sure, lots of it."

"Hard drugs? Or just pot and stuff like that? And how does it get here?"

"Lots of grass," Denis says. "Some hash. Some STP. A little LSD. There could be hard stuff, but I don't know about it. They could get it just like the other stuff. In Whitehorse. Or they could get it sent in by mail."

"By mail?"

"Sure. You just have on it 'McCleans.' Or 'Sears.' 'Handle with care.' "

"Anybody ever get caught? I imagine they're pretty strict about it around here. I mean, I wouldn't be surprised if they opened mail. And since the work is dangerous, I wouldn't think they'd want anybody going underground high."

"They don't mind if you're high. Ten guys just got fired who were smoking grass in Husky, but it wasn't because they had grass. It was because they were all sitting on the tracks with their head lamps out . . . That's a weird feeling to be high underground, in the dark. Especially on acid!"

I laugh. "I'll bet."

"You're writing a book," Denis says. "You really ought to talk to some of the old miners. Some of them are real characters. There's Pickin' Bill. He's in bunkhouse four. He saves junk—radios, magazines, guns, stereos, rocks, tin cans, anything. His room is so full of junk, he can't close the door. You know what he does? He takes the pins out of the hinges and takes the door off, goes inside, then he sets it back in place. They say he's been here ten years. He stays about two years and then he starts screaming and yelling, and then he goes on holidays for about two months and then he's back, normal as ever."

"Yeah. I can believe it. In general, though, I'm trying to avoid weirdos for this book."

"Then there's Tiny Tim," Denis continues, ignoring me. "You know what he does? Every Friday he goes and gets a big basketful of groceries at the store, just like he was living at home, brings 'em back, and just throws them in the garbage can in the bathroom. We watch him because there's always good things in the garbage can when he comes back—you know, crackers, cheese, lettuce, milk, a couple dozen eggs, a pound of hamburger—we get them out and eat them."

"Good God." I make a note of Tiny Tim. Apparently, from what Denis describes, the man is trying as closely as possible to simulate parts of a normal family life-style, including the weekly shopping routine.

"What do you suppose makes them that way?" I ask Denis.

"Maybe they miss women. No, a lot of these guys are here so long, I think they forgot. You'll see a lot of pinups in our rooms—you know, the young guys—but the old guys don't have any. I think they forgot."

"How about you?"

"That's simple. Whenever I want to get my rocks off, I just go to Mayo."

"And what do you do there?"

"You just check into the hotel for the weekend."

"You mean there are women in Mayo?"

"Sure. You can spend the whole weekend with them there."

I'm not sure I believe Denis. But it doesn't matter.

"Besides, we've got Bunkhouse Betty, and Gloria and Rhea. You heard about them didn't you? They're Indian girls. They live down the road here. They've been in every last room in these bunkhouses. They can tell you what guys are sloppy and what guys have stinky feet and what guys pick their noses in their sleep."

Denis goes back for another steak, returns. "One of the things I think I'd like to do next year when I quit is get a steady girl friend," he says. "You know, somebody to be with you all the time. That's nice, you know."

"Get out! Six-fifteen! Get the hell out!" Without warning, Horace suddenly bellows from behind the steam table at those ten or twelve of us remaining in the mess hall. He picks up his big serving spoon and bangs it angrily, repeatedly, on the stainless-steel table. "Go on! Get out!"

"Horace wants us to go," Denis says quietly. He rises, takes his tray with its half-eaten steak to the dish-washing counter.

"That's something else you do here," Denis adds parenthetically, as he dumps his steak. "I took that second steak and I didn't really want it. At first you think the food is pretty good here, but then it all tastes the same and you just take more than you can eat and throw it away, just because it's there. Right now, I'd really like to eat a hot dog that my mom cooked. That would taste good."

I want to finish my cigarette and coffee, and resent being rushed by Horace. I try to convince Denis to stay a few more minutes but he, instead, persuades me to leave. "We have to go," he says. We file out with the other men. No one voices any complaint about being tossed out.

Outside, there are a few miners standing idly about the yard. The other men, apparently, have returned to their bunkhouses. Though it is almost seven, the Yukon summer sun is still high overhead. I could stand another cup of coffee, or a beer, but there is no place to get either. The mess hall door is now locked and the beer parlor is not yet open.

"Well, what'll we do?"

We decide to walk to the company store, in the center of town, to see if we can buy a cold soda. Denis drops his cigarette on the dusty ground in the yard.

"That's another thing you learn here," he says. "To be sloppy. You start throwing papers and cans and cigarettes around. I used to be so neat. When I first came here, I used to spend so much time cleaning up my room. Now I just throw things. After a while you learn there's nobody to keep up an appearance for. Not even yourself."

We walk down to the store, but it is closed, as we expected. We walk over to the library, just to see it, but it too is closed. At my suggestion, we walk back to the coffee shop, to see if there is a magazine to buy, but its door is locked. These places have regular hours, I know, because I have seen the schedule posted somewhere. But probably, since each place is run by a part-time employee—a single-status miner or a miner's wife—the hours are geared somewhat to suit the daily schedule of that employee, and not to suit patrons. I begin to feel a little angry about it, as if the whole thing were part of a plot to make things inconvenient.

We walk outside and stand on the porch of the coffee shop. I ask Denis if he participates in some of the recreational opportunities the company provides, such as curling, softball, swimming, soccer. Denis says no, that only the married employees seem to participate in these things. "I wouldn't mind swimming," he says. "I like to swim. But the company pool is in Biggy Camula's backyard. You feel funny going over there." (Camula, apparently, is one of the high level married employees, lives in the married section of town.) "Besides, they have one set of hours for single-status employees and another for the families. And who wants to swim with the same guys you see in the mine all day?"

Denis hoists his lanky frame up onto one of the two-by-four railings that leads steeply down the ten-foot coffee shop steps, walking down it, balancing himself like a tightwire walker. The railing is fragile; it could easily break under his weight.

"Denis, you're gonna break your goddamn neck on that thing."

Denis stumbles over his own feet, falls off the railing, catches himself without getting hurt.

"You want a beer?" he says.

We go up the steps to the beer parlor. Eight or nine young men are now waiting. The door finally opens and we go in. It's good to get away from the sunlight. The beer parlor is a wood-paneled room, twenty by thirty, with a small bar at one end, a jukebox at the other, and with various posters on the wall, some serious, some satirical, ranging from a nude Playboy Bunny to a nude Burt Reynolds to nude Walt Disney characters—something for everybody.

Denis picks up one of the cafeteria-sized plastic serving trays. "I'm buying this round," he says. "Do you know how many drafts you can put on one of these trays? Forty-three."

He orders forty-three glasses of beer (a mixture of brands) and the bartender—also a mine worker—begins to draw them.

"Denis! What the hell are we going to do with all that beer?"

"This is a great way to get a lot of people over to your table," Denis says enthusiastically, but still without smiling. He slowly picks his way over to our table, puts the tray down, sets out one draft for him, one for me, and we drink, while the bubbles rise to the top of the other forty-one glasses.

During the course of the evening, probably thirty or forty men come in, some for one or two beers, some to stay all evening, some to buy a six-pack to take back to the bunkhouses. A few older European men come in, drink quietly, play a game of darts. The younger men play the jukebox. To my surprise, the jukebox has several new rock songs on it. Denis puts in a few quarters and beats out the rhythm on our table.

"That's another thing about up here," Denis says. "You get to learn all the words to the songs. Then when you go back outside, somebody says to you, 'Hey, how come you know all the words?' and you say, 'It's because I'm in the mine.'"

We sit without talking much. Four or five other young men sit down at our table: Tom Page, Paul Canter, Richard Fulmer, Dan Eliot, and two other men whose names I don't catch. Paul and Richard are here earning money for college. Dan Eliot says he came up with his married buddy, Ronnie. One of the other men came north to avoid making alimony payments. Tom Page ended up here when his car died and his money ran out in Whitehorse, and he took the first job he was offered. They are all from southern Canada.

"Jack was asking me about Gloria and Betty," Denis announces loudly. The heads of all nearby miners turn toward me.

"Already?" one says. "You just got here." Everybody laughs.

My face gets red. "No, not that. I just want to *talk* to them." Everybody laughs again.

"Watch out," somebody says. "Betty has crabs!"

"That's right," Richard says. "She does."

Somebody else says that I won't be able to contact the girls anyway; he has just received a card from Gloria, saying that they have all gone over to Clinton Creek—another company town—for the week. He takes the card out of his pocket and we all read it.

"How old are they?" I ask.

"Gloria is nineteen," Richard says. "Betty is sixteen. And I think Rhea is only fourteen or fifteen."

"Is this free? Or are they real business prostitutes?"

Again, everybody laughs. "It's free," Richard says. "They just like it."

"Doesn't the administration get worried about girls going into the buckhouses? Or do they even know about it?"

"Sure they know about it," Denis says. "But they know you need a girl, right?"

"Besides," one man says, "what can they say? When I used to work in the office, I used to hear them talking on the phone all the time. Tslvakis has a mistress in Whitehorse. Lowerre is sleeping with

Klepper's wife. He's over there every time Klepper is on exploration."

"That's the way you get promoted around here," Denis says. "Let your wife sleep with Lowerre."

"Or else buy him a case of CC," somebody else says.

"What about venereal disease?" I ask them.

"They're clean," Denis says.

"Well, maybe. But if they're over in Clinton Creek this week and back here the next, how do you know for sure?"

Nobody does know. I decide not to pursue that subject.

"So you never get kicked out for having girls in your rooms, then?"

"Sandy got kicked out, didn't he, Richard?" someone asks. "He was screwing Betty when that sonofabitch Walters from personnel walked into his room. He didn't even knock."

"Yeah," Richard says. "But that's only because Sandy was playing his stereo so loud. Somebody complained about the noise."

"Tell him about that time with the two of them in your room," Denis says to Richard.

Richard hesitates. "Go on, tell him," Denis says.

Everyone at our table listens attentively, except Dan Eliot, who seems to be thinking about a totally different topic. Richard relates the event reluctantly. "Betty and Gloria were both in my room. Gloria went out to the bathroom and I started getting it on with Betty. I had her clothes off but she was so drunk she passed out. Then Gloria came back in and I started with her and left Betty lying there. Just when we were both ready, I hear this knock on the door and it's Sandy and another guy. They clomped right in. Jesus. And like, they go at Betty, right? While she's still passed out. One from the back and one from the front. I couldn't get them to leave. They were drunk. So Gloria and I put our clothes on and walked out. That's all it was."

Everyone laughs. Now, with seven or eight beers, Denis seems in better spirits. He grabs Paul Canter by the breast and squeezes. Paul winces and grabs Denis's breast, and both men squeeze as hard as they can. Finally, Denis surrenders.

"Get away from me, you sex fiend," Denis yells in a sort of shrieking falsetto.

More men join us. When the original forty-three drafts are gone, each of us buys a round of beer in turn, and the more people who sit at our table, the more beer each of us is obliged to drink. We talk about the recent cave-in in 225 stope, about the broken shower head in bunkhouse 3, about the possibility of a trip to Whitehorse (if Paul can borrow a car), about the difference in alcohol content between American and Canadian beer. . . .

In a way, I like being here, just talking. The men are friendly, glad to explain things about the mine and the town to me. But at the same time, I know that if I were to stay more than two or three weeks, with nothing to do at night *but* talk, to the same men, about the same topics, I would go out of my mind.

One of the mine supervisors comes in, buys two six-packs, and leaves. Someone at our table remarks that the man has a severe drinking problem, often comes to work drunk. One of the married miners comes in, sits alone at a nearby table. Someone speculates that he is having trouble with his wife. The wife, he says, was seen in Mayo last weekend, with someone else. I am reminded that while it is difficult to lead a truly private life almost anywhere in the Yukon, this is particularly, painfully, true of the company towns.

I begin now to feel self-conscious, sitting here with my companions, visibly, conspicuously, having nothing to do for the evening. It is a little like being in a cage. Two young mine workers come in, quickly scan the room, then hurry off without sitting down to have a beer. They seem somehow different from the rest of us—better clothes? more sophistication? a different smile?—and I fantasize that they have somewhere to go that the rest of us don't know about. Perhaps a party. Maybe even a party with women. A strange feeling, one that I have not had since high school.

In fact, I know that the only difference between these men and us is that they have access to an automobile and are going off to the bar in Keno or Mayo, where they will spend the evening doing precisely what we are doing: drinking with other men. Still, it might be worthwhile going, just in case. . . .

"Do you know how to drink two glasses of beer at the same time?" Denis asks me.

"No. How?"

"Like this." Denis drinks from one of the glasses, holds the other above it, and pours its contents into the first glass as he drinks.

The evening wears on. The room warps slightly.

Tom plays the Jew's harp. At about nine, an attractive young woman comes in, looks around smiling, very aware that every eye in the place is on her. She is a newcomer, visiting a family in the married end of town. No one at our table speaks as she looks around. Then she walks over to a group of young men at a table near ours, sits down. Denis, theatrically, buries his face in Paul's shoulder, pretends to sob hysterically, moans something about being rejected. The rest of the men at our table pretend not to notice her. In a few minutes the woman takes out a cigarette and, for some reason, comes to our table to get it lit. No one volunteers. Finally, Richard Fulmer slowly reaches into his pocket, hands the woman a matchbook.

"Thank you."

Richard does not speak, points to the tabletop, indicating that the woman should put the matches down. She does.

"You mean nobody over there's got a match?" Tom says, annoyed.

At nine-thirty, Denis suddenly rises, stumbles a bit, announces that he feels lousy and is going to bed. The rest of us talk on. Tom plays the Jew's harp some more. At ten, Denis returns, forlorn-looking, announces that he has locked himself out of his room. The camp manager is not around. The personnel office is closed. There is no place to get a spare key. I look at Denis. For some reason, he seems almost on the verge of tears. Probably he has just drunk too much.

Tom Page gets up, puts his arm around Denis's shoulder, goes down to his bunkhouse with him, and breaks down the door. When Tom returns, we all have one more beer before returning to our own rooms, and bed. Since I have left my windows open, the room has cooled down some, but it is still too hot to sleep easily.

It is noon, and my third day at Elsa. The miners in Husky shaft are eating lunch in the underground lunchroom at the "100" level, 125 feet below ground, and I take the elevator down there to find Eddie Cardinal and Abe Heinrichs, the two men with whom I will be spending the afternoon in number 225 stope. A stope is an underground ore-producing pocket. Number 225 stope is at the "200" level, 250 feet below ground. There is generally good ground control in Husky, since most work areas are located in solid, unfaulted rock. Number

225 stope is an exception: A fault slices diagonally through our work area, and a cave-in occurred there two days ago, on the night shift, temporarily burying one of the miners up to his armpits in splintered rock.

I have been underground with Eddie and Abe before. Both men earn well over one hundred dollars per day, about half on wages, half on production bonus. They have worked as partners on 225 stope—Abe as miner, Eddie as miner's helper—for four months. They are very different people. Abe is thirty-nine, married, with children; he lives in Mayo and is devoutly—sometimes outspokenly—religious. Eddie is younger, probably about twenty-five. (When asked, he says, "I might be nineteen. I might be thirty-three. It's hard to tell.") He lives in bunkhouse 3 and has the reputation—not uncommon for a miner—as a drinker-curser-fighter-lover. Someone has told me Eddie was not long ago indicted on assault charges in Toronto arising from a "crime of passion." I don't know if that is true or not. I haven't asked him.

The elevator cage takes me to the 100 level. I exit from the cage and walk eighty yards down an unlighted tunnel to the lunchroom. I am afraid to walk alone underground. There are lights near the cage, but none in the tunnels, except the head lamps each of us wears on his hard hat. In the silent, black, eight-foot-diameter tunnels, with my head lamp lighting the grimy, wet timbers, I feel as if I am the only human being down here. I welcome the thin white rim of light outlining the lunchroom door.

No one greets me as I walk in. The room is twelve feet wide by eighteen feet long by ten feet high, with rock bolts and metal safety straps and mesh across the ceiling, and with narrow, plywood tables and benches against two walls. Eight of the shift's twelve men are here. Their faces and outfits are black from rock dust, and they look tired from the morning's work. The others, including Denis, have for various reasons missed the shift. All the men in the lunchroom, except Eddie, are dressed in their drab rubber coveralls, clumsy rubber boots, safety glasses, hard hats, and gloves—now laid aside for lunch—and wear yellow head-lamp battery cases strapped to their belts. It is hard to tell them apart. Eddie has on his old green flannel shirt and tight-fitting jeans tucked into his slim, rolled-top boots. Covered with black rock slime, his outfit does not look radically different from those of other men. But it looks a little different. Just as Eddie's above-ground outfit—his dungaree jacket with the word "Ed" in large, nail-stud letters on its back and the dog chain draped over his shoulder—is different from the clothes worn by other men here.

No one talks. Each of the men eats in silence, apparently with his own thoughts, oblivious to the others. Three of the men are asleep, stretched out on the lunch table, with their hard hats over their faces. Wet chunks of rock powder drop occasionally from their boots onto the eating surface. It is not really an eating surface, though, because every-one—except Abe Heinrichs—sits atop the table, boots resting on the bench, facing out into the room.

Only ten minutes of the lunch hour remain. I quickly eat my sandwich. Some of the sleeping miners wake, have a smoke, and exchange a few words. Dan Eliot, who removes the ore from Eddie and Abe's stope, asks Eddie if there will be any work for him this afternoon. Eddie looks at Dan, crushes out his cigarette, does not reply. Someone makes a sarcastic comment about Denis missing shift. Someone else kids me about "stope rats," enormous blood-thirsty creatures that devour writers: "Only one way to escape. When he gets you in his mouth, quick, take off your pants and shit on his tongue!" We all laugh, for different reasons.

Everybody is ready now. Nobody says, "Let's go." Just a quick glance around the room, and we all rise as one and file out into the dark tunnel and walk back to the cage, to be taken down to the 200 level. Eddie walks alongside me and we talk, keeping our head lamps out of each other's faces. Eddie is not especially tall, about five foot ten, but is rugged and has very dark, close-set eyes that seem particularly mean when he is angry, particularly warm when he smiles. He is unusual-looking, to say the least, part French, part Scotch-Irish, part Cree Indian.

"You gonna be wid us again? You never learn, do you?"

"Why?"

Eddie lights a cigarette. "We got it timbered pretty good dis morning, but last night dey had a little loose come down."

"What's 'a little' mean?"

"I tink he said four or five tons. So you just stay under the timbers." Eddie looks at me and smiles. "And don't let Abe get preaching. He's slow enough as it is. He belongs in a fuckin' church, dat guy, not in a mine wid me."

"How come you work with him?"

"Dat was my stope," Eddie says. "I was the miner. I took a little vacation and he's in dere when I come back. So he's the boss now. I got to wait now to get my own stope again. He belongs in a fuckin' church, dat guy. I knew the first day I was wid him he was no miner. He took all day to drill thirty holes. I could do it in two hours."

I laugh. "Well, he's a good guy."

Eddie spits in the dirt. "Oh sure. I respek religion. Fuck, I'm Catholic too, but it don't stop me from drinkin' and smokin' and fuckin' around wid as many women as I can. I ast Abe once: 'Abe, did you ever French kiss anybody but your wife?' He ran out and he didn't come back the whole afternoon." Eddie looks at me and grins.

Abe catches up with us. John Pollack, the cage tender, gets us all inside, jerks the signal cord, and we are dropped 125 feet farther down into the earth by the remote cage operator who is located in a building aboveground. Thinking of last night's cave-in, I am tempted, briefly, to ride back up in the elevator, to spend the afternoon where I can see sunlight.

At the 200 level, the various pairs of men slog off to their respective tunnels and work areas. Husky mine has a single vertical shaft running from ground level down to a depth of 375 feet, with three primary underground work levels at 125 feet, at 250 feet where we are, and at 375 feet. Men, ore, and materials—including dynamite, air drills, narrow-gauge railroad cars, mucking machines, timbers, and an assortment of hand tools—are moved down to and among these work levels by means of the cage and the "skip," a big bucket used primarily for ore. Each level has a network of interconnecting horizontal tunnels—either "crosscuts" or "drifts"—radiating out from the central elevator shaft.

Abe, Eddie, and I follow a set of railroad tracks 400 yards along a main drift in a roughly northeasterly direction, passing several junctions with other tunnels, each marked with directional signs. Though this is my third day underground, and despite the signs, I still suffer from a complete lack of orientation down here, rely upon my partners to guide me, and am almost paralyzed at the thought of becoming lost in this maze of tunnels. I am tempted even to accompany people to the toilet, rather than to be left alone in the dark for three or four minutes without the sight of a partner's head lamp. I am convinced too, even though the aboveground mine captain knows who is underground and where he is, that a cave-in will somehow separate me from other people and I will await rescue alone, forever. I dream about this. So, I am told, do all new workers.

Eddie strides quickly ahead, and Abe and I walk together in the winding tunnel. The beams from our head lamps bob up and down on the tracks ahead, on the soot-laden drops of water falling from the eight-foot ceiling and on the jumble of spruce timbers, bull horns, and rock bolts protecting the sides and roof of the tunnel. I somehow feel the pressure of 250 feet of earth and rock bearing down upon the timbered ceiling. It is chilly, about 40°. We slog through ankle-deep water now and water rains on our hard hats. The water, Abe says, comes from melting permafrost, and is not present in the mine in winter, when the ground above is frozen. In some of United Keno's other shafts, I know, permafrost is present even in summer, to a depth of 450 feet, and must be melted with hot water piped into the mine.

Here and there I catch the smell of dynamite fired at the end of morning shift. Our head lamps slice through the rock dust that fills the air. Everything underground is covered with the black slime of dynamited rock particles—the timbers overhead, tools, coveralls, gloves, ladder rungs, the plastic air lines, faces, everything. The particles of rock dust, after a time, also fill a miner's lungs and cause scarification of lung tissue—silicosis.

"Eddie says there was a cave-in in your stope last night," I say to Abe.

Abe smiles. "That's possible," he says. "You see, that is not good ground, but there may be a million dollars in there."

"Yeah, right. We'd have a fancy funeral."

Abe laughs. "This mine has a good safety record," he says. "There hasn't been a death here in years."

"Okay. Sure. But it could come down on you, couldn't it? Don't you worry about that?"

Abe smiles, stops, puts his hand on my shoulder. "No," he says. "I'm not worried. You would hear the timbers cracking if anything started to fall. And I know we are protected down here. We would be alerted. There is a protecting hand."

"God's, you mean?"

Abe nods. "Yes. I know it. I've experienced it and I'm grateful for this protection. A couple of times, for instance, I've been working in a place and a partner would say to me: 'Why don't you move? That's not good there.' And I would take his advice, and a little while later I might come back to that spot, and there's a couple tons of loose have come down there."

"Did that ever happen with you and Eddie?"

"No. But now you see, there's another example of God's influence. Eddie is sort of a wild man, isn't he? But he's controlling himself down here. This is a spiritual area. If one person feels spiritually, it carries, and another absorbs it."

"Sure. I guess. But I still worry about getting killed. I'm petrified all the time I'm down here. Aren't you?"

"No," Abe says calmly. "My death is of no worry. If anything happens, I know it's His will. And I know my destiny, because of my faith in Christ."

Strangely, though I am not really comforted by the thought of divine protection, Abe's own serenity does make me feel better. I hope, though, that he is not so serene that he won't hear the timbers cracking.

We come to a short ladder, on the left side of the drift, that leads up into the ceiling through a ten-foot-long metal chute about three feet in diameter. We climb the ladder and worm our way up through the metal chute, our boots slipping on the slimy rock powder. We emerge in a newly developed tunnel. This tunnel widens, one hundred feet ahead, into a roughly oblong chamber in the rock, about twenty feet high, twenty feet wide, and thirty feet long. This is our stope. Bright, silver-blue bands of ore —lead sulfide—show here and there in its walls as we move our head lamps around.

For some reason, I have come to think of the stope as a room, an unchanging place, and am surprised each time I enter to find that its "face" or foremost wall has been advanced another six or twelve feet. Today, its floor is covered to a depth of three or four feet with rock and ore fragments, "muck" blasted from the face and fallen from the ceiling. A new row of side timbers—seven- or eight-foot spruce logs—have been put up by Abe and Eddie. One ceiling timber, put up yesterday, lies on the muck, knocked down and splintered by last night's cave-in.

There is a sturdy wooden platform beginning about twenty feet from the face and extending thirty feet back to the point where the stope narrows into a tunnel. This platform, elevated five feet from the floor, has its own log floor and ceiling, eight feet wide, and a few of the ceiling timbers extend forward five feet or so beyond the platform, providing some protection from rock that may fall from the stope ceiling. But beyond these projecting timbers, there is no protection at all, and Eddie is out in this unprotected area when we arrive, chunking around with a pick, chipping loose fragments from the walls and face of the chamber.

Abe and I walk up on the platform and look down on Eddie. Eddie lights a cigarette as he sees our lamps approach.

"Jesus fucking Christ, where you guys were? I been here ten minutes already."

Abe does not respond. "We stopped for a hamburger," I say.

"Jesus fucking Christ," Eddie says, and returns to his work.

I now notice, on the face, a ten-foot-long white mark made with a can of spray paint, with the word FAULT printed above it. This, apparently, was done by one of the inspectors from the mine's geology office, and to me it seems a little gratuitous. Everybody knows it's there; why remind us? The rock in this area looks fractured, powdered, and I recall a geology professor of mine describing the tremendous, inexorable force with which faulted surfaces slide and grind against one another until the tensions in the rock masses are resolved. Today, I wish I were back in school.

"Hey, Ed, what are you supposed to do about that 'fault' mark over there?"

Eddie looks up at the wall, as if he had not noticed the spray-painted word before, then goes back to digging. "Fuck all," he says.

Abe and I walk fifty feet back from the face of the stope and sit down on a wooden cable spool near the eighteen-horsepower slusher motor. Abe wipes rock slime off the motor. The slusher is the mechanism that scrapes muck out of the stope. It consists of this motor—air-driven to avoid underground ignition—a large, five-hundred-pound forked bucket that looks like a small crane bucket, and a series of half-inch steel cables running under the wood platform and connecting motor and bucket. The bucket is up at the face, resting on the muck where Eddie is. Abe controls it from back here, with a series of levers. Long eyebolts are driven into the walls of the stope and have steel cables strung between them to guide the bucket around—sort of like a dog leashed to a clothesline run. In operation, the bucket shoves its way around the stope, scrapes up the fragments and blocks of rock, then hauls it back to a point midway between Eddie and us and drops it through a three-foot hole in the floor opening into a muck chute. The twenty-foot muck chute empties into a small chamber beside the tracks in the tunnel below us, where a mucking machine the size of a garden tractor scoops it up and loads it on muck cars, which are then periodically driven back and emptied into the skip.

I start to ask Abe a question, but my voice is

drowned out by the sudden roar of the slusher motor. It is a ripping sound and is deafening within the confines of the stope. Up ahead, looking beneath the wooden platform, I can see the bucket lunging around within the chamber. Within a minute, the rock dust raised by the bucket conceals Eddie from our view. For the rest of the afternoon, he and Abe communicate with shouts: "Ready?" "Okay." "Start?" "Not yet."

Eddie scrapes muck into the path of the bucket, hammers in the eyebolts that keep popping out of the wall, pushes big rocks down the chute, then steps aside to avoid being struck or pinned by the bucket as it grinds its way around the stope. Abe stops the slusher every ten minutes or so, runs ahead to help Eddie, then runs back, leaping over the hole that opens into the muck chute. I grimace every time he leaps; there's not much chance of his falling in there, really, but if he did, he would be smothered. The only protection over the three-foot hole is a sludge-covered two-by-six.

It is hard physical work, in a nightmarish swirl of dust clouds and head-lamp beams. The men work quickly to make their tonnage, not pausing for a rest or for conversation. There is nothing for me to do except look on in the murky half-light, and scribble my notes. The place where Abe and I stand, back within the tunnel, is heavily timbered immediately over our heads. Some of the spruce logs, I notice, are wedged firmly and neatly in place; some apparently are just stuck up there atop the bottom logs, to plug holes through which rock might fall. Looking up there now at that three-foot-deep pile of logs, I notice that one of the bottom logs is supported at one end by a vertical log that runs from ceiling to floor and rests on the wooden platform on which the slusher motor is mounted. Each time Abe starts the slusher, one corner of the platform rises and falls four inches, the vertical post rises and falls four inches, and the big pile of spruce logs above our heads rises and fall four inches.

I jab Abe in the shoulder and point above, train-

Gold

ing my head-lamp beam on the heaving pile of logs. Abe smiles and nods, goes on slushing.

"Isn't that dangerous?" I ask, the next time he stops the motor.

"It could be better," he says. "But you see, this is the nature of mining. We get paid by the volume of ore we make, so we can't take time to make everything perfect."

I leave my post by the slusher, climb the ladder onto the platform. In the darkness I slip climbing the slimy ladder and bang my shoulder into a four-inch spike protruding from a vertical supporting post. One of the things that would bother me as a miner, I think, is the fact that any pair of men in any stope must rely upon the two men in the previous shift, men you may not even know and whose safety precautions you may not trust. If you yourself cannot afford the time to make things safe, how much can you rely upon the previous shift? This problem is compounded, here at Elsa, by the rapid turnover of men, by the influx of new, young workers, and by the fact that you may not even speak the same language as the men upon whom you must depend.

I walk forward on the platform and look down at Eddie. He is on his hands and knees, close to the wall and facing it, digging at something buried in the muck. The big bucket, now stopped, rests on the muck three feet behind him, appearing as if it were waiting to scoop him into its mouth.

As he works, he calls something—which I do not pay attention to—over his shoulder to Abe, who then starts the slusher. Things happen quickly. The five-hundred-pound bucket rumbles up behind Eddie. Eddie must hear it, but is intent on his work and apparently thinks Abe is backing it off. I yell. Eddie looks back only as the bucket touches his foot—about to pin him against the wall—then leaps to the side. "Stop! Stop!" Abe stops the machine and comes running forward through the dust.

Eddie hurls his shovel against the wall. "Jesus fucking Christ!" He paws madly in his pocket, finds a cigarette.

"I thought you said okay," Abe says.

"Fuck! I said, 'I tink we have to blast,' not 'Start it'!"

"Oh," Abe says, "okay." He disappears back through the dust.

I am shaking a little. "That was close," I say. "You could've gotten squashed."

Eddie lights the cigarette.

"Oh yeah? You tink so, huh?" He paces around

angrily kicking at the rock. "In a fucking church he belongs." He finally picks up his shovel and resumes digging. I see two aluminum wires, about a foot long, protruding up through the rock fragments.

"What's that?"

Eddie does not respond, but keeps digging angrily, using the shovel like an ax, knocking rock fragments away from the wires.

"It's dynamite," he says finally. "We got a miss-hole."

The charge, a single stick of the thirty or so sticks in the round set by the night crew, originally sunk six feet within a drilled hole in the face of the stope, apparently did not get the current needed to explode it.

"Um . . . Ed? Do you suppose you ought to be hacking at it like that? I mean, it could go off, right?"

Eddie is amused by this. He looks at me and smiles. "God will proteck you," he says.

He now walks behind me, is gone a few minutes, returns with a blasting cap and tape fuse, gets down on hands and knees, and attaches it to the undetonated stick. I stand uneasily on the wooden platform, with as much of me as possible behind a spruce post—not that this would do any good if the stick went off. It occurs to me now that while every stope has at least two safety exits, neither of ours is really close enough to our work area to let us get away if the ceiling suddenly fell.

Either a tape fuse or an electrical charge can be used to ignite dynamite, but electric lines connected to a remote ignition device are always used to ignite an entire round simultaneously. This is done just prior to leaving shift, to permit the dust and dynamite fumes a chance to clear, and to give loosened ceiling rock a chance to fall, before the next shift arrives. Timed tape fuses—the kind used in old Western movies—are ignited manually, on the spot, and thus are impractical and dangerous for igniting more than one or two sticks at a time.

Abe drags forward a rubber air hose, opens its valve. The air hisses. This will blow out the dust and fumes before we return.

"Want to get warm, Jack?" Eddie says. He lights the tape fuse and its end sputters and sparkles in the darkness, a bright ball of blue-white light. Eddie slowly climbs up on the platform beside me.

"Now we run," he says calmly.

I do run, with Abe, back through the tunnel, past the chute, into a big, high-ceilinged chamber, whose ore has previously been removed, and part of whose volume has been refilled—for ground stability—with a mixture of mine tailings and concrete.

"Don't hurry," Abe says behind me. "But keep going."

We climb a ladder up to the top of the twenty-foot-thick concrete slab, run fifty feet more, and start down another forty-foot ladder through a hole drilled down to the tunnel below. This is our number two escape route.

"Where's Eddie?"

"I don't know."

"Is there time to check?"

"Yes. Sure. But hurry. I'm sure he's all right. Don't be standing on top when it goes."

I run back, look down. Eddie is smoking a cigarette, standing around the corner from the tunnel and a hundred feet away from the charge.

"Hey! I thought you fell down."

Eddie takes a drag on his cigarette, waves me away. "See you in paradise," he says. "Now go on."

I run back to the manhole, and am ten feet down the ladder when the dynamite explodes. One stick of dynamite, in fact, does not throw rock very far. But since we are underground, the impact is violent. The noise sounds right above us. Pebbles rattle on the floor up there, the earth and ladder tremble, and, in the confined space of the narrow manhole, it seems to me as if the walls will collapse.

We go on down the ladder into the tunnel below, to wait thirty minutes for the smoke to clear. In a minute Eddie joins us. Dan Eliot is there, sitting on a muck car. Another light comes down the tunnel. It is Louis Sweet, the shift boss, who regularly visits each of Husky's work areas to supervise operations. It seems to me that I recall reading in the safety rules book that the shift boss is supposed to authorize any blasting, except that done at end of shift, and I wonder if Eddie could have gotten Louis's approval when he came down for the fuse.

It occurs to me too that tape fuses are supposed to be seven feet long and are to be lit with igniter cord; ours, as I now fuzzily recall it, was half that length and was ignited with a match. I'm not sure, but I don't raise the subject. Anyway, Louis asks no questions.

We have a cigarette and relax. Louis asks Dan where Denis is. Dan says someone from 231 stope asked Denis to come over to help them. It is an obvious, needless lie, since Louis must already have checked aboveground to see who made shift,

but he lets it pass. Dan, perhaps to change the topic, tells Louis that rock chunks have lodged in the muck chute leading down from our stope; he cannot get it to fall down into the small chamber beside the track, for the mucking machine to pick up. Louis takes a scaling bar, squeezes alongside the mucking machine into the chamber, jabs his bar up into the overhead chute.

Muck comes pouring down, including one fifty-pound rock. Louis quickly leaps backward. A five-foot pile of rock fragments drops in front of the mucker and the big rock crunches down into the narrow space between mucker and chamber wall where Louis stood a second before.

"Thanks," Dan says.

"You just have to poke it good," Louis says.

He goes on down the track to inspect another crew. We have another cigarette before going back. While we smoke, with our gloves off, I notice that a joint of one of Eddie's fingers is missing.

Eddie smiles. "Didn't I tell you about dat? Well, I used to have a girl friend. Her father was a dentist, see? You know what the sonofabitch done? He put some false teet up her cunt to get me. . . ." He holds up his finger. "An dat's what happened."

We climb back up the ladder and inspect the ceiling for loose. The chamber is still smoky. I walk forward on the platform. From above, a pea-sized piece of rock falls and clicks on my hard hat.

"Don't stand there too long, Jack," Abe says. He points up. There is no timber above me. I move quickly.

Bloom! Suddenly, a dynamite blast rocks the ground. I leap from the platform, vault over the slusher motor, and am thirty feet down the tunnel before I realize that our stope is not caving in.

Abe laughs. "It's three-thirty," he calls. "Somebody's blasting in another stope."

"Oh. It sounded right here!" I walk back.

"Well, it wasn't too far."

"How do we know, though, if our ceiling is coming down?"

"You have warning," Abe says. "You hear the little ones come down before the big ones."

"What's a 'little one'? I mean, how do I know that little piece that fell on my hat wasn't a warning?"

"You know," Abe says.

"Yeah? What if the little ones start coming when the slusher is running, and you can't hear them?"

Abe smiles. "You have warning," he says.

n the decades following the Klondike gold rush, mining
echniques have ranged from dredging to the smaller placer
perations shown above. At left, a house-sized dredge rests

Above, Marion Schmidt conducts a sluicing operation on Dominion Creek. At right, dredges have left mammoth furrows throughout much of the Klondike landscape.

Eddie now yells for us to shut up and get working. Abe starts the slusher and again the stope is filled with dust and deafening noise. I am afraid to go up front near Eddie. I am afraid to stand on the platform. I look behind us, toward our exit route, and now notice that in several locations along the ceiling of the hundred-foot tunnel, long shanks of rock bolts are visible for a foot or more between the steel ceiling bands and the ceiling itself, as if the rocks once held there by bands and bolts have fallen out. That, Abe tells me, yelling above the slusher, is just what happened: several portions of the ceiling in this stope are sufficiently rotten that they cannot be held. For the rest of the afternoon, I remain near Abe, under the timber ceiling that heaves rhythmically up and down with the surges of the slusher motor.

Now we hear a series of dynamite blasts from other stopes, most of them sounding like strings of distant firecrackers, one or two rumbling the ceiling and walls around us, but none as loud as the one that scared me off the platform. These, Abe says, are on the 100 level, 125 feet above us. We will not set our round of dynamite today; there is not enough time.

Abe and Eddie work hastily, ten or fifteen minutes more. Then Eddie comes back near us, lights a cigarette, and sits down. Abe continues to run the slusher for five minutes, then shuts it down, waits for Eddie to finish his cigarette.

"Well, let's go."

We're done for the day.

We walk back the tunnel, slide down the chute, enter the main drift, and walk silently back to the cage. Dan Eliot has already started back. We see his head lamp ahead.

At the cage, other miners, trammers, and laborers are waiting. Everyone looks tired, but glad to be going out. Eddie speaks briefly with Roland LeDuc, and they decide to go to Keno City tonight. "I don't know, Roland," Eddie says as the cage rises through the ground. "What we fuckin' workin' for? Fuckin' tirty dollars a night over dere on booze."

Aboveground, we leave the cage and run to the dry to shower. I am surprised now to see that it is raining, pouring in fact. It was sunny and clear when I went down at noon.

Thursday night, after the beer parlor closes, Dan Eliot invites me over to his bunkhouse room. He and his roommate Ronnie have two warm six-packs, he says, and I am welcome to help drink them. I accept, and we wobble over to bunkhouse 6.

Dan is an unusual person, from what little I have observed of him. He is about thirty. Physically, he is rugged, tough-looking, yet he has a naïveté and innocence about him that do not seem to fit. He and Ronnie have been here only about one week.

"When you came down here, I bet you figured you'd run into a lot of rough tough guys working underground, didn't you?" Dan says as we walk.

"Yes, I did."

"And we're not, are we? I mean, there isn't much difference between us and anybody you might meet in New York, is there? Not muscle-wise, anyway. We're really just tough in the head."

"No, I think it's just the opposite. I think people here are physically rugged, but a New Yorker is probably psychologically tougher."

Dan has a laugh at this.

"What did you do before you came here?" I ask him.

"I lived with Ronnie in Edmonton. Me and Ronnie have known each other a long time, and now that I got no place to live, Ronnie lets me live in his house with him and his wife."

"How about before that?"

"I lived in Toronto," Dan says. "I was married then."

"What did you work at?"

"Well, I can do almost anything," Dan says. "I never worked as a miner before, but I bet I'll be a good one. You ever hear of claus—clausto—people who don't like to be closed in? Well, I'm just the opposite. I like bein' closed in. If I could go a million feet under the ground, I'd do it."

"And why did you come up here?"

"Well, see, Ronnie's wife is gonna have another baby. They got four already. So we figured we needed some more money. It won't take us long, maybe till Christmas. Right now, though, we're pretty broke. That's why Ronnie don't come over to the beer parlor with the rest of the fellas."

We enter Dan and Ronnie's room. Ronnie is lying on his back on the cot, writing, and Dan introduces me. Ronnie is a short man, probably about forty-five. For the most part, he does not join our discussion. Dan gets us three warm beers from under the bed. "I'm sorry it isn't cold," he says, "but it isn't."

We sit there for a few minutes, not speaking. Finally, unable to think of anything more imaginative, I ask the men how they like it here. Ronnie grumbles that the mail service is loused up, but Dan is more enthusiastic.

"Oh, I like it," he says. "I hear a lot of the fellas talkin' about how bad it is, but I think it's pretty nice. You know, they got a movie here. I love movies. I been down to the show. It's just like a real theater. They got a great big screen, and it's colored."

"What movies do you see?"

"I don't know," Dan says. "I only seen two, and I think one of them had John Wayne in it. Is that his name? John Wayne?"

I nod.

"And the food is pretty good too. I always think, gee, I gotta go back and get another pork chop. You can have as many as you want. Or, if it's not pork chops they're servin', then I think gee, I gotta go back and get another piece of whatever it is."

"And you don't find any lack of things to do?"

Ronnie complains about the lack of women, but Dan remains upbeat:

"Oh no. You can play pool and drink beer. You can watch television in that building they got down there. You can take a ride, if you know somebody who's got a car. Or you can go out and walk around wherever you want to. I know some of the fellas don't like it, but that's the difference between them and I."

"The isolation doesn't get to you?"

Dan shakes his head. "I don't mind being down here away from everything, 'cause I know I'll always come out and I'll have some money and I'll have a lot of fun. A lot of the guys here can't wait. But I can."

"You said you were married. Do you ever get lonesome for your wife? Or maybe for a girl friend?"

"Oh sure. I get lonesome. I guess I told you my wife and I got separated. I still miss her, though."

Dan points to the wall over Ronnie's cot, which is completely filled with pinups from *Penthouse* and *Playboy*. "See," he says. "We got pinups here. And this one . . . she looks just about like my wife. The wife I used to have, I mean. She had hair about down to there. She was real pretty."

"Do you have any pictures of her?"

"No. I don't have any of my kids, either, but sometimes I wish I did." He pauses. "I really did

Minerals are separated from ore by flotation.

At Elsa, underground miners drill to
set blasts for lead, zinc, and silver.

love them. But I'll never go back. I figure that once you leave, you better stay away. My wife said to me, 'Dan, I love you, and I'll always love you. But you're gone so much, maybe it's better this way.' And I was gone a lot, too. I just couldn't stay home. I tried to, but I just had to get out and move around. I guess I'm just not the kind of fella who settles down."

Another silence.

"Where did you get all those tattoos?" I ask finally. "I never saw anybody with so many of them."

Dan looks at his arms, which are filled with tattoos—"Mom," "Father," "Dan and Marcy," a cross, several sets of initials, a rose, a heart. Several of them are partially erased. "I got 'em different places," he says. "Now this one here is good. See, the bleeding heart? That's a symbol, you know. Or maybe it's a bleeding rose that's the symbol. Anyway, that guy was professional and he did a nice job. But some of these other ones guys just wanted to do for practice, and I didn't have anything else to do so I let 'em. But a lot of 'em didn't turn out so good."

"Is Marcy your wife?"

"No, she's a girl I used to run around with. My real wife wanted me to have 'em removed. I wanted to too, but I said, 'Gee, it costs five dollars an inch. I don't have that kind of money.' Sometimes now I wish I didn't have 'em. When I first got 'em, the girls used to go for that. But now I guess they don't like tattoos so much anymore, do they?"

"I don't know. I guess it depends on the girl."

Dan looks over at Ronnie.

"Are you gonna get your package in the mail, Ron?"

Ronnie grunts.

"Are you, Ron?"

"How the hell should I know?" Ronnie snaps.

Dan jerks his thumb at Ronnie: "This guy writes more than anybody I ever seen," he says to me. "That's nice though, Ron. It's nice you write to your wife like that. I wish I could. . . . Hey, I wonder how much it costs to call Toronto? Do you know?"

"No, I don't know."

"Probably millions," Dan says. "I better wait."

"Who would you call?" I ask.

"Maybe my parents. Maybe a girl I used to know. I don't know, just somebody. But I better wait. You want another beer?"

We open two more beers.

"Did you ever see any freaks?" Dan asks me suddenly.

"You mean like in sideshows? Sure. Why?"

"I seen one once. He was all frozen and they said he was dead five years but he was gonna be thawed out in 1980—no, maybe it was 1981—and then he'd be alive again. Do you believe that? Or do you think I got gypped?"

We talk on, like this, with long gaps in our conversation, drinking the warm beer until three in the morning. Outside, it begins to get light. Ronnie writes or reads a pinup magazine most of this time, but finally rises, looks out the window.

"C'mere," he says to Dan and me, grinning. "Now look at those mountains out there and tell me what they look like to you."

"It's just mountains, isn't it?" Dan says. "It's . . . what do they call it? A silhouette?"

Ronnie looks annoyed. "I said, what does it *look* like?"

"Like a woman's breasts," I say.

Ronnie smiles. "That's close," he says. "But it's not quite right. Now come over here"—he takes me by the shoulder—"now you see? It's a woman all right, but her head is back that way and we're looking right up her cunt. See? She's almost ready. Her right leg is bent back and her left one is all tight. That's her foot over there. She's just waiting now. . . ."

I laugh.

Dan smiles but does not seem especially titillated by Ronnie's fantasy. "Gee, Ron," he says. "You been up here too long already."

A light knock comes through the wall from the adjacent room. A voice says gently: "It's three o'clock. C'mon now, boys, be quiet." Then, without pause, the same polite voice screams out angrily, hysterically: "You sonofabitch! Shut up! Go to bed or I'll kill you!"

We look at each other.

"Well," Ronnie says, "I guess I'll turn in." He crawls under his blanket.

"I guess I should go too," I say. "It sounds like you've got a lunatic for a neighbor."

Dan looks uninterested. "C'mon, have one more beer. Don't worry about that guy. If he says that again, I'll go over there and throw him out the window."

Dan says this very calmly, but for some reason I tend to believe him. Apparently so does the neighbor, for he doesn't complain again.

"See," Dan says, "I don't get a chance to talk to a

guy like you very often. It's interesting to me, a guy who writes books. I thought that's what you did when I saw you down in the tunnel with your pencil and pad. I noticed that. I learned to notice a lot of things about guys that other guys don't see. What's it like anyway, to write books? You probably get to travel all over, don't you?"

I try to give Dan a realistic notion of what it is like to write—to collect material, to sit for hours alone at the typewriter, to try to sell book ideas. I try to emphasize the negative aspects of it, the long hours and little money.

When I finish, Dan nods. "It sounds nice," he says. "I sometimes think I should have done that 'cause I've had a lot of experiences that most people never heard about."

"You never did tell me what you did before you came here. What was it?"

Dan hesitates, looks down.

"I guess you spent some time in jail, right?"

Dan nods, smiles.

"What for?"

"It wasn't a big thing," he says. "I wrote bad checks. About two thousand dollars' worth. They put me away for it. . . . You prob'ly don't think that's very good, do you?"

"I don't know. I guess it depends on just how you went about it."

"I never wrote 'em on anybody poor," Dan says. "I always did it on people I knew had the money. And I always spent the money on nice people. I gave some of it away. I threw a party." He laughs. "I guess I never got to use much of that money myself."

I laugh too. "No, I don't imagine you did."

"Here," Dan says. "Let me show you. Write your name down on paper."

I sign my name. Dan looks at it for a minute, then copies it slowly, methodically, left-handedly, producing a signature that only vaguely resembles mine.

"It's hard to make that loop in the *J* the way you do," he says. "But you see, they never look very careful when they cash a check. They should though, 'cause guys like me are always tryin' to get away with it."

"It's a pretty good copy of my signature," I say.

Dan smiles. "Well, I'm pretty good at whatever I do," he says.

We both yawn. "I better get back to my bunkhouse," I say finally.

I know you want to talk to as many guys as you can," Dan says. "So maybe we won't get the chance to talk again like this. But I want you to know, I sure liked it."

"I liked it too. And if you get traveling around again, and get to New York, you're welcome to stay over."

Dan smiles. "Well, you better think that over," he says. "I got a record, you know. But if I do ever get to New York, we'll go out and have a good time. We'll have a few beers and something to eat, and it'll be at the expense of me. You remember that."

In the following days I go underground only once more, and spend most of each morning sleeping off the previous night's drinking. I am unsuccessful in my attempt to locate Tiny Tim, the miner who buys food to throw away. Somebody tells me he took a bus out to Whitehorse for a while.

I spend Friday evening with Denis, Tom, Paul, and Dan in the Rec Hall. There isn't much to do. Tom and Dan play darts, but the game is aggravating because there are only two darts. Denis and I want to play table tennis, but there is only one paddle. Dan wants to make his phone call to Toronto, but there is a sign above the phone: "Definitely *no* long distance calls," which deters him. We end up watching a movie on television.

Denis was right: The food is all starting to taste the same.

It rains on Saturday. The valley fills with clouds, and trickles of mud run across the parking lot above the mess hall.

After lunch, Tommy Pirano invites me to his room, on the second floor of bunkhouse 5, one of the older frame buildings. Someone has smashed the lock and kicked a big hole in the building's outside door, and it swings loosely on its hinges.

Tommy is twenty-four, works as an underground laborer, has been at the mine for almost two years, with one long vacation, and has lived part of his life in New York City. Our lunch today, when he came over and introduced himself, is the first time I have spoken with him at any length. I like him immediately. He is extremely intelligent, warm, open.

Tommy's room is different from any of the others I have seen. It has no pinups, but instead is decorated and furnished with his own wire and clay sculptures, art prints, a real armchair, a large and blooming African violet, and, most unusual of all, a bookcase. The books include works on or by Gide, Borges, Sartre, Camus, Miró, Dali, plus the *Bhagavad-Gita, The Naive and Sentimental Lover, The Pocket Oxford Dictionary,* and *Mining Explained.* A list of vocabulary words staring with "d" is pinned to one bookshelf: *deglutition, Dei gratia, delectus, delimination, deliquesce, deltoid, demimonde,* and a dozen others I have never even seen before. On his desk are letters he has written to a flower shop in Whitehorse and to Duffy's Book Shop in Vancouver.

We talk.

"My ultimate aim is to be a chef," Tommy says. "To own my own restaurant, and to write historical novels about cooking." He speaks slowly and carefully, almost as if he worries about how his words will come out.

I can't help laughing. "Historical novels on *cooking?!*"

"Well, maybe not with cooking as the central subject matter, but sort of interspersing cooking concepts throughout. And there is material there, too, if you look into it. For example, did you know that Catherine de Medici, whose family supported Michelangelo, brought five hundred chefs with her when she came to France?" He hesitates. "Though I guess you would know much more about writing than I. It's possible that I won't pursue the novel part of it. It might not work out in terms of income. But it still remains something I would very much like to do."

"How about the chef part? Can you cook?"

Tommy smiles. "Oh yes. I'm a natural chef. I started out in New York, in fact, at the Engagé Cafe on Tenth Street and Avenue B. All the jazz men used to come in there. And later I owned one of the prominent vegetarian restaurants in Vancouver."

"Really? I mean, with interests of that sort, I just don't see what you're doing here working as a mine laborer."

"Oh, that connection isn't an obscure one. My first job here in fact was bull-cook for Western catering. But more than that, I find this a very beneficial place. I really came here to get strong. I mean that both physically and spiritually. I was actually physically weak when I came here, but now I'm quite strong. Two years ago, I would have been frightened to death to be here with all these men, but now I get along better with people. Also, I'm gaining financial

power. I'm putting money away. And I like the concept of mining; it's like being a sailor or an astronaut. The mineral itself fascinates me beyond measure. I like the country, its power. I'm very much an animist, in that respect. I suppose I would call this place my dream center. I tend to be clairvoyant, and find this a good place to exercise those capacities."

"Well, fine. But did you just say to yourself one day, 'All right, working in a mine is the place for me'? I mean, how did you come to get here? And what happened to that vegetarian restaurant in Vancouver?"

Tommy smiles. "I was bought out in the restaurant. At that time I wasn't handling money well. And the immediate circumstances of my coming here were simply that I came to Whitehorse to visit a friend and drank up all my money. I needed a job, and so I just applied for one at a mine, and here I am. But in a year and a half, I'm going to Cordon Bleu, in Paris, to study cookery. I've already sent them six hundred dollars toward my tuition. It will cost seven thousand in total."

"Okay. So then you're essentially working now to put away money, to become a chef."

"Yes, but I'm flexible. I have other aims, other projects I would like to pursue. One thing would be to set up a hypoglycemia foundation, to determine the incidence of hypoglycemia and its relationship to crime and alcoholism and drugs. And another thing would be to unite the hypoglycemia foundations of the U.S. and Canada and Great Britain in sort of a worldwide front. I've already been in touch with the heads of the U.S. and Canadian foundations by mail and by phone, and with friends of mine in the medical world."

"You mean you've actually made phone calls to these guys?"

"Yes."

"Are you convinced that hypoglycemia is a significant phenomenon? I mean, it's my impression that it only affects a few people."

"I'm quite sure it's significant, from what I've read. In any case, cancer and heart disease are serious threats to life today, and they are directly related to abnormal intake of sugars. And it seems that sugars evoke in us a cycle of aggression and schizophrenia—it involves the thalamus and thyroid glands and the cortex of the brain—and produce abnormal social behavior—crimes, drugs, alcoholism,

79

militarism. I wrote to one doctor of neurology in Edmonton, and he thinks rock and roll music is also one manifestation of this. And you see, this would be a real battle of visionaries against corporate giants and government. It would produce a real and profound revolution, because the immediate effects would be the removal of sugars from household food products and from institutions. And of course, that's a multibillion-dollar industry."

"You mentioned that you drank up all your money when you first came?"

"Oh yes. I was a real alcoholic. I'm not drinking at all now, but I had d.t.'s and hallucinations. I think I may even have gotten cirrhosis, because my knee keeps swelling and that's one of the symptoms."

"Why or when did you start drinking heavily?"

"Well, I was a Buddhist monk for seven months, and when I gave up the vows I was very depressed and I started drinking at that time. My whole life, you see, has been rather filled with unusual experiences. I ran away from home at sixteen. I had only a tenth-grade education. I've traveled a lot—to India and Egypt and Crete and Greece—and by nineteen or twenty, I had had many more strange experiences than most people have in a lifetime. Drinking was just one more thing."

Each of Tommy's statements gives me four or five more questions I want to ask about him. Unfortunately, I can ask only one at a time.

"So you don't have any permanent home, then?"

"No. I consider this my home. And as I said, I love it here. Because when I first came here I came with a girl I loved, and so it was an initial loving experience. And it's a wonderful place aside from that. It has great potential. The management here could do wonderful things to help these young men without vision to have vision. One of my own visions is that they could establish some sort of a cultural exchange program. They could build houses, make it suitable to live. Or have young men live with families. They could raise sheep, for instance—I believe they would survive here—and they could hire young girls to do weaving from the wool. There are just so many things."

"What happened to your girl?"

"She went to Keno to be with another man," Tommy says, "and I stayed on at camp."

"Oh. That's too bad."

"Well, perhaps," Tommy says pensively, "but maybe not."

A silence. "Well then . . . um . . . Tommy, dammit, I've completely lost track of what we were talking about. . . ."

Tommy smiles understandingly. "Yes, people often have that trouble with me. I believe we were talking about the food industry, hypoglycemia, restauraering, things like that. Well, another thing I would like to do is to explore new concepts in restaurant architecture incorporating simple natural and human works. Sort of an Oriental approach. I would love to go to Kyoto and study both cooking and architecture—the simplicity of the East. I've written a couple of letters about this. For example, I would like to set up a vegetarian retreat incorporating plants and water and Miró drawings. Another thing I have looked into is the possibility of establishing a homeopathic hospital with vegetarian cookery used as an integral part of the treatment. I've researched this minimally, but I have looked into it with my mind. But if the concept of using natural foods in healing should take hold, that would be a formidable foe, as it were, to the popular concepts of medicine, and of dining out, and would meet with enormous resistance."

"Yes, I agree. Do you consider yourself a revolutionary?"

Tommy thinks. "Oh, I suppose so. I was a member of a Trotskyite party in Texas and a member of the DuBois Club. That didn't quite suit me because I am not really a very political person. I would not be surprised, by the way, to see either Canada or the United States fall into some form of paramilitary government."

He picks up some clippings from his desk. "I have here some information on people in the right-wing movements," he says. "I got these clippings from the *Manchester Guardian*. I think they might be of use to a discerning person, if there is a right-wing overthrow someday."

"Well. . . . Sure. I suppose they might be."

"Another thing I am very interested in," Tommy says, "is researching the sea as a source of future food. Vegetarian food, though, not fish. In fact, I would like to write a book on fish, to try to encourage sportsmen not to catch them. The book could use silk screen and lithograph and fine pen and ink drawings. And another thing I am committed to fight is the concept of killing animals for food. I was in the Indiana stockyards not long ago, and these beautiful young calves were there just waiting to be slaughtered. It was tragic. My heart went out to them." He shakes his head sadly. "I am also against trapping. I wrote a letter to the editor of the fashion page of the *Vancouver Sun* about that."

"Yeah, I don't like trapping either, because it's a painful death. But being here in the Yukon has changed my feelings about it a little. I can at least sympathize with the Indian people's trapping."

Tommy nods. "Yes. But unhappily, the native men just spend their money on alcohol. I've seen these young native males just pouring a hundred dollars a day down the drain on alcohol."

Again, I have lost the thread of our conversation, and ask the first question that comes into my mind: "With your vegetarian and organic interests, I don't see how you can stomach the food here. It's good, but it's hardly organic or vegetarian."

"Oh no. I find the food here very acceptable. I aspire to be a great chef, but I'm not a fusspot about what I eat."

"Tommy, I keep forgetting what we were talking about. Okay, I guess I would like to know something more about the plain facts of your life. You said you had had a lot of unusual experiences. What sort?"

Tommy nods. "Well, you already know some of them, and you can probably imagine the rest. Unusual sexual experiences, unusual associations— once I was stabbed in Tompkins Square Park and I ended up in Bellevue Hospital, then N.Y.U. Hospital, then Fairfield Hills Hospital in Connecticut. I was on drugs, of course—heroin. Previously, I was institutionalized for a nervous breakdown in Houston, Texas. My doctor in Houston, by the way, was Raul Fuentes, a very fine man who served twelve years in prison under Peron."

"Is that why you came to Canada in the first place? To get away from drugs?"

"Well, partly. I was arrested for possession—a narcotics agent planted that particular convicting quantity on me, by the way, not that I didn't have plenty of it myself. And I skipped parole. I also wanted to avoid the U.S. draft, so that was another reason I came up here."

"Un-huh. I see. And am I right in thinking you're also homosexual? Or bisexual?"

"Oh yes. I thought you knew that."

"Well, I guess I did. But it doesn't matter. I mean, I don't give a damn if you're trisexual."

"I'm not extroverted about it though," Tommy says. "I'm getting to the point now where my sexual needs are not compulsive. After all, I've had enough basic experience—sex, drugs, alcohol—to last me a lifetime. I do get lonesome for a woman's company every once in a while, but I can go to Whitehorse for that."

"Do you think you might ever get married and stay around here?"

Tommy thinks. "I may marry and raise a family sometime. And if I lived in Canada, this is where I would want to live. In the city, I feel overwhelmed. Here it is easier to have your own place."

"But I suppose maybe you would first want to get done with your schooling in Paris before you made any plans to settle down, right?"

"Yes," Tommy says hesitantly, "I suppose so."

"What's the matter? You don't sound so sure about it now."

"Well, I suppose I'm never really sure of anything until I do it. You see, that's the main reason I've sent them some of the money in advance. I can say to people, and to myself, 'I'm going to school at Cordon Bleu next year,' and then if someone tries to shake my conviction in going, I can say, 'Yes. I've already sent in the money.' "

I try a little pep talk. "There's no reason why you *shouldn't* go, is there? I mean, you're not going back to drugs or anything. . . ."

Tommy shakes his head. "No," he says. "I'll never go back to drugs and alcohol. That is, I *believe* that I won't go back to them, but . . . you see, it's a pretty constant struggle for me to stay on a positive path. And that's one of the reasons it's good for me here. I don't have nearly the pressures I would have outside. I have my room and my food, and my books, and my work to do. But I'm simply not ready to go back out. Not yet."

"And I guess you wonder if you'll ever be, right?"

Tommy smiles. "Yes, I guess that's so."

"Well look, you are working. You are saving. You have sent some money to the school. You're a nice, likable guy. You've been off drugs and alcohol quite a while. . . . I'd say things look pretty good, Tommy, really."

Tommy smiles and nods. "You're right, I suppose. But sometimes I wonder. I wonder."

Saturday night, I drive with Roland and Eddie—in Eddie's Ranchero, at seventy miles per hour—to one of the two bars in Mayo. The patrons,

as expected, are about 90 percent miners from Elsa. The other 10 percent are mostly young Indian people from Mayo who, the miners have told me, often pick fights with miners, or vice versa. There is some verbal friction tonight, but no real trouble. Aside from the woman tending bar, the only white woman in the place is an American girl from Keno City, who, because of her height and skinniness, the miners refer to as "Lesser Bonerack." Her somewhat heavier sister—"Greater Bonerack"—works in the Elsa coffee shop. Greater is a nice person and is liked by the men. Lesser is sort of condescendingly flirtatious with the miners, and is disliked. I observe now, about myself, that I am getting into the swing of Elsa life, because when Lesser asks cutely for a bite of my hamburger, I break off a chunk and throw it on the floor. Or is that only to amuse my friends, Roland and Eddie? Or is it because I am drunk? Probably all three.

In any case, we have a good time. Eddie says something like, "Jack, you worked wid us, you got drunk wid us, you're okay," which makes me feel good. Eddie and Roland also take thirty minutes to draw for me an elaborate diagram of a "square set" and a "round set," showing the order in which the thirty-four dynamite sticks are wired to the fuse to go off in proper sequence. I do not understand a thing about the diagram, even after they explain, but the nice thing is that they bothered to draw it. It is my last night here, but I don't tell this to Eddie and Roland. We stay until the bar closes at 2 A.M. and then drive back. To the bunkhouse.

At 7 A.M. I pack and eat breakfast. The bacon is too salty. Only three or four other men are in the mess hall. Sun streams through an eastern window. Across the room, two young men—a very tall, brawny guy and a short slim man—who have apparently stayed up all night drinking, begin to shout and to throw coffee and grapefuit slices and orange juice at one another while eating breakfast together. The big man throws the other one over his shoulder, carries him outside, drops him on his back, from a height, into a big mud puddle in the yard. The smaller man comes back in, goes behind the steam table, despite Horace's shouting, gets a handful of scrambled eggs, and pelts his companion. The scuffle continues awhile. What surprises me, I guess, is that I barely pay attention.

Outside, the yard is strewn with empty, half-empty, or broken liquor bottles. The wind blows a small spiral of dust down the road. Two old miners are asleep on the porch of the beer parlor. Tommy Pirano gets up and waits with me for my ride to catch the bus in Mayo. I'm to ride with Oskan and Joan Esak, a married employee couple, but they come a half hour late. They have been up all night too, at a married couples' party. I think briefly that I would like to see Denis and Dan and Eddie and Abe and Roland and Tom and Paul, but there is no time for that. Tommy and I say good-bye and shake hands, quickly, and we take off to Mayo, speeding, throwing up a shower of dust in the morning sunlight, with a bottle of rum, paper cups, and ice cubes set on the seat among us.

NEIGHBORS

EACH YEAR THE Yukon attracts many young or young-minded urbanites from southern Canada or the United States who intend, for want of a better term, to homestead. Yukon homesteading, bush living, may mean something as straightforward as clearing land and building a cabin (or inheriting one someone else has abandoned). But shaped by knowledge, pressures, styles, and ideals of the late twentieth century, it may also mean an attempt at starting an organic herb farm or a meditation center, and commonly involves an attempt at wilderness group living.

Most of these attempts fail, and most Yukoners are delighted to see them fail. However, since most stories one hears of them are secondhand, it is difficult to discover just what goes wrong in the average bush commune.

One of the most talked-about of such ventures took place in the south-central Yukon, four miles in the bush off the South Canol Road, about fifty miles east of Whitehorse. Duffy McCabe, a competent local cabin-builder, was enlisted by a young Vancouver Buddhist, or follower of Buddhism, to build a cabin later inhabited by groups of seekers from various parts of Canada. McCabe also built his own bush cabin, next to the one occupied by the young Buddhists, and lived there one winter before terminating his association with the group.

I find Duffy parked along the Alaska Highway, between Whitehorse and Johnsons Crossing, living in his schoolbus home. Duffy, about forty, is goodnatured, intelligent, energetic, talkative. He has worked as a truck driver, carpenter, laborer, shortorder cook, country-and-western singer, restauranteur, fisherman, and lumberjack, and has lived in the Yukon several years.

Duffy's life has had its ups and downs. His marriage has recently split up. He has been involved in unsuccessful business ventures. He was hospitalized for a prolonged period, after a barroom brawl with local miners, and during that time he lost his half share in a small Whitehorse diner. He is nevertheless clever and resilient enough to bounce back from each of these situations.

Duffy's schoolbus home is neat, but crowded with couches, cabinets, a bed, a table, a stove, two or three expensive hunting rifles and several amplifiers, electric guitars, microphones, tape recorders, and other equipment from his band, the Grizzly

Stompers. We sit drinking bourbon throughout the afternoon, sometimes going next door to a roadside gas station for ice or to use the bathroom, as Duffy gives his version of what happened between him and his Buddhist neighbors.

"The first thing was, Vince Honeywell approached me and wanted me to help him build a cabin back in the bush. I was suspicious all right. I figured, this guy is an operator. You've met him, so you know what I mean. The way he glides around. And that crazy stuff he goes for. I noticed when he ate chicken soup, he picked the pieces of chicken out of it! And you ask him why, and he says in that fluttery little way, 'Oh, meat causes cancer.' Well, I didn't go for that shit! But at that time he was reasonably new. He had a pretty glib tongue and he was always in the diner over there at the crossroads, floatin' around and talkin', and he impressed people.

"The deal was, see, with the Bikkhu's money Vince had somehow leased this piece of land way back in there at the end of that mining road, on the shore of the lake. He didn't know anything about building a cabin, and he needed me for that. So he and I would build one for him, and we would build another one for me and my family about seventy yards away, and we would have a place to live. I knew in winter I would have to drive the kids out and back every day to school over that rough goddamn road, but the government pays you for that.

"So he and I would be neighbors. And of course, we would live in peace and harmony and brotherly love. That's what Vince said. It would be our little Shangri-la, back in the bush, eh? He talked a lot about the harmonies of nature and men and the vibrations he was getting and all that shit, and I figured this kid is a little insane, but he sounded like a good neighbor. And he let it be known that he had backing, much bucks, from the Bikkhu back in Vancouver. He was—how did he put it?—the vanguard of a movement, up here. He had all these tools and a four-wheel drive, and I would be free to use them, so I figured, I've got myself a good thing here. Besides, I figured I'm an operator too. I can handle whatever comes along.

"And you have to realize too that I was desperate. Our marriage was shaky. I was broke. I didn't have a regular job. My wife and two kids and I lived in a tent out here by Marsh Lake. Before we came up, I'd seen one of those ads in a paper—'Men needed for pipeline, good pay'—so we picked up

stakes in Alberta and came up to Whitehorse and I went to see this guy who ran the ad. For two dollars he was supposed to give you all the information you needed to get a good job on the pipeline. Well, he didn't have any information. All he had was the biggest suitcase of two-dollar bills you ever saw.

"Anyway, I was desperate and I didn't have a job. So I grabbed Vince's offer and went back in there to look at the proposed location of our little paradise. All Vince had done in a month or so was to get three or four logs laid up—and right off I saw that they were green logs! And you know what's going to happen to green logs when they dry out? They're gonna split and twist, when you've got 'em spiked down, and leave big cracks in your wall. But I didn't say anything. We just got to work, and in thirteen days I had that first cabin done, the big one."

"Did you have any friction, working together?"

"Are you kidding? Sure. See, I had to just about teach him which end of the ax to use. He had all these ideas in his head, but they were crazy. He wanted to go a mile away from the cabin site to get our logs. Remember, these are green logs he's thinkin' about. They're heavy. Now keep in mind that when you're out in the bush, you don't have a lot of cranes and things to do your work for you. You lift these big logs yourself and set 'em in place. And of course, hauling those logs from a mile away helps to put more ruts in your road. And right around the cabin were a lot of dead standing trees, all dry and light. They're the ones to use. Besides, you want to get that dead timber out of there anyway, in case of forest fire. It only takes a fire thirty minutes to go ten miles, and if you've got a lot of dead timber around your cabin, poof! Good-bye, cabin. It's not like New York. Even in a four-wheel drive it takes an hour to drive that four miles in to the cabin. Well, I don't have to tell you. You were in there. There's no fire truck gonna drive in to save you.

"Anyway, I finally convinced him of all that. But then he wanted to chink those cabins with moss! He said it was 'natural.' Well, there's two things wrong with moss. First, it's got every sort of freakin' bug in the world in it. And second, it's gonna dry out and fall out of the chinks. And then where are you going to be when it's sixty below and your walls open up and you got nothing else around to plug those holes with? Now they used moss seventy years ago, I know, but they had nothing else back then. Anyway, we finally chinked it with okum.

"And he wanted all these goddamn windows. A picture window. A dormer window. And I said look, every hole you poke in these cabins means more wood we have to cut. Windows let out heat. We're gonna use up our local wood fast enough without asking for trouble. But he had to have his windows!

"You see, this guy was intelligent, but he had no idea, no idea at all, about how to survive in the bush." Duffy pauses to put on a country and western tape of "If You Loved Me Half as Much as I Loved You" and to pour us another drink.

"Well anyway," I say, "you got the two cabins built. And they're beauties, by the way, especially the big one that Vince lives in. I was impressed. I've never seen such a fancy cabin in the bush."

"Oh sure," Duffy says. "That's the fanciest bush cabin in the Yukon. Two stories, twenty-four by twenty-four, right there on that little lake. What's he got in there now? Has he still got that harpsichord?"

"Yes. It's really very elegant. He's got the harpsichord, some antique furniture, a big stove, lots of good wine, a chandelier, several bookcases. He's also got quite a bit of machinery—two snowmobiles, the truck, a tractor, a Rototiller, I think—"

Duffy throws back his head and laughs. "A harpsichord! That crazy sonofabitch! Can you imagine getting that in there?" He shakes his head, remembering. "You know, he wanted to build a monastery up on the mountain—that bald one back of the cabin—and then the Bikkhu would come up there and it would be a world center."

"I asked Vince about that. He said he never had any idea of building a monastery."

Duffy snorts. "The hell he didn't! He was gonna build this big monastery up there, and I said that's fine, but what are you going to build it out of? And how are you going to heat it? There's no trees up there. There's nothing but caribou moss. How are you going to get the materials up there? There's no road! See, he had these flowery ideas, but he just didn't think." Duffy laughs. "Oh my God, if the Bikkhu ever knew how much money I saved him . . ."

"How much *did* it cost to build the two cabins, by the way?"

"Four hundred eighty dollars," Duffy says. "And most of that was the extras—the windows, the spikes, tools, roofing. But let me tell you, we used the very best in materials. The Dharma was paying it all. See, like I told you, Vince was an operator. He had that old Bikkhu wrapped right around his finger. He had a lot of people fooled. He was a talker. He used to spend half his time up in Whitehorse flittin' around with the big shots. And he impressed them too, don't think he didn't."

"Well, despite all this, everything worked out for a while, right? I guess I don't see just what was the thing that made you enemies?"

"Oh, we're not enemies. We still say hi, and I would sit down with him and have a drink. I respect that sonofabitch. He knows where it's at. But you see, he started writing these letters to other Dharma people. Other Buddhists. Telling them how beautiful and serene and natural everything was. He was writing letters all over the world constantly. And then these groups started to appear. His 'followers.' *He* was the guru. These goddamn assholes from Saskatoon, Vancouver, every place. You'd just get one group run off, and there'd be another one. They came about a half a dozen at a time and lived in Vince's cabin, right next to me. You see, Vince was only there part of the time. He was always off in Whitehorse arranging some political deal. He had a place there, too.

"I said to him, hey, who are these guys you're bringin' in here? I thought this was gonna be some kind of sanctuary? And he said 'Oh, it's okay. They're spiritual seekers. We're all gonna be happy and groove on nature together and share and live in peace and love.' And all these guys did was lie in the cabin or down at the crossroads and meditate and fart around, and they never did a *thing*. Sometimes they would go inside and meditate for a month. Straight! And they'd put up a big curtain to keep out the light. And not too much sex, because that would do something to your spine, they said.

"And Vince was always after me not to eat 'flesh foods.' Hell, I didn't even know what 'flesh foods' were! But that was the thing. Here we'd be eatin' moose meat and right to your face they'd tell you how bad it was, while they sat there eatin' homemade bread and lettuce. And it was *our* bread and lettuce! These guys would come over and bullshit and you'd end up inviting them to supper. And don't forget, we were on welfare. But those goddamn leeches never had a thing for themselves. They just didn't seem to know what it was to be poor, and how hard it was to get supplies in over that road.

"See, one of our reasons for coming up to the Yukon was to get our family together. And here these guys had grass and hash and all that shit. I wanted my kids away from that stuff. And they'd push their religion on you, too. They'd say to my kids, 'Go tell your dad he oughtn't to eat meat.' And then on top of it all, Vince asked me to move out of my cabin for a while so the Bikkhu could come and meditate and be quiet. I said no fuckin' way, baby. I met the Bikkhu once, by the way. He was a nice old guy all right. He had a little beard. But like all preachers, he was a con man. He probably had thousands of kids all over Canada payin' him fifty dollars or so a year, just like the ones that came up here.

"And these guys were always saying, 'Oh, how great the woods are. How wonderful nature is.' And shit, they didn't know a goddamn thing about living in the woods. When you're in the woods, you've got to go along with the elements of the woods. I told Vince and them to keep the hell off that road during breakup, and other people around here told 'em too. You just *don't* go on a dirt road like that in spring and early summer, because you're gonna rut it and make it impassable, and then it'll *stay* rutted. You've got to respect a road when you're four miles out in the bush and treat it like it was your lifeline. What happens if somebody gets sick? You can haul in bullshit like harpsichords and you can drag logs from a mile away to build your cabin, but do it in winter, when it's solid. When it's soft, you only take a vehicle over that road when you absolutely got to. But no! None of them could stand it to be in there away from town, and they were always running back and forth and the road went to hell. Well, I don't have to tell *you*, do I? You were out there and got stuck and had to walk in.

"Anyway, none of these guys—or sometimes a girl, they were all in their twenties—could do anything for themselves. They couldn't change a tire. They couldn't sharpen an axe. I swear, they came from a square room someplace with nothing in it. Christ, they were dumb. Oh, they had brains all right. They just didn't know how to survive."

Duffy paces back and forth across the bus. He is theatrical. But at the same time, he seems to feel his experience with the Dharma people as keenly as if it were yesterday.

"See, what their contention was, they were gonna raise vegetables—self-sufficiency, eh? Now you were out there yesterday—and this is two years later, when they've had plenty of time to get the ground ready—and you tell me how many vegeta-

bles he's getting. None, right? Those goddamn broccoli plants never got up more than five inches. My God! Of course, you can't raise that kind of stuff in the Yukon. You plant in mid-June, and you get your first frost maybe in late August. If you're lucky! Or maybe you get two frosts in July. You can't count on the weather up here. Sure, you got twenty hours of sunlight, but that's not enough. Well, they had that vegetable idea so stuck in their heads that they were saving five-gallon cans to harvest vegetables in! They never got a goddamn radish when I was there."

"It sounds to me like the Dharma groups came from middle-class suburban homes and had no awareness of any other kind of life."

"You're completely right," Duffy says. "But my God, how long does it take to catch on? You know what they did? They got some boards somewhere and built a stand out there around a tree to put their tools on, and their grub. But the Yukon has much bears eh? Now all you have to do is spend sixty-nine cents and get a can of mothballs and scatter them around and no bear will come near. I told 'em that. But no. They just left their grub out and one night, a grizzly comes around and cleans 'em out. And you know what those idiots did? They threw a pail of honey at him to scare him away!"

"What did the bear do?"

"I don't remember. He probably ran in the bush and died laughing."

"Actually, from what Vince told me, I think he also got disillusioned with the groups and regretted the whole thing," I say.

"Then why didn't he get rid of 'em? You know why? Because he liked being their guru in the north, that's why. I finally got pissed off. I had some tobacco, and one night they just came over and bummed it, all the time laying on this rap about not eating meat. I went over and I took Vince right by the throat and I said, 'Those guys are gonna be out of here by tomorrow night!' And he said, 'This is my cabin and I'm gonna do with it just as I please.' And I said, 'It only took me a few days to build this cabin and it'll only take me about eight hours to burn it down. If those guys are here tomorrow night, you're all gonna be sleepin' in ashes!'"

"What happened?"

"They beat it home," he says. He shakes his head again. "But of course, more came in to replace 'em.

"You see, nothing went right. Don't forget, I was a lumberjack for two years, and I homesteaded before, in Alberta. I know a lot about tools. And those idiots didn't know a thing. Now everything was bought by the Dharma, so it was a little awkward. But we had just one chain saw. And when you're out in the bush, you learn to treat it right. You can't get a replacement part without a trip to Whitehorse, and maybe you can't even get it then for two months. So I figured I would hold onto the saw. But they wanted to use it. They were building this octagonal cabin—did Vince show you that? Oh, you missed something. That was gonna be a world retreat. It's right out in back there. It must be seventy feet across. If they'd ever finished it, it woulda taken half the logs in the Yukon. But they only got two or three logs laid up. Anyway, they wanted to borrow the saw one day, but I took off the chain and reversed it so they couldn't possibly cut with it. I knew none of them would figure out why the teeth weren't cutting, and I figured they'd get disgusted and give it back. But you know what they did? They took that thing out and used it steady for a half hour tryin' to cut *one pole*, and they burned the insides right out of it. So then we didn't have a saw. Oh God, I should've known."

"I guess I'm a little unclear why Vince came up here in the first place," I say. "He mentioned to me, casually, that the Bikkhu had specifically designated the Yukon as a place of retreat, and that a tidal wave was going to destroy the world but the Yukon would be protected by its coastal mountains. But I can't really believe that he believes that. I mean, maybe, like a lot of people, he just had to get away from whatever his life was down south, and invented a purpose for himself up here. . . ."

"His purpose was to infiltrate the government," Duffy says positively. "I think very definitely that his purpose was to infiltrate the government with Buddhists and their ideas."

"Oh bullshit, you don't really think that."

"Sure I do. They wanted to turn the whole place into a park. No killing animals. No cutting trees. All of this shit. Oh! And I forgot to tell you this. Vincent, with the Bikkhu's money, had already bought out two big traplines, up near Quiet Lake. Twelve-thousand acres! He controlled all that. And he said that's how it should be, that God didn't want any trapping, and he was gonna help Him, and just let the trapline lie idle. But you know, when you buy out a trapline like that, you prevent some Indian family from earning a living off it. But this guy

wanted to take over the place with ideas like that, and I'm completely convinced that they wanted to overthrow the government. I'm not the only one who thinks that either. You just ask around Whitehorse and see." He puts down his empty glass. "Hey, I'm hungry. I don't have too much here, but you're welcome to it. Let's get some eggs started."

Duffy fries the eggs. I think about the notion of government take-over by a group of Buddhists. It sounds like a joke to me, a cliché. But in the Yukon—23,000 population, conservative, isolated—I can see how a person with an apparently political personality, some followers, and some money, could create this worry.

"Well, I can see that you're going to write a good book," Duffy says. "You're interested in this shit. But that's what the Yukon is, shit like this. You're gonna do a good book, I know. I'm getting good messages. That's what Vince always said: 'I'm getting good messages.'"

Duffy paces. He leans for a moment on the corner of the amplifier and gets a shock from a loose wire. "Ouch! Shit!" He leaps away. "You know, the Yukon is a crazy place. And in a strange way, Vincent and his group fit right into it. You just drop some city nut in a place like this—seventy-below weather, gold miners, people eatin' caribou and beaver and moose meat, runnin' around with each other's wives—and in a funny way, he fits.

"But he was different too, from most of the people you'll meet here. Maybe I just can't explain it right for you to understand, but these Buddhists were just against everything anybody needs to do to live up here. And they were always layin' it on you to meditate and align your bed to get the right vibrations from space and to keep away from meat. They were always buyin' sesame seeds and lentils and all that shit. Thirty-six pounds of sesame seeds I brought in once from Whitehorse! Thirty-six pounds! That would keep a Chinese restaurant goin' for a month. But Vince said that he didn't want any meat on his property. And once, in November, I had these two moose hangin' from his rafters when he came in. Oh, he was mad! He said that God looks after that, and gives us vegetables to eat. Well, I said maybe He does, but when man is down here, runnin' things, then that screws it up and changes everything. See, we had to eat. *We* couldn't afford goddamn sesame seeds like he could. I had to get something to feed my family. . . .

"And that was a funny story too, because right after I shot those two moose I saw these two guys from the government settin' down on the lake in a chopper. They were from forestry. And I thought, oh-oh, I've had it now. I got two moose hanging up there, and I don't even have a license. Well, they came to shore and sort of poked around. Those moose weren't up so high that you couldn't see 'em. They were right in sight. But they said all they were lookin' for was fire safety hazards. I offered 'em a beer and we sat right there under the moose and drank it. And they never said a thing about it.

"But anyway, Vince was opposed to eating meat. He was opposed to guns. You said he's got a rifle now? And he's eatin' fish? Well, that's a change. He was opposed to trapping. Oh my God, Vince raised supreme shit when he found out I had deadfalls set around there. See, we were on welfare and I couldn't afford steel traps. I was tryin' to catch a few furs to sell. I saw this wolverine walking across the ice on the lake one day, and oh my God he was beautiful. You know, wolverines don't give a shit for anybody. I coulda shot him right then, but of course, that's not how you do it with an animal like that. That's too easy. You've gotta outsmart him if you're gonna earn his hide. And I never did, by the way. Anyway Vince raised hell and told me to spring all the deadfalls. Of course, I never did. I bet there's one set out there yet.

"And on this meat thing—not only didn't God like it, but you were gonna get cancer if you ate it. What horseshit! One night I asked him, what does a moose eat? He eats willows and the tips of bushes and things, and that to him is like spinach or something, eh? So now I go out and shoot this sonofabitchin' thing and it's just a big vegetable, 'cause that's all he eats. So how can you tell me it's gonna give me cancer!? You're just as crazy as hell."

I am laughing now, as this tale unfolds. "Well," I comment, "I think maybe Vince has learned something from his experience. I sort of doubt he'll get any more groups in there. He's all alone now."

Duffy snorts. "I hope you're right. Maybe the poor sonofabitch'll survive now. Because they did the dumbest things when they were all there together. There was this one group in there, six guys and a girl in that small cabin. And right in the middle of the winter, they took the chain saw and cut a hole in the roof for a window. They wanted to see the stars, they said! Well, shit, it's fifty below! Like I said, Vince wanted picture windows everywhere. Okay. So we had lots of standing firewood near the cabin right then. But later, when that's used up, you gotta haul more in. And then you're back to your road again. See, everything ties together when you live in the bush. Just what is that road like now?"

"Well, it's pretty deeply rutted. It's hard to get out, even with the four-wheel drive."

Duffy nods. "See, when I was in there, I used to drag a log behind the truck every time I went in or out, to keep those ruts smoothed down. But Vince didn't know enough to do things like that. I predict that in another year, he won't even be able to get in there."

"Vince said something to me about you setting off a charge of dynamite in the lake and killing all the fish. What was that?"

Duffy throws back his head and laughs uproariously. "Killing the fish, shit. You can go right out there now and catch a jackfish. So you tell me just what kind of harm that did. It was one goddamn stick of eighty percent dynamite. And you know that if you let one stick go, it's not going to get any fish except those right around it. But anyway, it was winter and I set it to clear a hole in the ice to get water through. Those assholes had let the water hole freeze up solid. Now in this country, when you go out to get water, you don't just cut a little tiny hole. You cut a big hole, four by eight, and you keep it clear, or it's gonna get smaller and smaller, and you're gonna have a helluva chopping job to clear it again. Well of course the Dharma people let it freeze shut. Oh my God, it was pathetic! They were out there on their hands and knees with a cup or some damn little thing, trying to scrape the ice away. It was like one of those movies you see with the guy in the desert lookin' for water! So I set off the dynamite. And they came runnin' out of that cabin like a war had started. I just figured I'd open it up for them."

Duffy laughs. "Oh Jack, they were pathetic. They just couldn't do a thing for themselves. It was midwinter. They ran out of firewood, and every once in a while you'd see one of them run out of the cabin and break off a little stick of wood here and there. Then a half hour later, another one would run out and get another stick. Those idiots would've frozen and starved if it wasn't for me."

"Does that mean they finally consented to eat meat?"

"Consented?! They were starvin'! There was seven of 'em, and seven dogs, and all they had was brown rice. But did you ever try to live on rice out in the bush at seventy below? They ate meat all right! My meat, of course, but I couldn't let 'em starve. Finally, one day when Vince came along, there we all were, cuttin' steaks off those moose with a power saw, and they were just droolin' for it. Old Vince couldn't take that. There they were, the Dharma people, his followers, eatin' moose, and lovin' it. That was quite a shock.

"And of course the dogs couldn't live on brown rice either. They were just skin and bone. To show you how hungry they were, I had been savin' the hides off those two moose to tan for gloves and mukluks and things, and those dogs found 'em and they ate 'em. Not only were those hides frozen stiff, but they ate 'em hair and all. There was hair-filled dog shit around for weeks. It was cruel. Finally I couldn't stand it anymore. I went over to Vince and his crew and told 'em that if those dogs weren't out of there by sundown, I would shoot every damn one of 'em. And I would've, too. But they took 'em out that night."

"What finally happened between you and the Dharma people?"

Duffy snorts with laughter. "See, we just couldn't stand each other any longer. And people around more or less sympathized with me. So I got this idea, and I went over to Don Preston's place, down the highway. He's got a typewriter see, and we made up this letter. It started out as sort of a joke, but then we got serious. It was supposed to be to me, from this rich American. He had every kind of a gun and wanted to kill moose. He was willing to kill two or three of them to get a good head. He'd got my name from somebody. He wanted to hunt over there at the lake, and wanted me to guide him. He knew about this fancy cabin I'd built, and he was willing to pay me seventy-five hundred for it! Then he would stay there and hunt, eh? He and his buddies. Many buddies. And we hinted that maybe his wife didn't know about the cabin, so, please respond to his letter by phone at his business address. And he wanted to effect the transaction quickly, so he would fly up to the Yukon, if I agreed. And we also hinted that there would be lots of secretaries coming with the men and lots of wild parties. Get the picture?

"So I took the letter back to the cabin and showed Vince. I watched his face as he read it and I could see it was working. His world was falling in, see? He just about goes crazy. It's bad enough to have just one nut like me shooting moose and eatin' flesh foods, but to have a whole club of drunken hunters next door . . . He was on his knees, beggin' me not to sell my cabin. And I said, well, I don't know, kid, I'm strapped for cash. But since I know you, and understand how you feel about this place, I'll move out and give the cabin to you, if you want, for only five thousand. And he said, 'Oh, I don't have that kind of money,' and I said, 'Well then, I'm sorry, but I've got to accept this guy's offer. I'll phone him today, because I need that money by next week.' And he said, real scared, 'Don't do anything! I'll be right back!'

"Well, he roared out of there, and a couple hours later he came back. He'd wired the Bikkhu. He said, 'I could only get thirty-eight hundred, is that enough?' And I said, 'No, five thousand is already twenty-five hundred less than this guy will give me. I'll take a twenty-five hundred cut because I know you, but no more.' I was gettin' a little worried now because maybe he couldn't really get any more, and I'd have to live up to my bluff. So real quick I looked around and saw that four-wheel drive Toyota he had, and I said, 'Well, okay, I'll take the thirty-eight hundred cash and the Toyota, but you gotta decide right now. I can't wait.' And he agreed. I took the money. I threw my furniture in the Toyota and drove off, and that was the end of it. I never went back."

I laugh. "What goddamn nerve you've got. You really pulled the perfect con job."

"Yeah," Duffy says pensively. "I took him all right. Though sometimes I think maybe it was the other way around."

CANS

I RIDE FROM Whitehorse to Watson Lake with three young Indian people. Stephen and Jimmy sit in front. I sit in the back seat with Alice, Jimmy's older sister.

We drink beer as we speed along. When Alice finishes her can, she asks me to throw it out the window on my side, into the ditch.

"I can't do that," I tell her.

"Why not?" she says. "The window's open." She looks at me as if I do not understand the simplicity of her request.

"I'm not talking about the window. I just mean that I never heave anything out of an automobile. You know, litter."

"Litter?" Alice says. The word does not seem to register with her.

"I don't believe this," I say. "I must be brainwashed. I always thought Indian people were a lot more careful than palefaces about lousing up their surroundings. Why don't we hold on to that can until we stop. Then you can throw it in a garbage can."

Alice, still holding the beer can, looks at me as if I have lost my senses.

I continue, trying to make a joke out of it: "I mean, didn't you ever see that TV ad of the Indian guy crying as he comes upon a pile of litter in the woods?"

"No," Alice says. She tosses the can past my head and it goes clanking and skipping back along the highway. "I never saw that ad."

(Jack Hope)

POWER

THE YUKON'S RIVERS hold vast hydropower potential. Estimates indicate that dams placed upon rivers flowing from the St. Elias Mountains and upon the Yukon River and its major tributaries, the Pelly and Stewart rivers, could supply the territory with ten thousand to fifteen thousand megawatts of electrical energy each year.

At this point, the territory's power consumption is only about sixty megawatts. About 60 percent of this power goes to the Yukon's four large mines —Whitehorse Copper, Anvil, Clinton Creek, and United Keno Hill—and about 40 percent is consumed by Yukon residences and retail establishments, most of which are in Whitehorse. The territory's power requirements are met by two small hydropower projects which generate about fifty megawatts—one on the Yukon River at Whitehorse, one on the Stewart River near Mayo—supplemented by fuel oil generators located in various communities. A third hydropower project, which will generate thirty megawatts, is nearing completion on the Aishihik River thirty miles northeast of Haines Junction, about seventy miles west of Whitehorse. Over 99 percent of the Yukon's hydropower capacity remains undeveloped.

An essential question in the Yukon today is whether the territory should seek to expand any of its available forms of electric power generation —and hydropower is the most likely form to be expanded—beyond its immediately foreseeable needs. The question is important, because the future of this wild, sparsely populated, only slightly developed region will be strongly shaped by the availability or unavailability of power. If the Yukon develops its hydropower slowly, the region will change slowly. If it launches an ambitious power development program, demonstrating a willingness to dam its rivers and generate hydropower in excess of its immediate needs, this excess supply of power will attract new industry—mostly mining—and new population, which could dramatically alter the Yukon's social, economic, biological, and aesthetic complexion within a decade or two. Some Yukoners view this potential change as an improvement; some prefer the territory the way it is.

The agency in charge of Yukon hydropower development is the federal government's Northern Canada Power Commission (NCPC), which is responsible for 90 percent of the electrical power generated in Canada's frontier regions north of the 60th parallel. The Yukon manager of this agency is Frank Mooney. I go to meet with him in his office in downtown Whitehorse.

Frank is a middle-aged man, talkative, dapper, with graying reddish hair. He is married, the father of six children. On his office wall are certificates of his graduation from Francis Xavier College in Nova Scotia and an engineering degree from the University of Toronto, and a color photo of Otter Falls, a small scenic waterfall on the Aishihik River, once pictured on the face of the Canadian five-dollar bill.

The Aishihik power project is still under construction when I visit Frank, and we begin our discussion with this topic. The Aishihik project will primarily service the Whitehorse area and Anvil mine, via a hundred-mile power line built from the project east to junction with an existing line that joins these two locations. It is a small project, but it does provide a basis for discussion of the Yukon's future power development and for an assessment of some of the attitudes toward that development.

Mooney explains to me, since I have not yet visited the Aishihik site, that the project includes small coffer dams to raise the level of two or three large lakes—primarily sixty-mile-long Aishihik Lake—plus a three-mile aboveground diversion canal, an underground set of turbines, and a return canal to lead water back into the Aishihik River, all set among the Ruby Range of the southwestern Yukon.

"The beauty of these lakes," Frank says, "is not only that they're big, but that they're high. We just divert the water into a gravity ditch, then drop her six hundred and thirty feet into the ground, over the turbines, then lead her back to the river. She's our backup. If our whole system here in Whitehorse went out, that old girl could handle us and Anvil too. And it'll only take one man to run her, once she's finished."

Frank points to the color photo of Otter Falls. "In simple terms, we just divert most of the water from that view you see there into the canal."

"Otter Falls will vanish then?"

Frank smiles and raises his finger. "Part of the time," he says. "But we're going to maintain it in summer as a tourist attraction. We've even done a little survey, and we know that the hours of ten A.M. to three P.M. give you seventy percent of your tourist travel out there. So if they want, we can regulate the flow to those hours."

This notion, of turning the waterfall on and off like a faucet for the sake of tourists, seems a little bizarre to me. But Frank is apparently serious about it.

"We figure that if somebody is out there at night," he says, "it's for a reason not related to the falls. Why the hell spill water over the falls when there's nobody there?"

I ask Frank what Yukoners have to say about this idea.

"You know," he says, "the funny thing is, we didn't get much interest in that falls before we announced our intentions to go ahead with this project. But once we did, then some of them said, 'No, no, you can't do that. NCPC's going to ruin the falls.' The falls suddenly became very important to them." He sighs. "But we're *not* going to ruin it. We will even improve it by reducing the upstream flow which will slow the natural erosion of the falls." He points to the wall photo. "We hope to be able to sell this project later as prettier than it was before. It's all scrub brush out there now."

"Do you really think you can sell that idea?"

Frank shrugs. "You know, these environmental boys are hard to deal with. They put all their emphasis on the values of a bird or a bee, and that's hard to argue. Now out there in the St. Elias Mountains, they've got ten thousand megawatts locked up in that Kluane Park. So we say, 'Okay, Mr. Parks, one of your rivers dammed herself a while ago when the Tweedsmuir Glacier retreated, so why not let us dam that river like mother nature did herself? She's already done a five-million-dollar clearing job along the shoreline with her glacier. So why not let us put a dam in there?' And Mr. Parks says, 'Ohhh, what mother nature does herself is fine, but what man does to her is not permitted.'"

Frank sighs, dreamily, leans back, and places the tips of his fingers together. "It's hard," he says, "to watch old mother nature waste her energy. But we can wait. Someday . . . someday, in thirty or forty years, when the crunch comes, I know we'll be harnessing those rivers."

The fact that Frank feels the way he does, I suppose, is not surprising to me. As the Yukon's leading power authority, he apparently feels frustrated by opposition to his plans. Also, he probably feels frustrated as he sits amidst a vast hydropower potential for which there is no existing demand.

But what does surprise me is his willingness to publicly air his notions of improving upon nature, faking a waterfall for the tourists, of "selling" the public the idea that the Aishihik area will be made more beautiful by a hydropower project. Any hydropower developer in southern Canada or the United States would work to avoid such comments. But of course, we are not in southern Canada or the United States: we're in the Yukon.

I remark that I am in general familiar with some of the aesthetic and biological shortcomings of power projects: the need for transmission lines and roads; the raising and lowering of reservoir levels, alternately flooding surrounding landscape and exposing muddy unvegetated shorelines; the impairment of river ecology and of fish migration, especially in rivers containing species such as salmon. I ask him to comment on any of these situations as they relate to the Aishihik project.

"I can assure you," he says, "that we've designed this project to get every bit of energy out of the old girl we can, while maintaining enough flexibility to give the environmentalists anything they want. We *were* going to run the power line over a mountain, but the Indian people told us it was a Dall sheep area, so we dropped her down and still kept it far enough away to be hidden from the road." He ticks off one finger. "Fish aren't much of a problem because the Aishihik isn't a migrating stream. But the fisheries boys told us there is some movement of whitefish and grayling between the lakes, so we built a fish ladder. As for the flooding and drawdown, we're just using small dams at Aishihik, and we're only going to drop her four feet below historic low and raise her four feet above historic high, so we're only going to have a variation of about twelve feet in the water level. We asked for a fifteen-foot variation and they only wanted to give us ten. Right now we're dickering over that. But we can live with twelve. We can live with it."

"Well, twelve feet doesn't sound like much to me," I say.

Frank nods dreamily. "No, it isn't. Because on our next project, we're going to ask for fifty feet."

"I recall that Ken McKinnon told me there's an Indian fishing village back at the head of Aishihik Lake, and the project might flood it out. Is that so?"

Frank smiles. "Your friend McKinnon is a good man. But his fears are groundless. I can assure you that we will not be allowed to flood that village. First of all, let me tell you that there's nobody actually living there. Nobody at all. There may be about a dozen cabins, and a few people go out there in summer to fish. But we're only going to raise

Aishihik Lake four feet above historic high, so probably we're only going to flood out two old cabins. When we were planning this thing, we made one visit after another out there to the village. We laid out a red line and a yellow line along the shore and we said, 'Now here's the lowest level we'll draw down to, and here's the highest level we'll raise her. It's not going to be raised any higher than that.' And they all *saw* it. But whenever you talk to any of the Indian people, now, they say, 'You flood mountains, eh?' Of course we're not *going* to flood out the mountains. They're a thousand feet above the lake or more. But you can't make them *understand* that."

"I think Ken also mentioned some archaeological finds out there along the shore."

Frank nods, smiles. "We can draw down the water level lower than mother nature herself," he says. "So even if we do flood out the archaeological finds, then we can drop her down when they want to do some digging and say, 'Go dig, boys.'"

Frank's phone rings, and one of his two secretaries calls in to him to pick it up. It is a local reporter who wants to get a quote from Frank on a small oil spill into the Yukon River from one of NCPC's Whitehorse standby power generators. I offer to leave the room, but Frank motions me to stay seated.

"Hello, Gerry," Frank says grinning. "So you don't want to talk about the boys going back to work at Aishihik, you want to talk about oil spill. That's right. That's right, it's the first oil spill we've had in my four short years in the Yukon. Fortunately it was caught in time to prevent further oil spill. That's right. . . ."

The conversation goes on for ten minutes, but it has reminded me of another question about the Aishihik project. When Frank gets off I ask it:

"I think I've also heard that the Yukon Indian people had some objection to the fact that NCPC didn't hire any Indian workers out at the Aishihik project. What about that?"

Frank waves his hand in annoyance. "We *try* to hire locally as much as we can before going outside. But out of three hundred and seven employees out there, I bet there's only a hundred fifty local boys and maybe only fifteen natives. The rest are from outside the territory. We just can't get the expertise here. You look for skilled work like welding, or concrete work or surveying, and you just can't find it in the Yukon.

"And you know how the native boys are. They

don't hold down a job. They work for two weeks and they say, 'Oh, I have to go fishing.' And they don't come back." Frank shakes his head. "We'd love to hire them for some job like clearing the shoreline, but they just don't stay. They're a totally different bunch here than across the border. Over in the Northwest Territories, at a little project we have there, we hired seventy or eighty Dogrib Indians to cut brush and they worked out just fine. They're a happy bunch, those Dogribs. They developed a competitive incentive system on their own, and they're competing against one another to see who can cut faster, and they're doing just great. But not here."

"Why do you suppose it is that the natives here don't work out?"

"I'd almost start with the premise that all men are not equal. Now the Indians can't grow a beard. They can't hold their liquor. I don't think their pain threshold is much different than ours," Frank says, musing, "but . . . it's a very basic question, and I'd like to throw it back to the medical boys. They're no longer a proud race. They say we've done that to them, and maybe we have. But whatever the reason, I think it's going to take a pile of money and a long time. I think they have to be forced, more or less, into restoring their pride."

While I ponder Frank's statement, which to me seems part compassionate and part racist, part liberal and part conservative, he excuses himself again and makes a phone call. When he returns, he gives me a summing-up statement on the Aishihik project. "Anyway, Jack, I can assure you that we have done our best to employ local labor at Aishihik, and we have done our best to locate it in one of the most ecologically acceptable locations in the Yukon. We studied this situation very closely before we began." He pulls a thick booklet from his bookcase. "Of course, the environmentalists didn't think our study was thick enough, so we had to do another one. We didn't think it was necessary to spend half a million on it when we could do it for ten or fifteen thousand. That's Yukoners' money we're spending. That's an awful lot of money to spend on the birds and bees."

"Who has to finally approve your hydroprojects?"

"The water board," Frank says. "And there are nine of them. They're a good cross section of Yukoners. Jim Sykes is on it. He's with Environment Canada."

"You mean he's a thorn in your side?"

"No," Frank says. "No more than he should be. We can work with him."

"What are the backgrounds of the other members?"

"Well, there's Bob Cutler. He's an engineer-hydraulogist. Craig Miller is a DPW engineer. Then there's another man in construction. Another one owns a store. Another one is with Energy, Mines, and Resources. There's quite a group of them. They're a good cross section."

I do not know any of these men personally, but it does sound to me as if the water board is heavily weighted with people whose backgrounds lean toward construction, commercial and industrial development. "You don't have any sort of organized opposition from environmentalists here in the Yukon, do you? I mean, you don't have an environmental movement like those in the States or in southern Canada?"

Frank raises his hand and grins. "Oh, we have them. We have them all right. Oh, we don't have anything like the Sierra Club. But we have environmentalists, and don't think they don't speak out individually." He smiles. "The last ten or fifteen years, the pendulum has been swinging in their direction. And environment will always have a place. It should have. But when this energy crunch comes . . . and with the price of fuel going up . . ." Frank again sits back, places his fingers together. "It's hard to sit by and watch mother nature pissing her energy into the sea," he says, smiling, speaking through his teeth. "But we can wait. All we ask is orderly development. One of these days, we might be harnessing that power."

"Well, where will the next NCPC project be then?"

"We don't know yet what they'll give us," Frank says. "We call it 'Project X.' It'll probably be one hundred megawatts, but we don't know just where. We've got a consulting firm working on a study for us. And we're going to hold public hearings on it this fall." He lists a dozen or more locations that NCPC has been looking at on the Teslin, Pelly, Stewart, and Yukon rivers. I am not familiar with most of the sites. But then he mentions the Five Fingers Rapids, about twenty miles north of the town of Carmacks. It is probably the best known, most photographed spot on the Yukon River. I question Frank about it.

Five Finger Rapids

"That's one we're going to ask for," he says. "We'd put a hundred foot dam in the rapids, and that would give us what we want."

"Do you think Yukoners would agree to that?"

Frank shakes his head. "I don't think so," he says. "But that's all right. We'll ask for Five Fingers first, then we'll go for a really big one out in the boondocks."

"Where?"

"Granite Canyon," Frank says. "On the Pelly, about fifteen miles upriver from Pelly Crossing. We'd put in a hundred-fifty-foot dam there."

"With these big dams, then, wouldn't any of the sites you have picked out flood a very large area, relative to anything that now exists in the Yukon?"

Frank nods. "The Five Fingers site would flood out Carmacks," he says. "But that's nothing. We could rebuild the town, and I think the people would appreciate it."

I laugh. "And the Granite Canyon site? What would that flood?"

"The water would be backed up seventy miles," Frank says. "But there's no towns or roads or anything up there, and that's what makes me guess that that'll be our next site."

Now that we talk of flooding, I am reminded of a tentative plan I have heard mentioned for placing a major dam on the Yukon—I believe near Lake Laberge—which would create an enormous reservoir impoundment that would flood out Whitehorse. I ask Frank about this.

Frank pooh-poohs the idea as only partly serious, but nevertheless displays enthusiasm as he briefly describes the project. "Now I'm not saying we should do this now. Why should we, when we have suitable alternatives? But I say we should be surveying these sites now, so in forty years, when we need them . . . Sure," he says, with a sweep of his hand, "we could build that dam, or a series of dams, and back up the Yukon. But you see, whenever you talk about big projects like this you get into international complications. The Yukon starts in Canada, but it flows over fifteen hundred miles through Alaska. And even if only two hundred salmon came up the river to spawn," he says sarcastically, "they still don't want you damming it."

We talk briefly about the effectiveness of the salmon ladders that hydropower projects typically install on migrating rivers such as the Yukon, and Frank tells me something that I did not know: that these ladders are only partially effective. Apparently, a reservoir impoundment slows the downriver movement of water and alters the current enough so that migrating fish have considerable difficulty in even locating the narrow ladder that will carry them around the dam.

In any case, Frank's feelings on the fish problem seem to be that since other deep-water fish—such as lake trout—could be stocked in the reservoir created behind the dam on any river, this will compensate for any loss of salmon or other river species caused by the dam. While he readily acknowledges the negative consequences of dam building, he seems to view them all as solvable problems, whether they happen to be the loss of fish or the flooding of a town.

"I wonder if you, NCPC, have any definite goals or aims with regard to power development?" I ask.

"Our goal is definitely to grid the north," Frank says quickly, matter-of-factly.

"Well, I guess my primary question then is whether or not the Yukon needs any more projects, after Aishihik. Do you foresee an electrical demand that will justify any of these big dams? Or do you hope to build them and *then* create demand for the power?"

Frank shakes his head. "It is our policy only to meet demand. We don't have to create it. But it's got to come. We're looking at a several percent annual increase in electrical demand in the Yukon. This so-called energy crisis has made us look at our resources here. And," he whispers dramatically, "with a rise of eight cents a gallon in the price of oil this year and maybe another ten to fifteen cents next year, electric power will be feasible for heating homes. On the basis of this, people are just going ahead and building homes with electric heating. I have a couple of friends who are doing it now. And people are using more electrical appliances."

"How about the mines? That's where most of the power goes, right?"

Frank nods. "The mines are expanding their use of power too. Anvil is expanding forty-five percent, and that's where most of Aishihik will go. Then, in five years, there will be that copper mine at Minto. Then there's the Bonnet Plume operation and two or three others that may open up early in the 1980s. And we have to anticipate these mines so we can get our projects approved and in operation by the time they're ready to use them."

Frank smiles. "Here, I want to show you something, it's no secret." He rummages around on his desk and hands me a letter from the Henry J. Kaiser Company, Oakland, California. "You read that and then ask me about demand," he says. "I've got to make another phone call."

As he dials the phone, a portly, young priest wanders unannounced into the office. It is Father Fred Kirkpatrick, from Haines Junction, near Kluane Park and the St. Elias Mountains. Frank stays on the phone but pauses to introduce us.

"We had Father working in the underground, pushing power in the park for us," Frank says to me, laughing. "Right, Father?"

Once Frank's phone party answers, he carries on a three-way conversation with the two of us in his office and the phone party, periodically addressing his remarks to each of us, mentioning each of us to the other, and apparently enjoying the confusion of the situation: "If we're smart, we'll get a sharp P.R. man here, have him explain the pros and cons, and then say, 'Okay, boys. Now go ahead and vote. . . .' I've got a man from New York in my office. He's writing a book. . . . Thanks for that invitation, Father. We'll take you up on it sometime. . . . Sure. If we can get a gal to do it, that'll keep the women's lib types happy. . . ." Father Kirkpatrick stays only a few minutes after Frank hangs up, reiterates his invitation for Frank and his wife to visit, then leaves. I go ahead and read the Henry J. Kaiser letter:

Dear Mr. Mooney:
Thank you for the excellent hospitality you showed me during my visit to Whitehorse earlier this month. As you know, I have a keen personal regard for the Yukon country. . . .

As we discussed, the Henry J. Kaiser Company is seeking on behalf of a client to identify a source of power for a large iron ore mine and pelletizing plant near Haines, Alaska. We are interested in the possibility that the NCPC could develop such a power source at Granite Canyon, on the Pelly River, or another Yukon site prior to 1980. . . .

"So you see," Frank says to me, "he's asking there for a firm seventy-five megawatt site with maybe another twenty-five maximum for a reserve. Now that's what I call the kicker. It's the kickoff for the Granite Canyon site." Frank again lowers his voice to a whisper. "Because if he wants one hundred megawatts, we can construct that thing to two or three hundred megawatts and build our own capacity. Then if he depletes his resource over there, we can cut him off and use that power too." He sits back with a pleased look.

"But do you want to sell power to the Americans? Do people in the Yukon feel they should be damming their rivers to satisfy foreign demand?"

Frank picks up the Kaiser letter and poises it dramatically in the air. "This guy is saying to me, 'Frank, can you help us?' and I'm going to say to him"—he lowers his voice to a whisper—" 'You bet your life I can.' Physically we can, and I think politically we can too. We haven't let a customer down in twenty-five years and we're not going to in the future. The chamber of commerce and the city of Whitehorse have indicated they would go for development of peripheral power [foreign sales]," Frank says. "I talked to the commissioner about this letter and he responded favorably. He's for it."

Apparently, Frank makes no distinction between the power needs of the Yukon itself and the power needs originating in places outside the territory's boundaries. It is all demand, and a reason for building another hydro project.

Also it seems to me, despite Frank's disclaimer, that this plan does in fact amount to creating demand for NCPC's product. Obviously, predictable Yukon power needs must be anticipated and accommodated; yet, building considerably excess supplies of power essentially creates new demand for that power, by attracting new industry and population to use the surplus. There is nothing inherently wrong with this approach, providing Yukoners want it and are fully aware of its pros and cons. But an interesting political aspect of this approach is that once surplus power exists, this provides great leverage to pressure the Yukon's people to agree to new development—even undesirable development—in order to prevent the surplus from being "wasted."

"So then, if and when Kaiser's demand for your power ended, you would transfer that power back here and use it, mostly for mines." (As I say this, it also occurs to me that supplying power to Alaska would require a long power line from the Yukon; would that line be left idle if the Alaskan demand was cut off?) "But wouldn't you then have far more power here than you need? Especially if you built your Granite Canyon site, or whatever site it was, to two- or three-hundred-megawatt capacity in the first place? I mean, it seems to me that since the Yukon has only four mines and such a small population—"

"That's now," Frank says. "But in the future, this Yukon has a capacity for a one to two million population. As I said before, we have new mines coming in. Every time you get a new mine opening up you get an employment of about five hundred and a new townsite of about fifteen hundred. We have to be ready for that."

"But a lot of these mines don't stay in operation very long, do they? I just heard a rumor that Clinton Creek is closing down in a couple years because they're running out of asbestos. And I know you've had several others like that in the past few years. So if you base your power expansion on these mines and their towns, and build new capacity and high-tension lines and all that, then there's a good chance it'll be idle, excess capacity in not too long. Right?"

Frank nods. "It is true that up to now, mines have come and gone. But I like to think it's going to get better. And if we get these new mines at Minto and Bonnet Plume, we could get a smelter at Carmacks. We could get other supporting industries. That's the best thing that could happen in the Yukon."

"Is it? I mean, another way to look at it is that the people of the Yukon should first plan whether or not they want another mine, or another six mines, or whatever. And if they do, *then* they can go about planning their power needs. And it may be that they don't even want mines. Maybe they want to expand in another direction, or maybe not at all. Those mines, after all, are dismal places to work and live. And I'm not sure that the mining population is any great asset to the Yukon."

As I talk, I realize that one loophole in my thinking is that Yukoners, due to their territorial status, have only a limited opportunity to plan their economic future. Most major developmental decisions are made at the federal level, in Ottawa.

Frank does not pick up on this, but picks up on my criticism of mining as the territory's economic backbone.

"But without mining," Frank says, "where would the Yukon be? Where would we be without Anvil? When you discuss employment here, you're talking first about mining. Besides, there's so many environmental controls on what you can do, there's no way the Yukon will become another Detroit. This country is so damn big. And yet they cry 'Don't build a mine! Don't dig a hole!' " He shakes his head. We have eighteen thousand people here today, and if you ask these people why they're here, they'll say it's because of Anvil, United Keno. . . . And the question I ask is, don't we have a moral obligation to let a few more people live up here and enjoy this country?"

It is late afternoon. Frank and I talk on for another hour, but say nothing new.

Two other men wander unannounced into the office before the day ends: Bob Elfstadt, a Whitehorse contractor, and William Cunningham, a member of the Yukon's twelve-man territorial council, its governing body. Both men are apparently allies of Frank's, for they lament the ten thousand megawatts "locked up" within Kluane Park. Mr. Elfstadt says "it's enough to make you cry." Mr. Cunningham and Frank discuss other Yukon sites suitable for development.

"The thing I like about that Granite Canyon site," Frank says, "is that it's right in the middle of the Yukon's future lode growth."

"Oh hell," Mr. Cunningham says, "it's nothing compared to what could be developed. That Pelly could be dammed in five places. At Ross Canyon, at Braden's Canyon, at . . ."

"The Yukon too," Frank says wistfully.

Frank returns to Kluane Park. "You convert that park's megawatt potential, and you get eight or nine million horsepower," he says dreamily. "That's a lot of power, professor," he says to me, raising his eyebrows, "and that's a very conservative estimate. All it's doing now is flowing away into the sea. But we'll never see it developed in our lifetimes," he adds, sighing, speaking to Mr. Cunningham.

"Oh no, not in our lifetimes," Mr. Cunningham says.

"Not until we're dead and buried," Frank says. He sighs and shakes his head.

A few days later, Frank makes arrangements for me to go out and visit the Aishihik project, near Haines Junction, on a narrow dirt road about seven-teen miles off the Alaska Highway. The site of the project is picturesque. The lakes involved, and the eighty-foot-wide Aishihik River into which they feed, are set among the cool green mountains. Otter Falls is still flowing, though at a reduced rate because of the work going on above it.

The project itself, the three-mile diversion canal, the broad bulldozed slope denuded of trees above the tailrace, the coffer dams, the roads and piles of gravel are, of course, not attractive. But, with the exception of the imminent removal of Otter Falls, it seems to me as if the project—just as Frank said—is being constructed with relatively little aesthetic damage. Then too the project—even now, with the construction, machinery, raw earth, oil drums and boxy camp trailers, storage sheds and bunkhouses covering the site—is dwarfed by the scenic landscape.

I spend two days there and am guided into the underground tunnel, to Otter Falls, to the coffer dams, to the site where the fish ladder will be constructed. I talk to many of the men who work on the project as engineers, surveyors, bulldozer operators, laborers, and ask them questions similar to those I asked Frank to try to get an idea of how these people, who are doing the actual work on the project, view its various social, biological, and aesthetic impacts. Probably predictably, in my small sample of a dozen or so workers, there is not an overwhelming concern with this.

A man named Irv Durston, from South Africa, an engineer and foreman within the tunnel, expresses an attitude that is probably typical of many workers. As soon as he learns I am a writer, he launches an attack upon the people who work for Environment Canada and who impose environmental restrictions upon the project.

"So, here you see the fuck-up of the ecology, eh?" he says sarcastically. "Those stupid bahstards," he says of Environment Canada. "They got a car and an office. They got to go around and do something. So they get on us. Those bahstards. And they don't even know what they're looking for."

When I ask him, as a supervisor, about the job's Indian workers, he is even more outspoken.

"Those bahstards," he says. "They got a few smart ones and they're just sitting back and they know they'll make money. Only one in ten of them is any good. They'll go and get a job and work like you and me and they're fine. But the others just sit around. They won't work. I was supposed to make them work. The chief said, 'Sure, we'll give you a couple of boys,' and they were boys all right. They came in and mucked around a bit with their shovels and they quit. Why should they work? They're on permanent welfare. The bahstards. They lean on their shovels and lahf at us. They lahf. They don't own the land any more than I do but they pretend they have this big attachment to it. They don't care about the land. Those bahstards." He disappears up the tunnel.

Probably the most prevalent opinion expressed by the men on the job is essentially no opinion. They have a job to do, and they do it. Jeff Austin, the job's young payroll clerk who takes me to Otter Falls, seems to me typical in this regard. Jeff, who is from Vancouver, has been on the job seven months and plans to work only two more weeks. He hopes to buy land somewhere, and has a British Columbia land catalog in his house trailer. He also plans to go on a long trip somewhere.

"I'd like to buy at least twenty acres," Jeff says. "Maybe I'd like to farm. I wish I could decide."

"Where are you going once you quit?"

"I guess I'll go to Vancouver for a week, then hop on a plane. I'll go to Europe first. Then I'll head east. Or maybe south."

"And then?"

"I don't know."

We look at Otter Falls, which is alongside the road, a mile or so from the construction camp. It is a small, broad falls, overhung with tall spruce trees and lined with dark moss, with its water crashing in two stages down over a forty-foot ledge of black rock. Its white spray catches the afternoon sunlight as it drifts out over the dark masses of water-sculpted rock and returns to the river below the boulder-strewn base of the falls. Jeff and Myra McClellan, a young secretary, also from Vancouver, who has been on the job one week, take Polaroid snapshots. Two puffy little birds—fledgling oozels, I think—hop about the big boulders five feet to our right.

I ask Jeff what is just above the falls, a two-minute walk from where we stand.

"I don't know what the falls is like up there. I've never been up there."

I walk up, look, and return, while Jeff and Myra wait. "Is the falls still as large as it was?"

"I think it's smaller" Jeff says. "I think they're taking water away from it now."

"The rocks are painted up on top. Is that where you're going to dig a channel?"

"I don't know. I guess so."

"Here," Myra says to me, handing me a snapshot. "Can you hold this till it dries?" Then: "Oh, why did that come out so light? That just looks like a blob, but it's a mountain. I always get those spots in the picture."

"Did it ever occur to you people that you may be working for a project that's damaging the landscape? Did you ever feel guilty about that?"

"Well, yes and no," Jeff says. "They do need the power. And the thing about this country is, it's so big that it doesn't make any difference. There's a hundred more places just like it."

"Oh? It's my impression that there are very few waterfalls in the Yukon. This is the only one I've seen."

"Well, I guess there aren't many waterfalls," Jeff says.

"They're trying really hard," Myra says. "They showed us a film. When they're done, it's going to be nicer here than it was before." She drops her cigarette among the rocks as we walk back to the pickup.

"Can you tell me what the Indian people will lose as a result of the flooding from the Aishihik dam?"

"No," Jeff says. "I don't know what they'll lose. It'll wipe out an Indian village, I know."

"They showed me pictures of that village," Myra says. "There were only a half a dozen houses or so. There was no direction to them. They just pointed all over. And they looked very unused."

"Did you ever talk to any of the Indian people? Did any of them ever express their opinions to you?"

"No," Jeff says. "Not really. When we went up to Mel's cabin one day, we met Eli—Eli—"

"Elijah Smith?"

"Yeah, that's it."

"He's the Yukon chief, you know."

"Yes. Somebody said that. I suppose they're being financially compensated for whatever they lose."

"But you don't know that for sure?"

"No."

"Do you like your work here? I mean, I wonder why you took this job."

"No," Jeff says, "I don't like the work. But you can get the money together here. That's what counts."

Only two men with whom I speak on the job have anything really negative to say about the Aishihik project. One is an Australian laborer, who approaches me as I sit on one of the coffer dams.

"I've worked on dams all over the world," he says. "But this is the fuck-up of all. They let all that muck go downstream. In Europe they would never do that. There, you can't disturb anything downstream. Not in Norway, anyway. That's where I was last. Six of us were working with wheelbarrows to do this kind of work. They wouldn't allow us to use bulldozers like we are here. But they still stopped us. The waterfall silted up and they saw it in town and we had to change our operation."

"I expect that this place will be restored pretty well, once it's finished," I say.

"Yes," the Aussie says. "But in Norway you can't even bugger it up in the process. You have to replace every little bit of earth and moss. Everything is step by step, neat and clean. They're so patriotic and concerned about their country over there."

"Not so here, you mean?"

"Are you joking?"

The last man I speak with on the job is Dave Conners, a young surveyor from New Zealand. I work with him one afternoon, helping him survey for the final dimensions of a coffer dam, and ask him about the project's environmental impacts.

Dave thinks a long time before he answers each question. "I don't know what this will do to the area," he says. "It'll muck up the fish a bit, because we're going to draw down and raise the lakes in just the opposite way from which it happens naturally. Probably overall it won't be too bad, but one thing is for sure: It won't be as pretty here as it was before."

"Just how much are you going to change the lake level?"

Dave laughs. "Nobody knows that yet. It depends upon an awful lot of powers that be."

"How do you feel about working here?"

"Surveying is a wonderful job," Dave says. "And at first I was idealistic about it. I thought I would go to work doing survey work for national parks and things. But I'm an economic animal, and a goddamn hypocrite, like most everyone else, and here I am, mucking up the environment."

"If you feel guilty, I wonder why you stay."

"I've thought about that," Dave says. "I think most people like to work at active sorts of things, things that shape the landscape. It's a real power trip. It's arrogant as hell, and it's so disgusting that we feel we control the land, because we are so goddamn infinitesimal and insignificant as far as nature is concerned. But that's what I think it is, a power trip."

After we listen to President Nixon's resignation speech over the radio in the cab of our pickup, Dave drives me back to the cookhouse, at the main construction camp, for supper. There we unexpectedly meet Hugh Race, head of NCPC throughout all Canada, Bob Bitwell, who is an engineering consultant on the Aishihik project, and Frank Mooney, who is guiding them around. They are about to return to Whitehorse by helicopter, and I get a ride with them, once we have finished eating. My stay at Aishihik is done.

The chopper rises from the ground and heads south, toward the Alaska Highway. Frank advises the pilot to follow the Aishihik River and to look out for a certain spot where he wants him to circle. Hugh Race sits in front. Mr. Bitwell, Frank, and I sit in the rear seat. The helicopter roars.

As we near the highway, Frank touches the pilot on the shoulder and tells him to go down low to the river. The chopper goes down and circles several times. Frank now speaks earnestly, animatedly, to Bob Bitwell, points below, and gestures with his hands. Bob and Hugh look down with Frank. The chopper is very noisy and I catch only a few words of what Frank is saying: ". . . husband . . . 'Let's take . . . in there . . . only a little ways . . . doesn't want to, but . . . an NCPC campsite . . . little sign . . . and . . . the kids get . . . fishing . . . fireplace . . . cook supper . . . end of the day . . . stay overnight!"

I shout, "What are you talking about?"

Frank leans across Mr. Bitwell and yells back to me: "Remember I was telling you about building another Otter Falls? It would be right down there." He points to the river beneath the helicopter. "Bob here designed it."

"No! You never told me anything about that."

Frank is impatient with me. "Yes, I did," he says. "You just forgot it."

Frank has mentioned several ideas for rearranging the Yukon landscape. But this one—duplicating a natural landmark—really seems strange. I refrain from asking if the duplicate would be made of rock or paper mâché, whether it would be called Otter Falls II, or whether it would perfectly duplicate the moss, the overhanging spruces, and the angle of sunlight through the spray of the real Otter Falls, seventeen miles upriver.

"You mean a duplicate? . . . a real duplicate?"

Frank nods. "We could back up a little lake behind it," he yells. "It would be close to the Alaska Highway. The other one is seventeen miles back in there. People could get to this one. The kids could see it from the car. If it was late in the day the wife might persuade the husband to stop. They'd go in and there would be a little NCPC campground. The kids could catch some fish in the lake. . . ."

I do not know what else to do, so I smile. "You mean . . . you might really build it?"

Frank smiles, shrugs, looks out the window. "We might," he says.

The helicopter circles once more and heads toward Whitehorse. Flying back over wilderness we pass over a scenic, serpentine bend in the Takhini River which, it now occurs to me, is not nearly as close to the road as it should be to give passing tourists a good look at it.

BIG GAME

"AH GUESS AH'D kill just about anythin' now," Lindley says.

Lindley owns beef cattle in Texas, and is up here trophy hunting. He is about thirty years old, considerably younger than the other hunters in camp, but apparently the enormous costs of a hunt like this are no problem for him. Like the others, he has laid out roughly $4,500 for the trip, including the outfitter's fee, license and trophy fees, and plane fare from the States, and will probably spend another thousand or two when he gets home, to mount, tan, or stuff whatever trophies he brings back.

So far he has been successful: He has killed a big bull moose, a big caribou, a Dall ram that is the largest yet brought into base camp, and, prize of prizes, a grizzly. But with two or three days of his two-week hunt remaining, he is planning to go out again, to try to kill something else.

"What else is there to shoot?" I ask.

"Ah guess ah could get a black bear or a wolf. . . ."

"Or maybe a wolverine," one of the other hunters says.

Lindley's eyes light up. "A wolverine," he says. "That would sure make an awful pretty mount. Ah'd sure like that. But Ah'll take anythin' Ah see. Bear, wolf. It don't matter."

We sit on a pole cache in the outfitter's wilderness base camp in the Cassiar Mountains east of Whitehorse, admiring the collection of antlers, horns, hides, and skulls just brought in by a party of three returning trophy hunters. Lindley is one of this party. Three new hunters who flew in yesterday from Nebraska are with us, anxiously awaiting the start of their hunt tomorrow, asking questions of the returned hunters.

"How big was your grizzly?" someone asks Lindley.

"Hell, Ah don't know. Maybe two hundred, two hundred fifty pounds."

"That's a pretty young one, then," I comment.

"Well, it's a grizzly," Lindley says conclusively.

"What's a good shot for a Dall sheep?" one of the new hunters asks. "Shoulder?"

One of the returned hunters nods. "Right. A good shoulder shot. It's too risky to shoot at the neck. And don't forget, if you're planning on a mount, a neck shot'll blow a helluva hole in the cape."

The new hunter nods. "I'm sure glad you told me that. I'm sure going to mount it."

The returned hunter picks up one of the sheep skulls from the cache. "And you don't want to shoot unless the tip of the horn comes up over the nose," he points out. "Not if you want to get in the record books. You have to be patient. Before we got this one—it's a thirty-seven or thirty-eight—we saw over a hundred sheep. One bunch had twenty-six in it. We crept up and glassed 'em but they were all thirty-fours, thirty-fives at most. There wasn't a decent one to shoot in the whole bunch."

"Damn!" one of the new hunters says excitedly. "I understand what you say about eyeballin' 'em all, but I just hope I can hold out."

"What if we see one from the front?" another asks. "How can you tell what the curl is then?"

"Leave that to your guide. These Indian boys don't use a whole lot of adjectives, but they're all good men in the bush."

"Funny. They can't hold their liquor though, can they?"

"No, they can't. But you don't have to worry about that in camp. Just don't offer 'em anything to drink."

"Are any of you bringing out any of the meat from the animals you shot?" I ask the returned hunters.

"Ah got all that beef at home," Lindley says. "Ah don't need any more." The other hunters laugh.

"We don't want any meat either," one of the new hunters says, puffing on his cigar. "We'll be glad to leave it here for camp."

"But not much of it gets used in camp, does it?" I ask. "Just a hind quarter now and then. The rest is left in the bush." One of the returned men nods. In my head I calculate that the three Dall sheep, three moose, three caribou, and one grizzly shot by the three returning hunters weighed roughly seven thousand pounds; their carcasses, minus horns, hides, and skulls, are back in the bush somewhere, rotting.

My comment creates a silence. One of the returned hunters speaks. "I agree with you," he says to me. "I don't like to see that meat wasted, but there's no way to get it out. You'd have to haul it all into camp, then hire a plane from Whitehorse to fly it out, then fly it back to the States. I guess I justify it . . . well, I don't really justify it, but to the extent that I do, I tell myself that some wild animals will be eating the carcasses."

The other hunters nod vigorously. Apparently though, this man—from Colorado—is the only one who has even given any thought to the matter.

"Thas right," Lindley jokes. "Prob'ly right now some big ole grizzly is stuffin' himself on mah moose. Or a wolf, maybe, or a wolverine. Sure would like to get me one of them."

"I think I would feel bad shooting something rare like a wolf or a wolverine," I comment. "There are so few of them left in North America."

"But not here," one of the new hunters says. "There's lots of wolves in the Yukon, right?"

(Photo Researchers, Inc.)

"Besides," another hunter says, "every one we shoot is one less that's gonna get at the outfitter's horses in winter." The others nod. Because I am outnumbered, I do not make the obvious point that if the horses were not here, for use by wealthy American trophy hunters, they would not get eaten by wolves.

"Are you one of these antihunters?" one of the men asks suspiciously as I take notes.

I shake my head. I explain that I once hunted a great deal, that I do not think hunting per se is a sin, and that I recognize that wildlife habitat destruction—though construction of new highways, housing developments, pipelines, golf courses, ski resorts, whatever removes wildlife food and cover —is a far greater threat to animal populations than hunting. Relatively, hunting does little damage. This seems to satisfy everybody.

"Thas good," the cigar smoker says. "I thought you might be one of those antigun nuts."

"I sometimes wonder," his partner says, "if these antihunters ever contributed a dime to wildlife research or habitat improvement. It's hunters who do that, with their license fees and ammunition taxes."

I nod in agreement.

"If nobody ever hunted there wouldn't be a game animal left," the cigar smoker says, carrying the point too far.

This is untrue, though the cigar smoker seems sincerely to believe it. I do not refute the statement, but just repeat my comment about habitat destruction, adding that it is the high standard of living and the high level of material consumption on our continent that destroy wildlife habitat and therefore wildlife. I cite the graphic example that our North American custom of having two cars for each family creates a tremendous demand for petroleum, which causes Alaska pipelines to be built, which destroys caribou habitat. As I say this, though, it occurs to me that most of the men I am speaking with—who have just jetted up to the Yukon for a two-week trophy hunt—are probably big consumers at home and thus contribute doubly to the demise of wild animals, by hunting and by the conduct of their everyday lives.

In any case, the point of my little lecture is clearly missed, or ignored, except, perhaps, by the one hunter from Colorado.

"Shit," the cigar smoker says, "we dropped three hundred and thirty dollars this morning on licenses. Now I'll betcha hunters like us contribute one hel-

luva lot to the economy. All this antigun stuff is communistically inspired anyway," he continues. "Or it gets into some 'ism' or other."

"Well," another says quietly, ominously, "Russia has said many times that she'll take America without firing a shot. And that's how it'll go if these antigun people have their way."

The others nod in agreement.

I am reminded that while there are many points that one can make in defense of hunting, hunters for the most part rely upon inane and irrelevant clichés—which they have read in hunting magazines—to defend their activity. It also occurs to me that it is stupid of me, even a little unfair, to challenge these hunters' highs, now, when they are in the field, celebrating recent kills and looking forward to kills soon to come. I keep quiet.

"Now that moose I shot . . ." one of the returned hunters says, changing the topic back to his own accomplishments, "I had to hit him right in the Adam's apple. All I could see of him stickin' up over the brush was his head and neck. He went down. Whum! O'course, I knew his neck was broken."

"You damn betcha!" the cigar smoker says excitedly. "That was good shootin'."

"From what we hear," his partner says dreamily, "we're pretty sure of getting our moose and sheep and caribou. But we hope, we just hope, that we might get a shot at a grizzly too."

"Ah'd sure be happy to get somethin' else," Lindley says. "Wolf, wolverine. It don't make much difference. Ah guess Ah'd kill just about anythin' now."

BUS RIDE

"I'M YOUR DRIVER, Bobby Lasovick. The trip to Dawson is three hundred and thirty-three miles and it takes seven and a half hours. It's a long trip, but it's pretty and I'll try to point out a few things along the way. We'll be stopping five times. The first place is Braeburn Lodge. They have good pie there, but it's only a ten-minute stop. I advise that you eat your supper in Carmacks. We make a twenty-five-minute stop there. If you need a few more minutes, we'll take it, but try not to wander too far away from the bus. We're supposed to get into Dawson by eleven-thirty, and I'd like to see what's going on tonight. Probably you would too. Don't forget, it's Discovery Days this weekend! I have no objection to soda pop, but don't leave any cans under the seats. It's awful to clean up. I don't know all the answers, but if you have any questions about things we pass, don't be afraid to ask."

I sit near the rear of the bus with Vinny Amendola, from Brooklyn, who is up here to visit his sister in Dawson. We laugh at Lasovick's informality.

"Imagine a bus driver talking that way on the trip up to Albany," Vinny says. "They'd think he was nuts."

We pull out of the Whitehorse station. This is Norline Coaches' "Moccasin Express." The bus is about half full, mostly young people, mostly whites, with a half-dozen Indians. I suspect that most passengers are going to the Discovery Days celebration. The event—ostensibly a commemoration of the Bonanza Creek gold discoveries in 1896—has the reputation of being the summer's biggest drunk. The last day of the three-day weekend is called Recovery Day by resident Yukoners.

I recognized Lasovick, our driver; he is one of two men who regularly make this run. He apparently recognized me too, for he smiled and nodded as we got on the bus. He is short, about thirty-five, with blond curly hair, dark glasses, and a cherubic face.

I alternately sleep and read during the first stages of the trip. The day is hot and the bus drones on, over the rippled gravel road. Lasovick identifies the points of interest, most of which are mountains or river rapids or sites of old forest fires. At Lake Laberge, not a regular stop, he halts the bus and lets off two women hikers. Near Fox Lake, a group of a dozen horses walks in the dirt road and we stop for them. At Carmacks, an Indian man lies asleep in the left lane of the road, and we go around him. During our twenty-minute stop at Stewart Crossing, another Indian man, about forty, is refused entry.

"No!" Lasovick says. "I just saw you in the washroom and you threw up in there. Now you're not gettin' on my bus and do the same thing."

"I gotta get to Discovery," the man says drunkenly.

"Not with me you don't."

"I'll be all right."

"You'll be all right right here. I'm not gonna clean up a mess in my bus! Now get outta the way." He slams the door and we drive off, beginning the final, hundred-mile leg of the trip. It is almost dark. Most of the passengers are awake. Lasovick now becomes animated, anticipating his own weekend in Dawson.

"Hey!" he yells out to the two or three passengers asleep in the back seat. "Why are you sleepin' back there?" He flicks the overhead light on and off several times, to wake them. The passengers wake sleepily. They are apparently not Yukoners and are surprised at this sort of thing. "You better get ready for the big weekend!" Lasovick continues loudly. "I just wanted to get you ready."

A few people laugh. Lasovick is encouraged. He tells a story, keeping an eye on the mirror to sense the audience's reaction:

"When I took this job they told me I couldn't take a drink for eight hours before driving! But they had it all buggered up! So what I do now is take eight drinks an hour before driving!"

A few laughs again.

"All right! How many of you are going to Discovery Days? Let's see your hands!" Most hands go up. Someone in front calls out, asking if Bobby intends to buy him a drink.

"Sure!" Bobby yells. "I'll buy everybody a drink! But I don't have any money so I'm gonna pass around the hat now and I want you all to put something in it. Ha-ha."

This gets only a small rise, but the driver is undaunted.

"We got any party people on here?" he asks. Three or four raise their hands, including a young girl near the front. Lasovick turns half around and points to the girl.

"Hey boys! You hear that? What are you doing sitting in the back? We got a live one up here!" There are a few calls from the rear.

"Jesus Christ was walking through the forest!" he calls out. "And he came upon some people who were stoning a man. He stands there and this little old lady chucks a stone at the man. Whum! Hits him right in the ribs. So Jesus Christ walks over to this lady who threw the stone and he says: 'Mother, sometimes you really piss me off!' Ha-ha. Hee-hee." He turns around to look at the passengers.

This joke gets most people laughing, though it isn't clear whether they are laughing at its humor or its absurdity.

Lasovick is now unstoppable. "All right! Who else knows a joke? I want you to come up here and tell it."

Looking in the mirror, Bobby sees Vinny and me laughing. "Jack!" he yells. "You come on up here and tell us a joke! Come on! Don't you know any good jokes?" He waves his hand. I shake my head. "He's not very funny. Let's get somebody else." No one volunteers.

"How the hell did he know your name?" Vinny asks.

"I've ridden with him before."

"All right then. Nobody knows any jokes. Then let's all sing a song. Everybody's gotta sing! Hey, back there. You're goin' to sleep again." Again the lights flick on and off. Lasovick breaks into "Oh Canada" and people sing along. Periodically, he conducts, taking one hand off the wheel and waving it in the air. "We'll sing this when we get to town," he says. "We'll be a big hit. That is, if anybody's still sober. Ha-ha." He then begins to whistle the hora. No one knows the words, so he switches to "Clementine."

The songs and jokes continue. The bus stops three times more before getting to Dawson. The first time, a man gets off—miles from any town—and walks along the dark road and back into the forest. The second time, Bobby drives a half mile off the road, stops and unloads several lengths of aluminum pipe at a mining exploration camp, chats with some of the men there before getting back in the bus. The third time is at a roadside diner, a small aluminum house trailer set at the back of a mud-puddled dirt clearing.

"This is Mike Lovegren's place!" Bobby calls out. "He's building some new motel units here. He's spent twenty-five thousand so far. It ought to be real nice, once he's finished. We'll stop here twenty minutes and you can get a sandwich. The roast beef is best. There may not be room for all of us in the trailer, so maybe we'll have to rotate a little."

We go in and are served ham sandwiches by a sullen woman in bulging black slacks. The roast beef is all gone. Two thirds of the small trailer is used as a dining area. There are only four tables and most of us stand while we eat, clearing the doorway when an attendant comes in from tending the gas pumps. Lasovick is used to the place. He stands behind the counter, in the cooking area, lifts the lids from kettles on the stove and peers in, chats with the woman.

We eat and leave. All passengers are awake now and looking forward to the end of the long ride.

"Well, we're almost there. We're gonna hit every bar in town, right? I'll be in the El Dorado at one o'clock," Lasovick reminds us, "so don't forget to come in and buy me a drink! Hee-hee. Hey! Who's goin' to Diamond Tooth Gertie's? Ohhh, the girls in that show. I like that little Joanne. She's always smilin'."

People begin to gather their belongings from the overhead racks. Bobby maintains a constant chatter, telling his last joke as we rumble across the bridge into Dawson.

"Hey! There's a black man and a white man standing on the street corner. Which one of them is the doctor?"

A few people make stabs at it, but no one knows the punch line.

"You don't know? Think about it. What's one of 'em got that the other hasn't got?"

No response.

"Hee-hee. It's the black man who's the doctor 'cause he's the one with a little black bag!"

Again, it is not clear whether the passengers' laughter is at the joke's humor, or lack of it, or maybe, in this case, at the driver's gall in telling it. The telling, though, is not accompanied by any apparent hostility, nor is it encumbered by the guilt or embarrassment that would attend such a joke told "outside."

"Anyplace else," Vinny says. "a driver would be canned for that. Or he'd get his throat cut."

I suspect Vinny is right. But this is not anyplace else.

We unload our gear. The town is quiet, relative to what I expected, except for a small, impromptu, outdoor band playing for a few apathetic dancers near the center of town. The Discovery Days celebration seems not unlike any other Friday night in Dawson, except that the bars are fuller and there are more empties sitting along the curb. After being propositioned once—but very halfheartedly—by a teen-age Indian girl, we search out a place to spend the night.

HIGHWAY

ON AUGUST 25 I ride up the Dempster Highway with Dale Israel, a young bush dweller. We use Dale's four-wheel-drive Toyota Land Cruiser. At the beginning of the highway, in the rolling country twenty-five miles east of Dawson, we cross the green steel bridge over the Klondike River, bounce through a water-filled pothole, and continue north on the hard-surfaced dirt and gravel road, past a stand of scrawny black spruce on our left and a big gravel pit on our right. There is a sign near the bridge warning truckers of the gross vehicle weights allowed on the Dempster's few steel bridges: 84,000 pounds at temperatures above minus 30°, 63,000 pounds at temperatures below minus 30°. The day is chilly and clear. Four days ago, the season's first storm dropped eight inches of snow here, in the westcentral Yukon, but most of that is now melted. Forty miles ahead, to the north, snow clouds shut out any view of the seven thousand-foot Ogilvie Mountains.

Dale and I do not know exactly where we are going on this trip. We hope to travel as far as we can on the still uncompleted Dempster Highway, to its end, someplace near the Arctic Circle. But no one we have spoken with knows just where that end is. The bartender at the Downtown saloon tells us that the road extended to mile 230 last year but has since washed out, in its last thirty miles. A friend tells us that he has heard that the highway has been pushed as far as the Eagle River, at about mile 236. Someone else says the passable road ends only a short distance beyond the last construction camp at mile 169. But none of these people has been to the highway's end. And without a shortwave radio, there is no way for us to call the road's northernmost construction camp to verify any of these stories.

In a way the notion of simply heading north to some indeterminate point—The End—where the frontier road fades into the tundra, is an exciting one. Now that I think of it, I have never known anyone who has traveled a frontier road ending nowhere, in the midst of wilderness, hundreds of miles from the nearest civilization. And this experience will no longer be possible once the Dempster is completed, in five or six years, because the highway will then have a beginning and an end.

The road climbs slowly, sticking to the west slope of the mile-wide valley formed by the north fork of the Klondike, which flows south from the Ogilvie Mountains. Several hundred feet below us, and a half mile to the right, we can see the sun

115

sparkling on the fast-moving river. Although there is snow on the ground, the leaves of the aspens and poplars near the river are still as green as in mid-summer. Wind blows through them, and their upper, shiny sides catch the sun. Their bright green color contrasts peculiarly with the black eastern slope of the valley, where the morning sunlight has not yet penetrated. Nearer the road, at mile 2, and again at mile 4, mile 7, and at short, regular intervals along the road, there are large borrow pits—one hundred feet by three hundred, and ten to fifteen feet deep—cut out of the earth to supply road fill. These are old pits, dug fifteen years ago when the road was first begun, but their raw brown surfaces have not yet grown new ground cover. A few sapling poplars have sprouted in them, but no grass or moss has yet taken hold. The near arctic growing season is short. It will be several decades before the cuts are regrown, and probably centuries before enough organic matter has broken down to replace the soil removed.

We go on. The sun shines warmly on the road and in the cab of our vehicle. Up ahead, the gray snow clouds around the mountains seem to have moved farther south, in our direction.

The Dempster Highway is being constructed by the federal Department of Public Works, maintained by the Yukon Territorial Government. It was begun in 1958, during the Diefenbaker administration, and was planned to extend from the existing Klondike Highway, near Dawson, 376 miles north and east, through the uninhabited northern reaches of the Yukon and across the Arctic Circle to the town of Arctic Red River (or just "Arctic Red"), near Ft. McPherson, within the Northwest Territories. The Dempster is the Yukon's biggest construction project, and is a major and high-paying source of employment for men from within the territory and from outside. Though it is only a two-lane gravel highway, it is currently costing about $100,000 per mile, due to the unusual construction problems within the sometimes mountainous, sometimes marshy, always frozen country through which it is being built.

Just why the Dempster is being built is another question, and a difficult one to answer, it seems. There are no commercial links between the small towns at either end of the highway, and the towns themselves are so tiny—Dawson, population 780, Arctic Red, 200, Ft. McPherson, 600—that it does not seem economic to join them with a multimil-

lion-dollar highway. Nor is there any human population along the 376-mile route of the highway, except for the small camps of two big-game outfitters, and two or three small cabins built alongside the road by private individuals since the road was begun.

One reason commonly given for building the Dempster was access to petroleum and mineral deposits lying in the permafrosted landscape of the northern Yukon. The road, initially, was included within the federal "Roads to Resources" program. But apparently, at the time the highway was begun, no one knew just what oil and mineral resources—if any—existed there. And if any existed, they were apparently not of critical importance, for two years and seventy-eight miles after it was begun, construction on the Dempster was halted, and was not resumed until 1969. Since then, the road has progressed steadily.

In recent years, new discoveries of oil have been made in the northern Yukon. But none appear to be exploitable at current market prices, further lending to the notion that this "road to resources" was a speculative, rather than a purposeful, venture.

More significantly, major finds of petroleum and natural gas have recently been made in the arctic delta of the Mackenzie River, within the Northwest Territories, near the northeastern Yukon border. And since the Dempster Highway will terminate just south of the delta and will there be joined by a hundred-mile highway running south from the new delta exploration town of Inuvik (population, 4,000), it is now said by some of the Dempster's proponents that the highway's primary purpose will be that of a supply route, bringing men and materials from southern Canada to the new oil fields.

But the same questions remain about the need for the Dempster Highway, because still another wilderness road, the Mackenzie Highway, which will also terminate just south of the delta, is being built by the federal government north through the Northwest Territories, roughly paralleling the Mackenzie River. This road would apparently serve the same supply function as the Dempster and is a more direct route from southern Canada. Since both highways travel through wilderness to reach the same point, it appears that one of the two roads —probably the Dempster—is not needed. And of course, it costs twice as much to build two roads as it does to build one.

Finally, as far as Dale and I have been able to

learn, men and materials are already being brought to the Mackenzie delta oil fields—apparently without difficulty—via airplanes and freight boats going up the Mackenzie River. And since pipelines—not roads—will ultimately be used to move oil and gas from the Mackenzie delta down to southern industrial Canada, there seems a very real question of whether either the Mackenzie or the Dempster highway is purposeful.

Dale and I discuss this as we travel. We plan to ask people, today, along the route, to help clarify the situation.

We go on, toward the front of the Ogilvie Mountains and the snow clouds. There is no traffic. We are the only ones on the road. At mile 21, we get a long view of the Klondike valley and stop to take a picture. The valley stretches out to the north, ahead of us, a big, wide, U-shaped and glacial-looking landscape, with bright green poplars in its center and dark green spruces curving uphill, finally stunting and fading out near the five-thousand-foot tops of the mountains on each side of the river, blending again into a bright green carpet of moss and grass which extends almost to the black, rocky peaks. All this landscape is brightly lit by a beam of sunlight which peeks in under the eastern edge of the snow cloud—like the beam of a movie projector—to light the whole valley. Where we stop, there is an empty bottle—Canadian Club Blended Canadian Whiskey, By Appointment to her Majesty. . . . —which, for some reason, has been left standing upright in the very center of the road. It seems strange to me to think that until the road was put in, probably no more than two or three hundred white North Americans had seen this place.

We get back in and go on, crossing a series of narrow wooden bridges without side rails. The gravel borrow pits persist, every four or five miles, at roadside. On the left, at mile 31, we pass one of the Dempster's three or four private residences, a small cabin with a sun-bleached set of caribou antlers stuck over the door. The owner has a big red "Private" sign stuck on a tree near the house. This seems strange to us, since the road has almost no traffic. Why the sign? And if the owner really wanted privacy, why did he locate right alongside the highway?

As we go farther into the Ogilvie foothills, the sides of the valley pinch in, and the road is forced down near the river. Clouds and fog close in over-head. The highway makes a series of right-angle turns, through a stand of black spruce, and a few minutes later, at mile 41, we come to the first of the Dempster's highway camps, a dozen or so aluminum house trailers clustered under the Canadian and Yukon flags in the narrow strip of land between road and river.

We stop. It is nine o'clock and the road crew is out on the job. At first, no one seems to be around. Then we see a young man, probably twenty-five or thirty, with close-cropped black hair, wearing sunglasses, emerging from the cookhouse trailer. He comes over to our van and introduces himself: Ben Wolf, head of a highway survey crew. We speak briefly with him, asking him, among other things, if he knows if the road has a purpose.

"It's going up to Inuvik."

"Is there a purpose in going to Inuvik?"

"Well, there's oil up there."

"I thought that the Mackenzie Highway, or the river barges, would bring up all the equipment they need."

"Maybe. I don't know."

"I guess I question whether the money and the environmental costs make it worthwhile for the Dempster to be built."

"Are you guys environmentalists?"

"No. We're just writing a book. We're not environmentalists."

"Good. Because I think this environmentalism is a lot of bullshit. Or a good deal of it anyway."

"Why?"

"Well, if we didn't have a road up here, then nobody would ever get up here to bitch about it, right?"

This guy has a firm grasp of the obvious. "Of course. I mean, if there were no road, then naturally nobody would complain about it. But I don't see the point you're making."

"I mean, unless those people down south are just willing to sit home in Toronto and be told that the Yukon is beautiful . . . how are they going to see it without roads?"

"Who says they have to see it? We have been sitting down in Toronto or New York ever since the continent was settled without seeing the northern Yukon, and it hasn't hurt anybody yet."

"Well, I think the people of Inuvik will be glad to get a road access to the outside."

"I guess I would raise the same point: The Eskimo people up there have gotten along for ten thousand years without a road. And as far as the new oil people up there are concerned, the Dempster isn't going to do anything special for them, is it? The nearest town on the road will be Dawson, and that's still 500 miles from Inuvik. So I still say, why build the road? That's tax money, after all."

"I don't know about all that. I just think that this environmentalism is a lot of bullshit."

"You're not sure, though, if the road has a purpose?"

"I just don't want to get into all that."

Wolf makes uneasy, preparing-to-go movements. We switch back to more neutral questions. He gives us a few facts about the road; tells us that his crew is surveying to straighten out curves in the first seventy-eight miles of highway, which were apparently built incorrectly in 1959 and 1960; mentions that the road trucks kill many ptarmigan, because the birds sit in the road and are "too stupid to fly"; confirms the bartender's story that the last thirty or so miles of the road were destroyed last winter. Before he hurries off in his pickup, he tells us too that the person to see at road's end is John Hudson, project manager at mile 169, who is essentially the federal government's on-site representative for the highway, and who has been in charge of the road's planning and construction for the last two years. He warns that John is a talker, not a listener, and so I should not be pushy with him, then drives off. Dale and I go inside the cookhouse trailer to see if there is any coffee around.

Inside, we meet Ludwig Hoppe, camp chef, who invites us to sit down for coffee and a piece of his cake. No charge. Half the forty-foot trailer is a kitchen, with generator-run refrigerators and a big flat-topped stove. The other half is the eating area, with benches for the federal and territorial employees who work here. We sit down there, and talk.

Hoppe is a stocky man, fifty-three years old, with thick graying hair combed straight back. He smokes a big pipe and speaks with a thick accent. He is a German immigrant, lives with his wife in southern Alberta, and, he tells us, takes high-paying jobs like this one ($2,000 per month, with overtime) for a few months each year, then returns home.

"It's the money, then, that brings you up here?"

"Sure. Vat else? Vy should I come up here in de schticks if I don't get good money?"

I tell Hoppe that Ben Wolf has just been telling us that his crew is taking curves out of the road

originally put in wrongly. I mention that this implies a certain sloppiness in the original road building —especially in one done as recently as 1960—and ask Ludwig if he knows the reason for this.

He snorts annoyedly. "You tell me vy," he says. "But dat's de vay it is wit roads. Even ven dey finish, so called, dey keep on vorking. Take out a curf here, a curf dere. A vaste of money. But it gifs people chobs, and dat's vy dey do it. It isn't really needed."

"What do you think about the Dempster in general? Is it needed?"

"Of course not! Dere chust copying de Americans: Progress! More roads! More concrete. More schteel. More glass. Longer! Vider! Bigger! Anyting bigger is better! But I tell you, as soon as it connects to Inuvik, dere vill be hundreds, tousands uf tourists traveling dis road, trowing beer bottles, trowing tin cans. . . . A mess!"

I laugh, partly at Ludwig's thick accent, partly at his straightforwardness. "Well, one of the questions I want to get answered is why they began this road in the first place. Some people have told me it is designed to give the people up there a highway access to the south. Some say it was to get the oil out of the Mackenzie delta. But no one really seems sure."

"Vell, it certainly vasn't for de people uf Inuvik. Or McPherson. Dey don't need it and dey vouldn't do it chust for dem anyvay. And it vasn't to get de oil out, because dey didn't effen know it vas dere. You know how dey build roads: If dey started it in 1958, dat means dey had it planned years ahead. And it vasn't until a few years ago dat dey knew dere vas oil up dere. So dat means dey chust building a road for de sake of building a road."

"A multi-million-dollar project just for the hell of it?"

Ludwig relights his pipe, shakes his head. "No. I mean it vas a political ting. It vas de prime minister's baby and it still is. Dey say, vell, ve'll create six hundred chobs for you by building dis highvay, and people like dat and vote for whoever votes for de road in Parliament. But vat dey don't tell you is dat, sure ve gif you six hundred chobs, but ve haf to blast avay dat mountain for two hundred uf dose chobs, dam dat river for anudder two hundred, cut across de caribous' place for anudder two hundred, and so on. Dey ruin de landscape! Now I'm not vun uf dese environmentalists, but dat's vat it is."

"Do you talk like this to the people here in the camp?"

"Sure! I'm not afraid. I don't need dis chob. If I

don't vork here, I vork someplace else. Or if I vant, I go home and tviddle my tums."

"How about other men here in camp? Do most of them think the road is a good thing or a bad thing? Do people talk about it?"

"Not much. But dere's only a few here who disagree vid me on dis. I can tell by dere faces vhen I talk about it. Most uf de vorkers here are young men who are returning to university in de fall. Dey are intelligent. And no young man or voman could miss de implications uf a road like dis. A vaste of money, and a blight on de landscape."

"Do you know anything about the Mackenzie Highway, in the NWT? We were wondering why they need both that one and the Dempster, because they're leading to the same place."

"De Mackenzie Highvay vas a boo-boo. Dey vere building it and den dey chust schtopped it, as far as I know. Ve don't hear anyting about it dese days. Chust anudder political ting."

"You're saying the Mackenzie is unnecessary too, as far as you know?"

Ludwig nods and puffs. "Chust more 'progress.' To get votes."

"I've spoken with some of the people in Dawson, mainly storekeepers, and some of them seem to feel the Dempster is a good thing. Either that, or they just assume it's a good thing because it's being done. . . . In fact, they seem to get a little hot under the collar if you question it."

Ludwig gets angry. "Sure. Vat do you expect? Dey stand to benefit from it financially, vid de tourists. And whoever talks out against it, dey call dem 'hippies,' because dey are opposed to 'progress.' Dey call dem 'hippies' and make dem outcasts, because nobody likes hippies. And den nobody listens to dem. But 'hippies' is chust a convenient term. Many uf de kids haf better insight into vat is going on dan de politicians and businessmen. And dey know dat governments are corrupt and are chust doing tings like dis to make people vote for dem, and to help de big companies get de oil. It's not for de people demselves."

"You may very well be right. But maybe it's also true that Canada needs the oil."

"Vat I ask," Ludwig says, "is vy do ve even need all dese highvays? Vy not chust a pipeline? Ve are so rich dat ve could build a pipeline to de sun, so to schpeak. If ve veren't such a corrupt society, ve vould be developing the nonpolluting energy of de sun. In Chermany I bought a little cooker dat vould

use solar energy. It vorked vid a magnifying glass. You could cook a hamburger or boil vater vid it in minutes. Now ve know it is possible to do dis on a big shcale. Ve need researching on it. But *dat* is vat ve should be schpending our money on. Not on dese roads dat destroy de landscape."

"You seem to feel very strongly. I wonder if you are actively involved, up here, or at home, in campaigning for this sort of thing?"

Ludwig relights his pipe. "No," he says. "Let's put it dis vay: In a group, people can accomplish much. But alone, vun man can do nutting."

Dale and I finish our coffee, thank Ludwig, and drive on. A short distance north of the road camp, the road crosses the north fork of the Klondike on a small wooden bridge, then begins its long steep climb up into the Ogilvies, mounting the east slope of the valley. Below us and to our left, the Klondike valley widens again, and the land tilts to the west, sloping uphill to a ring of gray snow-covered peaks five miles away. The river separates into the rivulets that form its headwaters, and these streams disappear into the mountains. From where we are, halfway up the east side of the valley, the tilting of the land creates an optical illusion. It seems to me as if the land is strangely folded and that the mountain we are climbing is about to topple into the valley's center. The country is powerful and ominous-looking. The sky is low and gray over the peaks. Big wet flakes of snow start to fall. Back at the base of the mountains, where the road crosses the river, the territorial government has erected a small tourist picnic ground, with a bright green table and garbage can and two bright green fiber-glass toilets with yellow fiber-glass roofs. They seem out of place in this rugged, gray land.

We climb upward, passing over a narrow gorge on a steel bridge mentioned to us by Ben Wolf. For some reason, the bridge is installed upside down, with its side rails sticking down below the road surface. It is snowing regularly now, and we cannot see more than a hundred yards from the road. To our left, a big black raven sits huddled on top of a tourist sign that points out Tombstone Mountain, a tall, slab-sided peak across the valley.

Once on top, we ride along the crest of the mountains for a time. There are no trees up here, just a low scrub, some caribou moss, and the gray, hazy stone peaks sticking up out of the snow that surrounds them.

After thirty minutes, the snow quits suddenly

In the Ogilvies.

and it is sunny again. We are now in a strange new place, on a high, treeless plateau, stretching miles to the east and west. The mountaintops are different from the sharp rocky spires a few miles back. Here, suddenly, they are casual rounded mounds, grassy, protruding lazily above the surface of the surrounding plateau. They are covered with new white snow, bright in the late morning sun, while the surrounding amber tundra does not look as if snow had touched it. I have never seen country like this. The mountains—probably five thousand feet above sea level—rise only four to five hundred feet above the plateau and remind me of the rounded lumps of butter on top of a pancake. The sun's warmth is friendly. Yet, without a single tree or shrub in sight, this bleak still place seems utterly deserted, unwilling to support life.

And yet, this is not true. In a month or so, hundreds of thousands of caribou will be ambling through here, or not far from here, moving south and east in their paths of seasonal migration, munching the fibrous, slow-growing moss that makes up the bulk of their food supply.

No one has a very clear idea of how the Dempster will affect these peculiar gray and white animals. The road cuts directly across the traditional migration route of the continent's second largest caribou herd, the Porcupine herd. Now, apparently, the animals cross it. Biologists report, though, that in other locations, after a road has been in place for several years, the animals—for reasons unknown—often stop crossing it and wander about the countryside seeking out other directions. In the Dempster's case, however, there is no other direction. There will be no way around the road, once completed.

Environmentalists have severely criticized this highway, because no environmental impact analyses were done by the government prior to the project's initiation. In 1972, after much criticism and after the Dempster was already about 150 miles along, the federal government commissioned a consulting firm—Schultz International, Ltd., of Vancouver—to make an evaluation of the road's impact. The firm's report is critical of the haste with which the highway has been pushed forward, states that construction errors and undue environmental damage will probably result from this haste, and urges slowing or even postponing the project. It also notes that the highway's major negative impact will result from the increased human presence and activities it will introduce into the area—traffic, hunters, oil and mineral exploration—once it is completed. The road has already brought in some human activity, but

120

since the major impact will not be felt until the future, it is virtually guaranteed that no one will be held responsible, because by then the federal government will be able to point out that the highway was built during a former administration.

Most significantly, the firm's report notes that "the decision to complete the construction of the Dempster Highway appears irrevocable." Apparently, the Schultz group felt that the government would not be willing to halt the project, even if it is demonstrated that the road is environmentally and aesthetically disastrous. This would seem to indicate pretty clearly that any impact analyses are essentially token gestures to the public.

We drive on through the still flat landscape, punctuated by the lumpy white peaks, and cross a bridge over a dark, thirty-foot-wide stream. Something about the stream strikes me strangely, and I again have the feeling that the earth is tilting peculiarly. We ride on alongside the water, and suddenly it dawns on me: The stream is flowing in the wrong direction! It is moving north. I get out the small tourist map, the only one we have. As far as I can figure out, this is the Blackstone River. Following it with my finger to the Peel River, I find the obvious answer: This water is flowing toward the Arctic Ocean. Right now we are at a place where something truly irrevocable happened, several million years ago, when these nearby mountains were buckled up by some force from deep inside the planet. The result of that buckling is that half the sky's water in this area now flows south and west into the Pacific, and half flows east and north, into the Mackenzie River and the Arctic.

The road parallels the Blackstone for several miles, just a few yards away from the water. At about mile 75, we stop and get out for a drink of water. Outside the truck I feel the loneliness and moodiness of this bleak, sun-drenched landscape even more strongly. It makes me uneasy. The Blackstone is the only thing moving, the only thing living, for miles around. We lie down on a patch of moss beside the river and drink. The water is clear and very cold—like normal water with a mint in your mouth. On the low bank beside the water there is a discarded violet-colored Fanta Cola can.

We go on. Here in this flat terrain the river does not always remain in its bed, and in several places the bulldozers have pushed gravel up out of the Blackstone's bed to form dikes alongside the road to keep the water from undercutting the highway. We

now begin to see small oil or mineral exploration camps far out on the tundra, miles away, tiny glimmers from white tents and aluminum-sided shacks and oil barrels and drilling rigs. At this distance the small clusters of buildings look insignificant and harmless.

We see only one vehicle throughout the morning, the pickup truck of a caribou hunter. The hunter is perched on top of the cab, scanning the countryside with a pair of field glasses as we drive by. We exchange waves. It's still too early to see many caribou. I don't know of anyone who has shot one yet, but a few people from Dawson have been driving a hundred miles or so up the Dempster each weekend to try to get their winter's meat within easy dragging distance of the road. In two places, there are posted corridors where hunters are prohibited from shooting animals within one mile of the highway. But these corridors are short, covering a total of only twelve miles along the highway. And I can see, too, from my own hunting experience, that even if you hunted within the no-hunting corridors, you would run only a slim chance of getting caught. There isn't enough traffic on the road to worry about. The Yukon has only a handful of officials to enforce the game laws, and they can't be everywhere at once. And in this country everybody knows where they are anyway. Illegal hunting is already widespread; the Dempster spreads it a little wider.

The country has changed. We have dropped from the treeless plateau down to a valley more heavily forested with white spruce and with poplars whose leaves are beginning to turn yellow. There are rocky cliffs along the road, strange fingerlike spines of limestone with crumbled piles of their own remains at their feet. The road stays close to the river for a time, following the natural passageway made by the water. Since the river and its gravel are nearby, there are no borrow pits cut into the land; the road fill, varying from about eight to thirty feet in depth and from twenty to fifty feet in width, has all been removed from the riverbed. In one spot, it looks as if an entire river island has been removed, leaving only a single poplar standing lonesomely erect in a remaining patch of gravel. Why did they leave that little patch? It looks as if someone was amused by the weird look of the mound with its single tree.

The landscape retains its lonely, otherworldly character. At mile 96, we stop, turn off the engine, and listen. It is perfectly still, except for the sound of

Dall sheep in the St. Elias Mountains.
(Wayne Towriss)

Wolverine
(Photo Researchers, Inc.)

Caribou herds migrate twice each year across the northern Yukon
and still provide a primary source of meat for the region's Indian people.
(Yukon Government)

(Photo Researchers, Inc.)

(Photo Researchers, Inc.)

The lynx (above) and the wolf (below) are sought after by Yukon
rappers. The lynx preys on ptarmigan and varying hare, the wolf

Ptarmigan
(Wayne Towriss)

Spruce grouse

Fledgling hawk

Female grizzly waits for salmon.
(Photo Researchers, Inc.)

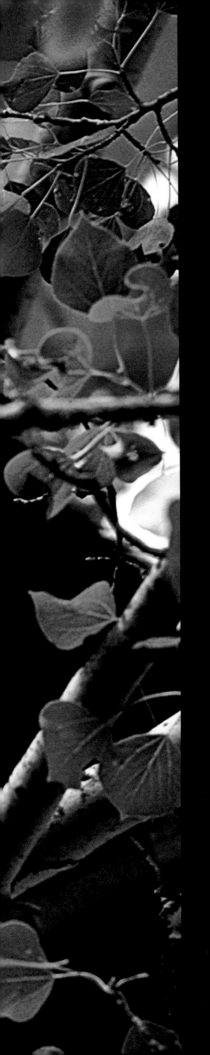

Black bears often visit bush camps . . .

and are killed for both their pelts and their meat.

Robert Frisch, veteran wilderness traveler.

a small, distant stream off to our left. We cannot see the stream, but we know that it must come from the slopes of two treeless, snow-covered peaks about two miles from the road. But the stream does not reach the road. Strange, because the way the land tilts, any water flowing from those peaks would have a straight downhill course to where we stand. It is eerie to look at the two cold white peaks, to hear the sound of the water, but not to see any sign of it. As we stand there, it occurs to me that there may be no stream back there at all, and that the sound we hear may be nothing more than an echo, left over from a time ten thousand years ago, coming forth now only because someone stopped to listen for it.

At noon, we reach the Ogilvie River, mile 123. The river is wide—about eighty yards—and is crossed by a graceful steel bridge. Just across it there is a driveway to another highway road camp, set in a pretty spot within some spruces along the river. We go into it and enter the mess hall trailer. Again we are offered coffee and some good-tasting fruit tarts by the camp cook, a man of about seventy named Theodore Shabad. Again no charge. We offer to pay, but Theodore waves it away. "No pay. This is government. Everything free."

We look around while Theodore pours our coffee. As in most remote camps, there are many men's magazines around the lunchroom. There is also a television set. There is no reception up here, but this one uses cassette tapes that carry both the audio and visual portions of films. Theodore tells us that the camp rents the tapes and plays them at night for the men. "No fuckin' womens," he says. "Gotta have TV or everybody go crazy."

Today, though, there do happen to be some womens here, three college students from Calgary—Elaine Kile, Jane Brandt, and Miriam Roos. They are the only people in the mess hall, and we sit down with them. The women are up here for the summer, working for one of the many mineral exploration outfits that have set up summer camps along the Dempster. Miriam and Jane are working as geologists' assistants and Elaine is the cook. Their camp has just closed down for the summer, and they are now on their way south. They are enthusiastic, feeling good about going home and about having spent a summer in this beautiful country.

When we come over, one of them is joking about being awakened this morning by gunfire.

"That was the earliest I got up in a long time," Jane says. "Five o'clock."

"What was it," I ask, "a big-game hunter?"

"No," Miriam says. "A grizzly came into our camp and they had to shoot it."

"How come they had to shoot it?"

No one seems to know.

"Was the bear in somebody's tent?"

"No. He was outside."

"I wonder then why they had to shoot it. Especially if your camp is closing down and everyone is leaving anyway."

"He was just a little one," Elaine says.

"Well," Miriam says defensively, "it wasn't such a little one. They said he was two years old."

"How did they know how old he was?"

"I don't know. They knew."

"And he was all mangey and skinny," Jane says.

"Did he look mangey and skinny to you?"

"They told me he looked mangey and skinny."

"Who? Some of the men in camp?"

"Yes."

I have heard bear stories before. And even though the grizzly is a formidable creature, it is my guess that the animal in question was not posing a threat. More likely someone in camp had a gun, wanted to kill something before going home, knew of the common dislike and fear of grizzlies, and used that as a rationalization to shoot. This is fairly common in the remote camps. It is unlikely that anyone will report you, and if the story is leaked, either the bear becomes skinny and mangey or it was about to attack the shooter.

"Then you don't really know if that bear was posing a threat? You took somebody's word for it, right?"

"Well . . ."

The girls and I are off to a bad start. I am annoyed that they—two of them at least—are unthinking enough to accept a clichéd and secondhand story as truth. We talk for a few minutes about a neutral topic—how grand the country is here—and I then ask them if they have any regrets about contributing to the country's demise, by working for a mining company.

They are indignant. "We're not hurting anything," Miriam says angrily. "We're just taking samples."

"What are you taking samples of?"

"Lead and zinc," Jane says.

"Did you find any?"

Miriam nods.

"We're not allowed to say," Jane says. "It's secret." They giggle.

"Well, assuming your finds are rich enough, what do you suppose your company is going to do to the place where you made them?"

A glimmer of light. "You're saying that this is one of the last great wildernesses and it should be left alone?" Elaine says.

"Well . . . I'm not sure that 'left alone' is my attitude. But I'm amazed that you don't see that the next step after exploration is to dig the stuff up."

Miriam is angry. "There's no way mining is going to hurt this country," she says. "The Yukon is one of the last great unexplored wildernesses."

"And you're helping to explore it, right?"

"Mining is helping to open up this country," Jane says defensively. "I think that's good."

"Why is it good?"

"It's just good, that's all."

"But why? You speak as if there is some inherent good in opening up the country. But that's just a cliché. What's your evidence? Who is it 'good' for? How do you even know it isn't inherently 'bad'?"

This seems to be a new idea to the girls. They sit without answering for almost thirty seconds.

"Well, like in Mayo," Jane says. "They need jobs. And mining gives them jobs. And Faro is the second largest town in the Yukon, and it's all due to mining. So I think that's good."

"Is it? Look at it this way: Before the mines were there, not so long ago, there were no people in either of those locations, right? So you can't say mining gives them jobs, because there was nobody there to give a job to. So your statement doesn't hold up . . . unless you can show that having towns and people in those places is somehow better than not having towns and people. Just like here. Can you convince me, or yourself, that it would somehow be better to have a mining town here than to have it the way it is now?"

Another pause. This too is apparently a new concept. I feel pompous and patronizing toward the girls. But I can't help it. I'm annoyed at such shallow thinking. Especially in college students. It sounds to me as if the girls are simply echoing things they have heard around the mining camp, without really thinking about it themselves.

"The Yukon wants jobs," Jane persists. "I think it would be good if all the towns had mines. Old Crow. Dawson. Industry provides jobs, and there's no industry."

"Look, the Yukon only wants jobs if it wants more people. And nothing you've said so far is proof that more people are better than fewer people. Second, even assuming that more people are preferable to fewer people, didn't it ever occur to you that people can work at jobs other than mining jobs, industrial jobs?"

"But a miner can earn good money," Jane says less securely. She looks at the other girls.

"I don't know," Miriam says. "Remember those guys we talked to? They were miners. But they didn't have much money."

"Well, a miner *can* make good money," I say. "And they earn it. But that's another thing to consider, if you're talking about 'good' and 'bad'—the nature of the job. Were you ever in a mine?"

"Mining today is pretty safe, isn't it?" Miriam says. "Don't they have all sorts of protective ceilings and things?"

Before I can answer, Elaine asks what Dale and I are doing up here. I tell her we are writing a book, writing down what people have to say about the Yukon. That does it; the girls volunteer no more opinions. They talk suddenly about baking bread. When Dale and I are ready to leave, we express an interest in seeing the carcass of the shot grizzly. But they are onto me now. "Oh, they took it away and buried it, I think," somebody says.

"What mining company did you say you were working for?"

"We didn't say," Miriam says.

"Don't worry about things up here," Elaine says. "There's no minerals up here anyway."

"Yes, there are," Miriam says. The girls giggle.

We return to the truck and drive on. The country changes again as we go north leaving the Ogilvie Mountains. We travel through a valley, then climb the valley's west slope to an elevation of maybe 2,000 feet. The landscape is rolling, and from now on the road sticks to the tops of ridges, giving us a view of sixty to seventy miles to the east and west. The poplars disappear and the spruces become stunted. It is bleak on top of the ridges, especially now in early afternoon with the dreary bleaching sunlight and a steady breeze from the north. Far to our right there is a finger of blue, snow-capped mountains.

Perhaps they are a northern spine of the Ogilvies; or is it the Richardsons? We try to estimate their distance, but since we can see forever, we cannot decide if they are five miles away or twenty.

The wind blows steadily, moving the short spruces and the scrubby plants of the tundra. The trees are bent from the steady push of the wind, and are peculiarly tilted, not growing straight up. It now occurs to me that some of these tiny twisted spruces, though they are no taller than four-year-old spruces I have planted back home, are probably forty or fifty years old. Maybe more. Everything is slow here.

I notice also that the exposed soil in the cuts along the road is dark brown and black and is not tightly packed as clay or silt would be. It looks loose and unstable, as if a man's weight on the bank above the road would bring down a muddy slide. It has no

vegetation, not even the seedling poplars like those a hundred and thirty miles south. This part of the road is only three or four years old, and we are now within sixty miles of the Arctic Circle.

Along the highway we see many exploratory oil rigs—in use or abandoned but not yet removed —plus the flimsy-looking aluminum buildings, dumps of blue and orange oil drums, and occasional airplane landing strips.

These dirt landing strips were built by the oil and mineral exploration companies, and typically incorporate some of the road as part of their runway. There is little enough traffic so that this can be safely done. The strips, I have heard, are "turned over" to the government after the company no longer needs them. That is, they are simply left.

At mile 148, we begin to see seismic lines and/or

125

winter roads. I cannot tell the difference between the two. Both are perfectly straight ten- or twelve-foot-wide swaths cut through the forest, stretching out as far as we can see to the east. The seismic lines are cut by oil exploration crews to form a grid across the land, along which seismic blasts are set off and readings are taken to detect the presence of oil far beneath the surface. The winter roads are bulldozed to transport men and materials to oil and mineral exploration areas up here. Since the earth here is wet, spongy, unfirm—especially in the low areas—it cannot be traveled by vehicles in summer. But once frozen to the surface and topped with a packed layer of snow, even large trucks can be slowly driven over the winter roads. One of the roads in this area leads through the wilderness from here back to Mayo, 200 miles to the southeast. One leads to the oil exploration area above the remote Indian village of Old Crow, 150 miles northwest. The seismic lines and roads reach out to the horizons, slicing with supreme indifference through everything in their paths, creating a geometric pattern upon the rolling landscape that will still be here a hundred years from now. Dale remarks that they illustrate perfectly the story of North American civilization—the shortest distance between two points.

Strangely, while I dislike the lines, I am not disturbed by the piles of oil drums, galvanized sluice pipe, bits of abandoned machinery, or the occasional papers and tin cans scattered along the road. These are more immediate, more human. This is a lonesome place, and this human disarray is somehow comforting. It reassures us that if we break down or blow both our spare ties, we will not be stuck out here. Someone will be along. I recognize, of course, that if there were no road here we would not have wandered so far from civilization in the first place and would not need the comfort of litter.

Up till now the Dempster has been regularly marked with mile posts, but now, at mile 154, we see the last mile marker, a tin sign leaned casually against a tilted black spruce. We go on, riding the ridge now, past another abandoned oil camp. Then, several miles ahead, we see the glint of house trailers perched on the tundra. This must be the last road camp, mile 169, the place where we hope to find John Hudson, the project engineer.

The camp is a sterile-looking place, situated on a patch of bulldozed muddy ground alongside the road, with white, boxy house trailers—offices, cookhouse, dormitories—and a variety of big machines sitting around. Three or four ravens sit upon the cab roofs of scrapers and bulldozers, rasping and cackling, watching for a scrap of bread or lunch meat to be tossed onto the ground. The doors of the trailers are fastened with heavy freezer locks, against the wind, and are joined together—something like old New England farmhouses—to eliminate the need for going outside in winter months.

We find Hudson in his house trailer office. The camp is in disarray when we arrive, because it is being moved, building by building, from here up closer to the end of the road. Hudson apologizes for this, tells us he has already heard that I will be visiting him, and, after a brief orientation lecture, takes Dale and me out in his crew-cab pickup to show us the last stretches of the highway.

The primary question in my mind, still, is the purpose of this highway, and I hope to get some information from Hudson, or impressions that will clarify the government's decision to build. However, he speaks primarily about the technical aspects of construction in this arctic region. What he says is interesting, and I realize that this is the first really technical information we have obtained. For a time, I put aside my queries on the road's reason for being.

The primary construction problems here, Hudson tells us, are the permafrost and the high content of organic matter in the soil. Together, they make arctic road building a very different enterprise from similar construction in the south. No one, he says, has yet learned how to build a road successfully using organic material. It is not a stable material; the particles do not cling together, as in clay or silt. Here, the weather is so cold for so long that the dead leaves, moss, sticks, and other plant material do not decay; the organic matter accumulates in the surface layer faster than it can be broken down.

As an illustration of the slow rate of breakdown, he tells us that trees cut out of the highway's path are not disposed of by burning—as might be done farther south—but are simply thrown onto the roadbed and covered with soil. Down south, this would be impossible: The trunks would decay, leaving holes in the fill. But not here. Hudson estimates it will be a hundred years or more before the trunks deteriorate.

Permafrost is a bigger problem. No one knows for sure how deep the frost is here, he says, but one oil company reports that their core drillings have brought up frozen earth from a depth of 2,200 feet. During July and August the upper two feet or so of earth thaw, then become soft and mushy. This is the "active layer," and the arctic road builder's main problem is to protect the permafrost, keep it from thawing, and thus minimize structural changes in the active layer to keep the road surface from sinking or collapsing. The permafrost is naturally protected by the surface layer of moss, which is a good insulator. Whenever possible, the moss is left in place and road fill is added on top of it. The fill itself also insulates, but not as efficiently as moss.

Before we drive up the road, John shows us a hole—four feet deep and two feet in diameter, with an oil drum thrust into it—in the earth parking lot just outside his office where the moss has been bladed away. The soil in this spot has thawed and collapsed, leaving the hole. This is what happens to the road when its permafrost melts.

We speed along, with John driving at sixty miles per hour over the rough road. He maintains a running monologue, making technical comments about the road, seeming annoyed when I interrupt with a question, calling out "point of interest" and coming briefly to a halt whenever he wishes to show us something. He slows abruptly for ruts and for the working trucks, bulldozers, and scrapers. In winter,

Abandoned cache along the Dempster.

127

John says, diesel road machinery in the field is kept running, day and night, all winter, to eliminate the time-consuming chore of getting it started each day in weather 60° or 70° below. Trucks are sometimes shut off at night, if they are in camp, where their electric engine block heaters can be plugged in.

John is highly intelligent, serious, businesslike, and aggressive, qualities that have gotten him far in Canadian civil service. He is only thirty, but is the Dempster's Deputy Project Engineer, has built most of the road during the past two years. He was graduated from Glasgow University in Scotland in 1966 and was hired from there for highway work in Canada. He seems older than his thirty years.

It occurs to me that from the government's point of view, John Hudson is the perfect person to speak with media people. He is all facts, knows his work backward and forward, talks constantly and forcefully, permitting few questions, and never ventures a value judgment of his own, except on matters strictly confined to the mechanics of road building. I make some attempts to solicit his personal impressions, but he either evades the question or changes the topic:

"Do you think the value of the road is worth the environmental costs it creates?"

"We'll go survey the situation, and then you can draw your own conclusions."

"What do the environmentalists say about the Dempster? Do you get any trouble from them?"

"I am not directly involved with them. Most of their dealings are with the people in Ottawa. I suggest that you stop and talk with the people there on your way back to New York."

"What would you say is the real purpose of this highway? To attract tourists? To supply men and materials to the delta oil fields? To help the mining companies?"

"It will certainly do those things. It's a developmental road. It's being built to sixty-mile-per-hour specifications, and it will certainly handle the traffic. Though I don't advise people driving that fast, because they may end up stuck in the mud. We spend a lot of time hauling out tourists who have gone off the shoulder."

The one thing that does seem to engage John, and that evokes spontaneous comment, is road machinery. I ask some questions about the various vehicles we see, and after that he comments en- thusiastically on each of the vehicles we come to, noting that a certain truck can carry a load of 57,000 pounds, that an A-frame hoist can lift the front end of a "631," that a certain scraper blade is twelve feet wide and can sweep the road in two passes.

We go on up the road. John talks of cuts and fills, likens a cut to "putting money in the bank," since it supplies the road builder with excess dirt and gravel that can be used in the roadbed, and compares a fill to "taking money out of the bank," since it uses up the material. Here, the road is routed along the ridgetops; cuts are few and thus he has to resort to borrow pits to get the several feet of fill needed to build the roadbed and to properly insulate the permafrost.

"We saw a lot of borrow pits back in the early stages of the road," I comment. "They looked like they would be a long time in healing."

John brakes abruptly. "All right then. Point of interest. Look back there. See that borrow pit? Behind those trees? We've got them out of sight here. Who's going to see that one, unless they look for it?"

He puts the truck in gear and we speed on.

"Will those pits revegetate?"

"In three or four years, there'll be petunias growing in that thing," John says buoyantly.

Sure there will.

As we proceed up the road, the various construction and survey crews recognize John and get out of our way. Occasionally he halts briefly, gives instructions or gets information, advises a surveyor to keep his chain tight. The road, despite the care taken to protect the permafrost, is rough and pitted, and in several locations we slow almost to a halt to go through grooves or potholes where an underground ice lens has melted, caving in the road surface. At mile 201 we see a place where the permafrosted soil in a cut through a steep slope has melted and slid away into the stunted spruces nearby, covering their trunks three feet deep in mud. It looks as if a fifty-foot section of the road simply displaced itself, moving twenty feet to the side.

I ask John if there are any plans to pave this road or, for that matter, any of the Yukon roads, all of which are dusty in dry weather, slippery in rain, icy in winter. John seems to take offense at this, tells me he sees nothing wrong with the dirt surfaces, then says that in temperatures of zero or below—which is most of the time—ice has the same coefficient of friction as asphalt and therefore is just as safe as a road surface. No, there are no plans to pave this road or others.

Finally, at mile 203.5, John whips the truck over to the side, shuts off the ignition, and is out before the engine rumbles to a stop. Dale and I follow. This is it, the end of the road. The road pad, John says, goes on another ten miles or so, but the negotiable road stops here. A few feet in front of us, another partially excavated cut has become a soupy mass of mud, flowing out from the road edge, though not as dramatically as a few miles back. The mushy road winds ahead and disappears among the blue hills in the distance. Close-by, a set of tire tracks leads out into the mud; it looks as if the vehicle stopped there and was hauled back.

"We didn't make those tracks," John says emphatically. "A tourist did it. We had to pull him out."

Dale and I each get out our cameras to take a picture of the Dempster's end.

"I'd rather you didn't take that photograph," John says coolly.

"Are you serious? Why?"

"I'm serious. Someone who doesn't understand it could see it and get the wrong idea."

His tone is so insistent that we have no choice except to force a confrontation—which might end the interview—or consent. We consent. John gets back in the truck and we follow. We start back down the road as fast as we came up.

"A couple of people have told me that you got the road built to mile 230, but then it washed out and now you're back to where you were last year. What about that?"

John bristles. "No no. That's not so! The road did not wash out."

"What happened to it then? I mean, I heard you got as far as mile 230. And now you're at 203 . . ."

"We built a stretch in October and November of last year," John says. "It was early winter and there was already snow on the ground. In spring, it took me five hours to drive twenty miles on that stretch. But it did *not* wash out, as you heard. We did not have a washout!"

I do not see much practical difference between what John describes—a road that cannot be driven—and what a layman might describe as a "washout." But since John is touchy on the subject, I try to tread carefully.

"Was the road rendered impassable because of . . ."

"It was never completely impassable," John says.

"All right then. Was the road rendered almost impassable because you went ahead with construction during winter, when there was snow on the ground? Would it have been better to wait? That is, was there . . ."

John interrupts. "You have two choices in winter," he says aggressively. "You can sit around your bunkhouse and sulk, or you can get out and do something. I chose to do something."

We speed on, heading back toward camp, but are halted by machinery in the road. John comes to an abrupt halt and points to an enormous bulldozer. "Look at this D-9," he says enthusiastically. "If we ran into him at forty miles per hour, the driver would never even feel the bump."

"I believe you. You don't have to demonstrate."

John ignores my attempt at humor. "They've been known to run right over an automobile without even knowing it!"

The machinery clears and we move on. It occurs to me that if I were in the arctic road-building business, John is just the man I would want to have in charge. Mistakes or not, I'm sure that nothing stands in his way. It is my guess, too, that Hudson is as competent as they come; any of the mistakes that may have occurred under his supervision are probably due to the peculiar and unfamiliar conditions of the north and would have occurred under any supervisor.

In a way, though, this is just the warning made in the Schultz group's environmental report: Given our lack of experience in northern road building, the haste of any project like the Dempster inevitably creates a more adverse environmental impact than need be created.

I ask John something along these lines, wording my question as diplomatically as possible. He answers very firmly and self-assuredly:

"If we were talking about building something down in New York, where there is a long history of road building, then we would have, say, three hundred years' experience with soils, freezing, whatever, to guide our decisions. But in the Yukon we have only a couple of decades' experience. And right here, along this arctic ridge, we have only my two-year experience. All right then, what do you do? Hold up the whole project for years and get a lot of scientists around to gather data on it? That would be ridiculous! We've got to get on with it."

We bounce through a rutted few feet of road. "That used to be a smooth stretch," John says.

"How fast, how many miles per year, are you building this road?"

"It varies. South of here they moved fast. But down there it was easy. The river was right alongside them. It was just a matter of belting in loads of gravel every day—bang! bang! But on this ridge I've had to go to the borrow pits. . . . If I could remake this country up here, I'd build it with a thousand cubic yards of river gravel every few hundred feet of road."

"I get the impression that you're moving along pretty fast anyway, right?"

John smiles, nods.

"I've heard the government is building another highway—the Mackenzie—that's supposed to meet the Dempster around Arctic Red," I say. "But I heard something today that made me think they'd halted construction. Is that right?"

"Not as far as I know. They're moving on."

"Well then, they're moving a little slower than you are, right?"

"Right," John says snappily. "And they'd better hurry it up, or they'll be calling it 'the Dempster.'"

We hurry on. John maintains his running commentary. Using different words, I re-ask my question about the environmental damage that may result from hurrying the project.

John is short with me.

"I will give you the same answer I did before. Now if you have, say, a one-hundred-mile road to build, you have two choices. You can build it all now. Or if you want to do everything just so, you can do ten miles this year, ten the next, and so on for ten years, and build every ten-mile length according to what you've learned on the last length. But then you run into other problems: What's going to happen to the cost of labor and materials during that time, for instance? You know what will happen. And since a part of my job is to save Canadian taxpayers' money, I know I'll come out ahead by moving forward right now, even if we do encounter some problems. Because the cost of curing those problems will certainly be less than if we did the road ten miles at a time."

John's statement makes perfect sense to me. Assuming, that is, that the hypothetical road he talks of is needed in the first place. The Dempster isn't, from all I've heard so far.

John again pulls the truck off to the side and leaps out. "C'mon. I'll show you something." He takes a crowbar from the back of the truck and bounds out into the moss alongside the road. We follow. It's rough going. Walking in this spongy, mounded mat of moss is like trying to walk in dense cotton. Weird stuff. It looks solid from the road.

"Here, sink that bar into the ground as far as you can," he instructs, pointing to a small patch of wet soil. I lift the bar and plunge it, expecting to bury it almost out of sight in organic material. But it drives in only about 20 inches, thuds against something hard. The surprise must show on my face.

"You didn't believe me?" John says. "That's not a rock. It's permafrost. And that's the farthest away from the surface it gets. It's melted its maximum. In another few weeks, it'll be frozen all the way back to the surface again."

I drive the bar in again, three feet away. Same thing. I have been here in the Yukon for months and have never even thought of trying this experiment before.

The demonstration over, John bounds back to the truck, starts the engine, while Dale and I struggle after him.

"Anything else you want to see?"

"You mentioned before that there is a hill from which you could show us the location of the Arctic Circle. I'd like to see that if you've got time."

John nods, slaps the truck in gear, and we speed down the road. John explains now that the presence of permafrost, so close to the surface, with its unstable active layer above it, is the reason for the "drunken forest" we have seen along the road, the strangely tipped black spruces; the root systems penetrate only to the top of the ice, and the shallow-rooted trees tip easily in the unstable soil.

"On your way back," John suggests, "get off the road and take a flying leap at one of those trees and you'll see. You'll knock it right over."

We pass another survey crew, all young men, and I ask John about the morale of the troops in this remote work camp. He tells me, as I expected, that there is high turnover. Not as bad as in some other remote Yukon locations, though, because the men are given several consecutive days off each month, which gives them enough time to get to Whitehorse, have a roaring drunk, and get back.

"Are they rehired if they stay longer than the allotted number of days?"

"Sure. But we don't call it rehiring. They're not *unemployed* when they stay longer. They're just *not working.*"

"How do you personally like your work up here?"

"Well, you have to like your work in the north country, don't you? Or you commit suicide."

Even this answer, I can't help notice, is stated in the abstract. I do not feel that John makes a conscious effort to conceal his own feelings, to be indirect. Rather, I suspect that his way of talking is simply a language one learns, without trying, after enough exposure to the civil service.

We zip past the camp. A raven drifts across the road, right in front of us. John mutters something angrily under his breath, does not try to miss the raven. The bird is shaken by the wind of the vehicle, barely makes it past the front end of the truck. I like ravens; I used to have a crow for a pet—the raven's smaller cousin—and know that they are comical, intelligent creatures. At the same time, they are fearless and pushy, and I can see how, living up here in this outlandish place, followed and peered at by these aggressive, ominous-looking birds, you could get to hate them.

We go several miles past camp, heading toward the hill from which we will see the Arctic Circle. We pass an abandoned oil camp with its forty-five-gallon drums scattered about.

"Those aren't our oil drums," John says. "They belong to a company that was exploring here. Some of them still have oil in them."

"What company was that?"

"We have several outfits along the road," John says, "but they prefer to remain anonymous. This one left a long time ago."

"Have any of them found oil?"

"I don't know. I suspect they will, because the formation of the land looks to me like the kind of place oil is found. But if any of them have found it, I don't know about it. They keep it secret."

We pass a spot where someone has emptied an auto ashtray on the shoulder of the road.

"I see you're getting all the hallmarks of a regular highway, even litter."

John shrugs. "Tourists. I don't like it. But maybe if it gets bad enough, they'll finally start to enforce the litter laws."

I glance at my notes again. There's not much there, except some question marks, some "didn't says" and "ask laters." Not one solid expression of John's opinion.

". . . And what again did you say was the purpose of the Dempster? My notes seem a little unclear on it. How do you view your mission up here, in building this road?"

John responds quickly. "I would say that my mission up here is to design a road—no, to design and *build* a road, in accordance with design standards."

"Um . . . okay . . . 'to design and build a road.' I've got that. I'm not sure that was just what I—"

"To design and build a road *to design standards,*" John interrupts impatiently. "And in the process, to minimize degradation of permafrost."

"Well, then . . . maybe you can tell me how *you* see its ultimate purpose?"

John hesitates, the only time I have seen him do it. But the hesitation I think is not because he is concocting a company answer, but because the reason for the road is so obscure that it escapes even him. "Uh . . . uh, I would say its purpose is to generally access the north."

"Okay. 'To generally access the north.' And by that, I assume you mean for oil and mineral exploration, for access to Inuvik and McPherson, for material supply to the delta . . . ?"

"It has always been a developmental road. And now that we've gotten this far—and we've done a good job, even if I do say so myself—we could access the Bonnet Plume area without much trouble."

"Bonnet Plume? That's a hundred and fifty miles to the southeast, right? You mean with another road, then?"

"Yes."

"I see. Well, do you think that building a road to Bonnet Plume would be a good thing? I'm asking for a value judgment here, I guess."

"I'm only saying that now we could do it, with less trouble."

"Let me ask you then, considering all the pros and cons, if you feel the Dempster is a good thing or a bad thing. I mean, it seems to me that the decision to build this road . . ."

"To make that kind of a judgment, one would

have to do just what you are suggesting, add up all the pros and cons, assuming you could even identify them. And I think you're in just as good a position to do that as I am."

"Well, what would be your reaction, for instance, if they, in Ottawa, suddenly decided to halt the Dempster just where it is? Would you agree with that decision?"

"I suspect that that decision will not be made. But if it was, I imagine they would have a reason for it."

It's no use. There is a way to use the language so that you never open yourself up. We go over a bump.

"And what do the environmentalists say about it? What do they think about this project?"

"Those damn environmentalists!" John says angrily, cursing for the first time. "You never know what they'll say. I went to a meeting once in Whitehorse. This woman got up and wept. She actually *wept*, right there in a meeting!"

"She was an environmentalist, you mean?"

"Yes. And we had a surveyor working here. He was another one. He was going to go off and live in the bush and commune with nature. And I said to him, all right, but you tell me how you're going to live out there without society. It's ridiculous."

That's all John has to say on the topic. I don't argue its relevance or nonrelevance to the Dempster. It is nevertheless an opinion, the first I have heard him express.

We reach the hill. John stops the truck and strides out onto the tundra, points out a hill beyond a hill, perhaps thirty miles away. That's it, the Arctic Circle. We look out there for a few seconds, at the rows of blue ridges stretching our forever. The country is big enough and open enough so that, if the cartographer's Arctic Circle were superimposed upon the land, we could see its curve. The country is regular and rolling. There is nothing dramatic about it, nothing different from the scenery we see all around us, but it somehow feels special to be within sight of this coldest of climatic zones. There are no promontories or unusual features that would give you any idea which way was north and which south. For a minute I wonder what it is inside a caribou that tells him which way to go, in spring and fall.

My daydreaming is short-lived. John seems anxious to get back. I pick up a small red berry from the tundra and ask if he knows the name of the plant. He doesn't. He eases back toward the truck. I am sort of reluctant to go. I casually remark that a friend of ours, Bob Frisch, walked one hundred fifty miles northwest from the Dempster to Old Crow, autumn before last.

"That's impossible," John says authoritatively. "No one has done that."

"Oh sure," I protest. "He's known for his hiking. He's taken a lot longer trips than that."

"I think he was pulling your leg," John says. "I find it very very hard to believe that anyone could make that trip. Especially in fall."

I don't have the energy to argue it. I change the topic. "Do you ever get out to hike?"

"I can't afford that luxury," John says.

"How about hunting? Do you get out to hunt?"

"I'm a legal hunter," John says.

I look again at the country to the north. I regret somehow that I have not gotten out there. Not because it is scenic, but because it is so endless. In this country of wildness and bigness, this block of land is the biggest and wildest; if you walked due north, from here to the Arctic Ocean, you would not find one other person. The space is powerful.

"It's sure some country out there," I remark as I turn back toward the truck. As I say it, I realize that right here, where we stand now, was "out there" until a year or so ago, when the road reached this point. And not many years before that, everything north of Dawson was "out there."

John stands with his back against the truck, waiting. He seems a little impatient, or maybe embarrassed, by my enthusiasm. He points to the tire of the truck.

"This thing has seventeen-inch wheels," he says.

We get in, drive back to camp, and eat supper with John. After dark we begin the long drive back to Dawson, slapping our own faces to keep awake. On the road we see a big covey of white ptarmigan and later a young bull moose and his cow, who stand staring at us as we grunt to them from fifty feet away, trying to speak moose. After three or four minutes they tire of our inept attempts and trot across the highway. Late in the night the white silent Ogilvies gleam strangely in the blue moonlight, and just a glimmer of the northern lights shows in the sky as we drive south.

133

DAWSON

WITH LAST NIGHT'S rain, Dawson's streets have turned to mud. It sticks to my boots as I walk through town. Overhead, the sky is gray and somber. The air is chilly and still. Most summer tourists have departed. A green pickup truck turns off the new strip of asphalt on Front Street and rumbles into the center of town, but otherwise the place is quiet.

The little town sits on the flat, bordered by the blue Klondike River on the south, the big, gray Yukon on the West, and the arc of hills on east and north. It is a peculiar mixture of new and old, restored and abandoned, earthy and plastic. Space along the boardwalk-lined main streets is shared by old general stores and new motels, metal house trailers, takeout hamburger stands, and old clapboard gold-rush buildings with their rusting, corrugated tin roofs. Here and there an old one-room log cabin, with a gray plume of woodsmoke rising from its stovepipe chimney; here and there one of the government's modern low-cost houses, painted bright blue or yellow or pale green, with fuel oil tank and TV antenna, a bleached set of caribou antlers and a dismantled snowmobile sitting in the grassless yard. Nearby, the attractively restored Palace Grand theater with its brown wood front; up the street, prefab motel units with aluminum siding, and a three-story apartment building, tacky-modern and sterile.

It is difficult to imagine the town as it was three quarters of a century or more ago, a thrown-up tent and clapboard city of thirty or forty thousand. But despite its mongrelization, Dawson is still the Yukon's nicest town, settled-feeling, almost cozy, without the bland uniformity of Whitehorse or the just-ripped-from-the-earth look of the new mining towns. Logs and dirt and wood still hold the edge over aluminum and asphalt and fiber glass. It's a slim edge, though.

After getting groceries I cross the street and go into the Downtown saloon for a beer. In addition to a few late-season tourists, there are six or seven familiar faces in the long, dimly lit room. Three or four local Indian people sit to the left of the door. Two of the area's older gold miners sit at one of the small tables. One has a little Bayer aspirin bottle filled with gold dust, and he shakes it occasionally for the tourists to notice. One man sits alone at the bar, with a lynx pelt draped about his shoulders. Another man, about thirty, sits alone in the rear, near the washrooms and TV set. He is Jean Lenoir from

135

Dawson

Montreal. I have not seen him in two months. He signals and I join him.

Jean has been up here since early June. The last I knew, he was living a sort of semibush, semi-suburban existence with his woman friend in an abandoned cabin not far from town, next to the cabin shared by Bob Frisch and Hans Algotsson. This is Jean's second stay in a Klondike cabin. The first, last year, did not work out; he was driven back south by the weather. When I saw him last, he was determined to remain in his cabin throughout the coming winter, to avoid a repetition of last year's experience.

But things have changed. His woman has left. His savings lasted only through July, and his unemployment checks from Montreal have been arriving irregularly. He has sold his car. He has worked as a gold miner's assistant and as a carpenter on a new government building in town, but both of these jobs have somehow evaporated, for reasons he does not make clear.

Nevertheless, these turns of fortune do not seem to have diminished his enthusiasm for staying the winter.

"I figure I'll have a lot of free time this winter," Jean says. "Once I've got my firewood and my moose, there won't be a lot left to do, eh? So I think I'll do some trapping, for extra money. Maybe thirty or forty traps. I might need some dogs for that, so I'm going to see if I can get some of Sven's pups."

"Well, first things first, I guess. Do you have your wood in yet?"

"No. But that's not going to take me very long. I need maybe three cords to heat the cabin, and I'm fast at it. Now you probably think Bob is a pretty good bushman, eh? But the other day he and I were splitting wood together, and I noticed I was splitting up four pieces for every three of his."

"Oh? That's very good. But you probably want to get your wood in pretty soon. You're going to have a foot of snow here within the month."

Jean nods, but does not hear me. "I figure this is the place to be," he goes on. "This is the last frontier, eh? You've got to be strong to live here. You've got to be a real bushman. But if you are, you've got it made. If you live in a cabin like I do, you've got your fuel free. If you can shoot, you've got your meat. I figure I won't have to spend more than, oh, two hundred dollars the whole winter."

I nod. "Sure. I don't know if you'd get by on only two hundred, but I imagine you can get off fairly cheaply."

"And this is no place for women, eh? Not in winter. I think if you have a woman, it's probably more trouble than if you were alone."

"I don't know. I think if I were going to live here for the winter I wouldn't want to live alone. Of course, your cabin isn't really in the bush. You're near the road, so you can at least get into town now and then to see people. And you've got Hans and Bob for neighbors."

"You may not think my cabin is in the bush now. But wait till winter. You know, that road is snowed in. If I want to get into town I'm going to have to walk six miles on snowshoes to the corner, then get a ride in. It's the same as being in the bush, eh?"

"Well, maybe. Anyway, I was just going to remind you that there are several women living successfully in the bush. Right on your road there's Mickey and Liz. Then out on the river there's Mary, Rosemary, Donna, Mrs. Burian . . ."

"But they're all living with their husbands," Jean says authoritatively. "I don't think they could take it alone, eh? And not many of those young couples will stick out the winter anyway. You have to be rugged. They're all city people."

"Well, you may be right. It is true that most bush couples don't make it. But I don't think being from the city has too much to do with it. For that matter, you're from the city too, right?"

"I've lived in the bush, though. I spent a winter alone in a cabin. It was a beautiful experience. Beautiful."

"I didn't know you'd done that. Where was it?"

"It was, uh, in northern Ontario. It wasn't the whole winter. It was about a month. But I got to be a good bushman. It was beautiful."

I nod. "Sure. I imagine that spending a winter alone, or even two weeks, is one of the greatest experiences anybody could have. It's something very few people get to do in our society. I'm glad there are still a few places left where it can be done. Like here."

Jean nods enthusiastically. "That's valuable experience to have. Not many people have it. And you never know when you'll need it. If I were in an airplane that crash-landed in the wilderness, I'd probably survive, eh? While everybody else might die."

I laugh. "Well, I really doubt if there is much likelihood of getting marooned in the wilderness. But I do think that being alone in the bush can give us some perspective on our everday lives. Like, it's good to be reminded every now and then that water doesn't originate in a faucet. Or that heat requires fuel. Things like that."

Jean nods without hearing. "And it makes you into a good bushman. Now you see, what I am going to do is very, very difficult. But it's not difficult if you learn the tricks of living in the bush, eh? Now I'm going to have a lot of spare time because I know how to work fast in the bush. So you know what I'm going to do? Order a lot of books from the library and read them through the winter. I'll return them when I come out in the spring. You can do that if you know the tricks."

"Well, maybe. But my observation is that it's not so much tricks or toughness that makes a successful bush dweller as it is steadiness in the head. I mean, you have to get along with yourself, or with whoever shares your cabin. And you have to have a steady work routine. Like the Burians. They keep plugging away, summer and winter, every day."

"That's probably the nicest thing about the bush, eh? You're your own boss. You don't have anybody to give you orders."

"Yeah, but it's hard to discipline yourself to, say, cut wood in summer when you don't have the immediate need for it. But if you don't, and keep putting it off, then you get caught when it turns cold."

"But it won't take *me* very long, eh? I'll need two or three cords of firewood and I can cut that in a week. I'll probably start it tomorrow."

"Why not today?"

Dawson, nestled at the junction of the Klondike and Yukon rivers, held a population of 30,000 in 1898. The town's 780 residents now live among the remains of the gold rush era.

Dawson's saloons and gambling hall are the centers of its summer social life.

Yukoners

Sod roof and chimney cover

An abandoned gold rush dwelling.

"I'm waiting for a pogey check from Montreal. And I want to be here when it comes in. I thought it would come in Saturday but it didn't. So I got a ride in with Sven to wait for it."

"Well, okay. But you could've spent the time getting firewood. I think you're going to need seven or eight cords, by the way. Not just three or four."

"Did you ever live alone in the bush? In winter?"

"No. I think the longest time I spent alone in the woods was four or five days."

"Then you don't really know how much wood I'll need, do you?"

"Look, dammit, I'm just trying to give good advice. Now Bob and Hans's cabin is precisely the same size as yours, and they burn seven or eight cords a winter. So I think you'd better face the reality of how cold it gets here. You'd better plan on cutting a little more wood."

"Do you think you could stick out a winter here?"

"In a cabin alone? I don't know. Physically I could do it, but I think I might not have the patience and regularity to do all the routine chores. My tendency would be to let the fire go out, I think."

"You see, that's why you'd never make it."

Jean's arrogance annoys me, but over the past three months I have met several people—people attempting to convince themselves to remain in the bush—with attitudes not unlike his.

We order another beer. Despite the dozen or so people in the Downtown, the place is quiet. We can overhear the gold miners talking at their table. They are discussing a short article on the Klondike printed several months ago in *The New York Times*. I have heard them discuss this same months-old article three or four times before. They are critical of the article, and of the local gold miner who was interviewed for it. They do not feel that he gave the correct impression of what the Klondike is like.

"This is the last frontier, eh?" Jean repeats. "We're right in the middle of it."

"You mean Dawson?"

Jean nods. "Dawson, the Klondike, the bush . . . And probably the nicest thing about it is, if you know how, you can use it to your advantage. Now this winter, I'll be working just for myself. I'll be doing what I want. You can be yourself here, eh?"

"Well, maybe. Certainly you have the physical space to try new things, like building your own cabin or living off the land. But as for 'doing what you want,' I think you're answerable to a lot of people here, just like you are in any small town. People know other people's business, and you have to behave yourself. You don't have a lot of privacy, or social freedom, or whatever you want to call it."

Jean is adamant. "Oh no. People don't care what you do, as long as you don't bother them. You can do what you want."

"Can you? I think you've got your eyes closed for a guy who's been here all summer. Look at Jeff. It bugged people here that he didn't work, and spent all his time hiking, until Arnold told that story about his being an eccentric millionaire. So now we hear everywhere that Jeff owns a beef ranch and that somehow entitles him to hike, in their eyes. But the point is, it bugged people, until that story came along. They wanted him to work at regular jobs, like they do. In a small-town atmosphere, there's pressure to conform."

"Then you ignore it, eh?" Jean says glibly.

"Oh yes? What would you say if I told you that I've already heard four different versions of the split-up between Cathy and you? Even before you told me about it. And I've only been in town one day!"

Jean's expression changes with this news. I feel momentarily guilty, but only momentarily. He bounces back:

"Look at the people who founded Dawson. Those old guys were independent as hell. They weren't conforming. They were real bushmen. They were wild when they came into town. Gunfights. Broken bottles. Everything. They did what they wanted. And they more or less set up what the place would be like in the future, eh?"

I shrug. "I don't know. I wasn't there. But all I've read about the gold rush makes me think they were a pretty subdued bunch. Or maybe depressed is a better word. Did you ever look at Bob's book of old gold-rush photos? There's not a smiling face in the bunch. Not one. As far as the glamour of the gold rush goes, I think that was mostly created in fiction. I don't know where you got that stuff about gunfights in Dawson. There weren't any. The mounties had an iron hand on the town. People weren't even allowed to carry guns."

Jean seems surprised. But undaunted.

"Well then, how did they get to Dawson in the first place if they weren't real bushmen? They *had* to be tough, those old gold miners, eh? Why did they come here in the first place?"

"You mean were they hairy-chested men? Who

knows? They certainly went through an awful ordeal getting here, over the Chilkoot Pass. Though I think most of them learned their toughness on the way. They weren't bushmen to begin with. As for why they came, I'll bet it was some combination of wanting to find gold and running away from something in their own lives. You know, something like a bad marriage or the inability to get along with people or to keep a job. Something like that."

Jean gives me an uncomfortable look. "Oh no. They were tough. They weren't running away from anything."

I shrug. "Well, I'm no student of the gold rush, but from what little I know, I suspect there were a lot of neurotics and misfits who left home to take part in it. I mean, the obstacles to getting here were tremendous. There was a good chance of losing your life. They lived under filthy conditions. They ate lousy food. They spent the winter in tents. They had to haul all that stuff over the Chilkoot Pass. And for all that, the chances of anybody finding gold were slim. I think the people who turned back were the sane ones. They sized up the situation and saw it wasn't worth it. They made a good decision. The

ones who came on to Dawson didn't. I think that they were driven by something stronger than gold. Like I said, something in their own lives. Or in their own heads."

Jean seems upset. "Is that right, eh? Well, I don't think too many of them were running away from anything. Maybe they were just the strong ones, eh? Maybe the ones who turned back just didn't have what it takes."

"Okay. Maybe. I don't know what you're looking for. But I think the core of Dawson society was created by merchants and entrepreneurs, not by these wild and woolly gold rushers you picture. I really think that a lot of them were just unhappy people, looking for some kind of magic in a new place. They didn't find it, and they left."

We get another beer. Jean seems somehow troubled by what I have said. It dawns on me finally that his conception of what it means, what it takes, to live in the Klondike today is strongly linked with his romantic conception of life during the Klondike gold rush of 1898. But I have heard other Yukon people—newcomers, even longtime residents—express an almost identical view of the Yukon's gold-rush beginnings. A strange pattern emerges from this: Yukon gold rushers—mostly Americans—were attracted to the Klondike by a myth, or by a promise thin enough to be considered a myth. Since that time, we have created another myth out of gold-rush life. And for many people, this second myth apparently continues to serve as an important attraction of the Klondike. People like Jean have gone one step further to assume that somewhere smoldering beneath the surface of the Klondike is the experience of the gold rush, magically unchanged by passage of time, to be relived, today, by the faithful.

The man at the bar now begins to talk to his lynx pelt, inserting his hand into the pelt's head and moving it, puppetlike. He orders a beer for himself and one for his friend and dips the lynx's head into the foamy glass. The two carry on an animated discussion of sex, politics, and bear hunting. I can't tell if he is drunk or if this is something for the tourists. Outside the sky is darker. Light comes through the windows and falls on the floor in long, gray rectangles.

Jean's mood has changed, perhaps from things I have said, perhaps from thoughts of his own. He looks toward the window for a long time and finally speaks.

"You were alone in the bush for four days, eh?" he says.

"You mean that time I mentioned? Yes. Four or five."

"You were lonesome, eh?"

"No. Not really. Because I knew I'd be coming back in a few days."

Jean nods. "And how much wood do you think you used in that time? Of course it wouldn't be anything near a cord, eh? But what part of a cord?"

"Well, some was already cut when I got there. And I spent maybe an hour each afternoon cutting enough for night and morning. Oh, maybe a fifth of a cord in all. But that's just a wild guess."

"A fifth of a cord. That sounds about right."

"That was upper New York State. It was November. But it was nowhere near as cold as here. If you're trying to figure how much you'll need, I wouldn't use that as a guide."

"Oh no. I just wanted to know. I would figure about twenty percent more though, eh?"

"Oh hell, I don't know. For you, I think the important thing is just to get at it, now, and cut your wood before snow comes."

"It won't take me long though, eh? I figure I'll need about seven or eight cords for the winter. I should be able to cut that in two weeks."

"Look, all I mean to suggest is that you get at it. That cabin of yours has been occupied for decades on and off, and there's no dry timber right nearby. So you'll have to find some, trim it, cut the logs into lengths, and get it to your cabin. Once you get it there, you can cut it up at your leisure. But you've got to get it there. You may not have to haul it far, but you'll need somebody's truck. Maybe you can borrow Hans's."

"You know what they say about firewood, eh? It warms you twice. Once when you cut it. Once when you burn it."

"Jean, believe me, at thirty below—"

"Did you have a gun when you were in the bush?"

"Yes, I did."

"I think a good gun is something important to have in the bush. For your meat. And in case something comes around. Like a wolverine. Even a grizzly is afraid of a wolverine, you know."

"I've heard that, but I don't really know."

"They can come right down your chimney. And if they do that, you want to kill, and kill fast. So you have to have a good gun. And you should be able to use it."

"I guess so. Though Bob takes those long trips through the bush and he doesn't carry a gun with him."

"He doesn't, eh?"

"No. Bob and Hans will be good neighbors for you, by the way. They've lived here several winters. If I were you, I'd ask their advice about things. And Hans has the truck, so you'll be able to get into town for groceries. Maybe you could even cook some of your meals together."

"I wish they didn't live so close by," Jean says. "It's better to be all alone if you're going to spend a winter in the bush, eh?"

I nod. "I know what you mean. But maybe for your first winter it's a good idea to have them nearby. Then maybe next year you might decide to move really out in the bush. That is, if you decide to stay."

"Oh, I'll stay all right." He thinks a moment. "That's one of the nice things about the bush, eh? You get this fantastic appetite. You're hungry as hell in the morning. So you jump out of your sleeping bag and start the fire, and then when the cabin's warm you get up again and cook yourself some bacon and eggs and homemade bread."

"Sure. If you've got bacon and eggs and homemade bread."

"What do you mean?"

"Oh, I was just trying to picture living here in the winter. I mean bacon and eggs are super-expensive in Dawson. And you can't buy any homemade bread. And unless you get into town pretty often you probably run out of things. If I were here, I'd probably be too impatient to shop correctly. I'd probably end up eating that goddamn bannock all the time. And then my teeth would fall out."

"Your teeth!"

I laugh. "Oh, I just mean that bannock is all the gold rushers ate. And their teeth fell out. They got scurvy from lack of vitamin C."

Jean puts his hand to his mouth.

"Don't worry about *your* teeth. Scurvy is a long-term thing. You have to go without fruit for a long time. But if I were you, I'd buy a bottle of vitamin pills and make sure to eat greens and fruit once in a while this winter."

"I notice a lot of people have bad teeth here," Jean says. "I wonder if that's scurvy, eh?"

"No. I doubt it. But it probably does have something to do with diet. And probably the lack of dentists. Is there a dentist in Dawson? I don't even know."

Jean shakes his head. "I think the doctor looks at your teeth. I think the dentist is in Whitehorse."

I nod.

"They say it's dark here in winter, eh? It isn't dark all the time, is it?"

"Oh no. It's light enough to be outside five or six hours every day."

"That sounds nice though, eh? If it's dark I'll have lots of time to read. Once I get my moose, I'm going to get a lot of books from the library."

"Well, first things first. I keep saying this, but I think if you've really decided to stay the winter, the first thing you should do is to get your wood. You should get right on that before anything else. Do you have a saw?"

"No. But I can borrow Bob's Swede saw."

"Sure. I'm sure he'd let you use it."

"You know, we already had one snow," Jean says. "It came right through that hole over the bunk."

"You don't have that fixed yet?"

"No. But all I have to do is put some plywood over it, eh?"

"I guess so. I think there are two or three pieces of plywood out there in the little shed behind your cabin."

"Did Bob and Hans tell you about the guy who lived in my cabin last year? He'd come over every day or so to visit, and then he'd say something like, 'Oh, while I'm here, I wonder if you've got a couple of sticks of firewood.' " He laughs. "Can you imagine that, eh? He never got in his own wood. That kind of person doesn't last long in the Klondike, eh? They run him out of town on a rail."

It is 2:00 P.M. Most of the tourists have now left the saloon. The gold miners are still here. The man with the beer-drinking lynx is still here. One of the local motel owners comes in for a drink, talks about his next year's plans for expansion and about the added tourist business that will be brought to Dawson once the Dempster Highway is completed.

I turn back to Jean. "You know, I think you should really ask yourself whether or not you want to stay here this winter. And if you don't, then maybe you should spend your money on a plane ticket back to Montreal."

"I did that last year," he says grimly. "I said I'd stay this year, and I'll do it."

"Okay. But don't feel compelled to do it just because you said you would. People often have to change their plans. Maybe you should just figure on coming back next summer. Give yourself more time."

"I'll do it if it kills me," Jean says.

"Did you have a job in Montreal? Maybe it would pay to go back, save up some money, and come back next year."

Jean waves his hand impatiently. "If I went back to Montreal, I'd have to work for my father again."

"You don't get along?"

"When I left, I told him he could go to hell before I would work for him again."

"Do you hear from your family?"

"No."

"Who forwards your unemployment checks?"

"My wife."

"Oh. I didn't even know you'd been married."

"It's in the courts now. It didn't last long."

"Couldn't you work for somebody back there besides your father?"

Jean shrugs. "I could work for somebody else *here* if I wanted to. I don't like to take orders. This is a frontier here. A man should be able to work just for himself here, eh?"

"Well, a few people here do, just like anyplace. But most people work for someone else. Just like anyplace."

"That's strange, eh? People work at regular jobs here. Electricians, post office, schoolteachers. I thought they would be different."

"You mean trappers and dog mushers?"

Jean shrugs but does not answer. He looks at his watch and suggests that we go to the post office for his check. We pay, and leave the Downtown, walking back toward the green rectangular government building in which the post office is housed. The town is quiet. The gray sky is lower, heavier, with the feel of approaching weather. Out on the street, I see a young couple with backpacks and a cardboard hitchhiking sign: SOUTH.

In the air, Jean's spirits seem to improve, and he talks again of his plans for winter:

"Once I get a moose, I should be able to go the

winter without buying any more meat, eh?"

"Sure. A moose weighs a thousand pounds. Half of it is meat. That ought to keep you for a while. Just don't shoot it too far from the road. . . . I guess you've decided to stay, then?"

"Oh, I'll stay all right," Jean says.

Frank, the postmaster, gives us our mail, also the mail for Bob and Hans and Sven Holmberg, making his usual suggestion that I should get my own box. Jean's check has not come. The next mail will arrive in two days. We go back outside. On the post office steps someone I do not know asks me if it is true that a friend of mine owns a beef ranch. I say yes.

"Do you want to go back out to the cabin?" I ask Jean. "I'll give you a lift."

"No," Jean says glumly. "I want to be here to wait for the check. I've been waiting for it a week."

"A week? Here in town? I thought you just came in this morning."

Jean shakes his head. "Whenever I go back to that cabin I start to feel bad. The walls feel . . . funny. Cabin fever, eh?"

I laugh uneasily. "It isn't cabin fever season. I don't think you should worry about it. But I do think you should think seriously about returning south for the winter. Unless your feelings change."

"No. I'm not going back this winter. I'm going to stick it out. I think I'll feel better once I get my firewood and my moose. Then I'll have things under control, eh?"

"Do you want to go back out to the cabin this afternoon, then? I'll give you a ride."

"No. I'm going to wait here for my pogey check."

"Okay. I'm going to be heading out."

"Do you know what the plane fare is to Montreal?" Jean says.

DREAMS

"WHEN I SHOT that moose," Jimmy says, "I hit him in a good spot. Right here." He points to a spot on the side of his own chest, behind the arm, where an entering bullet would strike either the lungs or the heart. "When a moose gets hit there, he dies. But this one got into the lake and swam. I followed him in the boat. He got out on a point. How do you say it . . . a peninsula. And before I could get steady to shoot again, he throw up his head like this, and he calls. A long call. And then he falls.

"I killed plenty of moose, but it was the first time I hear a moose call after I shoot him. And we have this story—I guess white men would call it a story—that when a moose calls like that, it's bad luck for the hunter or somebody in his family. Something bad is going to happen. I knew that story but I didn't believe it. I didn't even think about it. I just cut him up and put him in the canoe. And I didn't tell anybody about it. Two days later, when I was back to the village, my little brother fell off the roof and killed himself. He was playing up there. Then I remembered that moose and I thought: 'My God.'

"You think that's a story, don't you?" he asks me.

I tell him that I believe those things actually happened as he told them, but that the whole thing could be coincidence.

"It happened to me one other time," Jimmy says. "This was just last year. I was hunting with my brother and his wife, up the lake. They were visiting from Fort St. John. Willy and I shot. We hit the moose in the neck and in the chest. A big fat cow. She threw up her head and let out that same call and fell down. This time I was scared. Right then I told my brother and his wife about the story and about the other moose. And I told them to be careful. I was

careful too after that and I told my wife and children to be careful. Nothing happened for two weeks and so I thought again, 'Well, it's just nothing and that last time was bad luck.' But on Saturday I got a long-distance call from my brother's wife. She was crying and I said: 'Mary, what's the matter?' She said her brother had just committed suicide. He shot himself through the head. She said: 'You warned us about that moose.' "

We sit and drink our tea. The sun is not up. Jimmy is waiting for daylight, to go hunting, and I am waiting for my ride from here—Watson Lake —back to Whitehorse. The cabin is dark and over-heated. The shadows cast by the kerosene lamp play across Jimmy's dark angular face. He looks far younger than his forty-five years. I ask him if he has had other prophetic experiences. He says no, except for the fact that he can tell, in advance, whenever he will have a successful hunt.

"How do you know that?"

"I have a dream," he says. "And it tells me I will shoot something tomorrow."

"You mean you see yourself shooting a moose or a caribou or whatever it is?"

Jimmy nods, thinks, takes a sip of tea. Then he shakes his head. "No," he says. "I don't see myself shooting anything. It's not that kind of dream."

"What is it then?"

Jimmy looks down, takes a cigarette, looks at the window, where light is just beginning to show. "I've never told this to a white man," he says, smiling.

"If you don't want to tell me, don't. But I'm not going to laugh at you whatever it is."

Well," Jimmy says, "it won't hurt. We're both men. We can talk." He lights his cigarette. "I don't know if you had these dreams," he says to me. "Probably you had them when you were a boy. Maybe you even have them now. These wet dreams?" He raises his eyes to see if I understand. His face is very serious. I nod quickly. Jimmy seems relieved by my confirmation. He smiles briefly. "Well, I have them. And whenever I do, I know I'll kill a moose the next day."

"How about when you're not even planning to hunt?"

"When I'm not hunting, I don't kill anything."

"But when you're hunting . . . ?"

"When I'm hunting, I always have that dream before I kill something."

"Always?"

"Always. And if the girl is really fat and beautiful, and she really loves me, I know the moose will be fat and good eating."

"And that never fails?"

"Never."

"Who is the girl?"

"I don't know. I don't remember her face. I think it's different girls."

"How about when the girl is not beautiful and doesn't love you?"

"As long as I have the dream, I get the moose. But maybe I'll have some problem if the girl doesn't love me. Maybe I'll wound it. I had one dream like that and I shot the moose in the belly the first time. I had to chase it for a mile. And if the girl isn't beautiful and fat, then the moose is skinny."

"Does it work just with moose?"

Jimmy shakes his head. "It works with anything. Sometimes I don't know what I shoot. But I know I'll shoot something, and I know how it will be. Two years ago I had the dream when we were hunting caribou. The girl was really good, but when we were done, somebody was trying to pull me away from her. I think it's her father. So I know I would have trouble the next day and need help. I asked Billy Jerome to go with me. He did but he got tired and came back. I was walking alone on the trail and I met two grizzlies about a hundred feet away. Then I knew what the dream meant. I thought: 'You damn fool, why didn't you turn back too?' I stopped, but one of them ran at me. She was screaming. I shot her here, in the neck, and she fell down right in front of me. The other one—it was her cub, but he was already big—he came right over the top of her and ran at me. He was screaming too. He wanted to save

his mother. My gun was a bolt action and I just had time to get another cartridge in and step aside. I shot him like this, to the side, when he went by. I didn't even aim. I didn't even know what was happening. I came so close to getting killed. He ran into the bush and I ran back down the trail. He was dead when I came back. Then I got some men and we brought them back to town. Edna Buckshot tanned the big one for a rug."

Jimmy's simple and undramatic relation of this event is impressive. I ask him if he wasn't extremely lucky to kill the two grizzly bears so quickly.

"Yes," he says. "You empty your gun into them sometime. I knew I would kill one of them, because of the dream. But I didn't know whether I would kill the other one or whether he would kill me. That's why I wanted Billy to come with me."

"I thought you said you didn't know you were going to meet bears?"

Jimmy shakes his head. "I just knew I would kill one animal and that I would have trouble. I didn't know what trouble. I guess I thought I might fall or have an accident. I didn't know it would be bears, until I saw them."

Outside, the sun rises across the lake.

I think aloud, trying to relate the dream to the event, in symbolic terms. "I guess one might say that one of those bears was trying to pull you away from the other, as in your dream."

Jimmy smiles. "I guess so," he says. "I never thought of it like that. But they never pulled me. They didn't get their paws on me."

"Have you had any more dreams like that?"

"I always have them."

"But I mean . . . where the real event might be related to some detail, some unusual detail, of the dream. Do you know what I mean?"

Jimmy nods. "Four years ago . . . no, five. I went hunting with Peter John. You know him. He can't hunt. He can't shoot. He spent too much time in Vancouver. So if I go with him, I give him the poor spot and I take the good one, because I'll get the moose and he'll miss it. This time I started to have that dream. The girl was really beautiful. But then she left me and went with somebody else. So the next day, I wrote on a piece of paper that Peter would get a really big moose by the end of the day. I didn't show it to him. I just put the paper in our teapot and set it in the front of the boat. Before lunch we saw a beautiful moose swimming to shore. He had horns like this, and when he got out of the water I could see his body was really big too. And I said to myself: 'I'm going to shoot that moose and eat him.' I told Peter to go into the bush and walk back to shore. I got out of the boat and walked along the shore. I told him: 'You can't shoot as good as I can, so you chase the moose out to me and we'll get him.' I didn't know if this was the moose Peter would get but I didn't want to take a chance. We needed the meat. So Peter went in. He was clumsy and noisy and I thought he would chase the moose to me. In five minutes I heard one shot and then Peter yelled. He was excited. He said: 'Come on. I got a big moose.' So I took the good spot but he got the moose anyway. He was just a kid and he couldn't shoot, but he shot that moose. If you asked people in town who would get that moose, they would say Jimmy. But Peter got it. We cut it up and carried it to the boat and I said: 'I knew you would get that moose.' I didn't tell him how I knew. Then I showed him the paper and he was scared. I think he still has that paper. You should ask him to see it. Now he wants me to hunt with him all the time. He thinks I'm magic. But I'm not. A lot of the old people see things just like I do."

"Do people see things as often as they used to, let's say, before phones and radios and helicopters and other things the white man brought in?"

Jimmy shakes his head. "No. When I was a young man a lot of people had dreams. Some of the old people still have them, I know, but they won't talk about it. They wouldn't sit down with you and talk like this. The white man thinks it's crazy, you know. So they're embarrassed. I think I'm about the only person my age who has them. I'm forty-five. I don't know any young people who do. Like Peter. He'll never have them. Well, I don't want to say he never will, but I don't think he will. I was raised in the bush and I heard people talk about seeing things. He wasn't. I don't think we'll have these dreams much longer."

It is nine o'clock and daylight.

"Are you sure you can't hunt today?" Jimmy says.

"I'd like to go with you, but I really have to wait for my ride. He should be here pretty soon."

"That's too bad," Jimmy says. "If we went together, we would get a moose today."

A LOSING BATTLE

AT NINE-THIRTY, the morning sun begins to light the black southeastern horizon. I am the only passenger on the Dawson-Whitehorse bus, and I sit in front and talk to the driver. He was a concert violinist, he tells me, before coming to the Yukon. Outside, the cold blue-gray hills move by. There are ten inches of snow on the road, and the limbs of the spruce and aspen trees are coated with crisp white frost crystals. It is only 20° below, warm for late fall. At Stewart Crossing, we pick up another passenger, a young man from Australia walking off his job at United Keno Hill Mines. He tells me he is recently divorced, came to the Yukon to forget, but could not take the isolation of Elsa. He is now going to Africa, he says.

Just south of Pelly Crossing we see the Land Rover, off to the side of the road. This is my man, John Lammers, who lives twenty-five miles in the bush, alongside the Pelly River. Lammers's bush residence has no phone. I arranged this highway meeting by leaving a message with the radiophone operator, to be later conveyed to Lammers's radio. Until this moment, I did not know if he had gotten the message, or if he would show up. The bus stops and lets me off. Lammers helps me load my gear in his truck. We turn the Land Rover and start down the twenty-five-mile wood road that leads into his place.

I feel relaxed, now that I have made my connection. I take out a cigarette.

"No smoking in this vehicle," Lammers says, smiling. "We'll stop after an hour and eat lunch. You can smoke then. But not in here."

He means it, apparently.

John Lammers is the Yukon's environmentalist. He is not the only Yukoner with feelings for the landscape. He is, however, the one Yukoner who regularly, publicly, takes the "environmental position," and is known across Canada as an ardent and articulate conservationist.

Born in Holland, in 1921, Lammers is an agronomist by education. He worked in the anti-Nazi underground during war years, emigrated to Canada in 1947, finally reached the Yukon in 1953. Since 1965, he has made his living running summer wilderness river tours, and is the the only Yukon resident to do so. In 1968 he founded the Yukon's only environmental organization, the Yukon Conservation Society, and is a director or adviser for

149

several other environmental organizations in Canada and the United States.

Physically, Lammers is a big man, about six three, bowlegged, sharp-featured, with graying brown hair and beard. Like many educated, foreign-born North Americans, he speaks English with almost perfect diction and grammar. In fact, as I spend more time with him I realize that he speaks in complex paragraphs, with the precision—and sometimes the length—of an encyclopedia entry. He is good-natured but sharp-tongued. Among many of his fellow Yukoners, he has the reputation of being stubborn, independent, a little outrageous. Before meeting Lammers, I heard several stories about him. One of these had to do with his refusal to let the entourage of Canada's governor general visit his property during a recent northern tour, and I now mention this to him.

"Who told you that?" Lammers says annoyedly.

"I think it was somebody in Tourism and Information. The story I heard indicated that the governor general's party was just across the river from your place—twenty or more people, bodyguards, secretaries, the whole bunch. They called you on the radio and asked permission to visit. But you would permit only the governor general to come over. The rest had to spend the night on the west bank."

Lammers shakes his head in a way that seems half angry, half dismayed. "My God, it gets weirder all the time. You see, I lead a lonely existence here. Not physically lonely, because I enjoy that, but emotionally, spiritually lonely. I have this reputation of being impossible, and people do their best to perpetuate it. Every fact of my life gets distorted, innocently or intentionally. Now, for your information, that story is complete rubbish. What did happen, in fact, was that Tourism and Information, without even consulting me, put my place on the governor general's itinerary. They wanted to send twenty people out here. The first I heard of his proposed visit was on the radio news. I called Tourism and Information. I was angry that they had done this without consulting me. I told them that we could accommodate only about six people, and that we simply couldn't accommodate more, even for the governor general. But anyway, after a supreme hassle with Tourism, we arranged that he and his wife would come with two aides. They did come, and

John Lammers
(Jack Hope)

stayed for two very enjoyable days. It wasn't a big thing. There was never even the hint of a riverside incident like you mention."

I am not quite sure that I believe Lammers. "The story I heard was very specific."

"Well, who do you believe, them or me?" Lammers says, only half joking. "Because if you believe them, you can get out and walk."

We bounce along. Snow clings to the dense wall of spruces that overhang the narrow wood road. We see moose and lynx tracks crossing our path, in the snow. Lammers tells me that several times he has gotten stuck between the highway and home, and has had to walk ten or twelve miles, one way or the other. He tells me too that he has a propane heater, sleeping bags, snowshoes, food, and extra clothes for us in the back of the vehicle, just in case. He tells me that typically he gets out to Whitehorse only two or three times each winter, for mail and supplies. During breakup—April and May, when the road is mushy—he does not come out at all.

After an hour and a half, and still three miles from Lammers's home, we stop on a promontory overlooking the confluence of the Yukon and Pelly rivers. Lammers's cluster of cabins—the Palisades Nature Retreat—is visible far below us, on the bank of the frozen, snow-covered Pelly, across the river from a black palisade cliff. The landscape here in the central Yukon is not as dramatic as in the southwest, or in the Ogilvies, but is still, somber, and stretches unbroken to the horizon. It is now about 1:30 P.M. To our left, the hazy ball of the sun rests atop the rolling blue line of hills. We get out of the Land Rover and eat sandwiches and drink tea from the thermos.

"Now you can smoke that cigarette," Lammers says. "By the way, we don't allow any smoking in our house either. So if you want to smoke while you're interviewing me, you'll have to go outside."

"It's twenty below," I remind him.

"Yes, I know. Maybe your lungs will thank me, by the time you leave."

While I smoke and look, Lammers steps behind a clump of spruces. Within two or three minutes I hear the rip and snarl of a two-cycle engine. Lammers reappears, riding a yellow snowmobile with a long toboggan hooked to the back.

"What the hell is that?"

"What the hell does it look like?" Lammers says. "We're going to take this thing the rest of the way

and leave the Land Rover here. You're probably thinking that no self-respecting environmentalist rides a snowmobile. But let me tell you, it's not a toy with us. It's a necessary evil. Besides, if it snows while you're here, we'd never get back up this hill with the truck. Come on. Help me load up."

We remove our small amount of gear from the Land Rover and strap it onto the toboggan. I get onto the machine, behind Lammers, and pull my wool hat down over my forehead.

"Do you always do this?"

"We normally walk down," Lammers says. He smiles over his shoulder. "But since we had a tenderfoot coming to visit, we figured we'd better get out our limousine. Hold on!"

We lurch ahead, over the narrow snow-covered road notched into the hill. The snowmobile bumps and slides over the uneven surface. The land falls away sharply beside the road and I do not look at the scary drop-off. About halfway down, Lammers halts the snowmobile and points to a bulldozer slash cut into the hill, above the road. Soil has slumped from the slash, into the road, narrowing it a little.

"We were visited recently by an errant bulldozer operator," he says sarcastically.

"Errant?"

Lammers nods. "He was on his way to the Minto copper exploration area, which is twenty miles from here, in the opposite direction. There is a turnoff to Minto from this road, ten miles back, but this joker ostensibly got lost and pushed on ten miles in the wrong direction, with his blade down, pushing up dirt and trees all the way. That soil he loosened keeps washing and dropping down into this road, and we have to clear it away if we want to keep it negotiable."

We continue downhill and in five minutes reach the spruce- and aspen-covered flats near the river. It is warmer here, away from the exposed hillside. Lammers drives slowly, and we talk above the chug of the engine.

"You used the term 'ostensibly,' " I say loudly. "I assume that means you suspect that the bulldozer operator knew how to get to Minto, but came down your road for the purpose of aggravating you."

Lammers smiles. "You said it, not me. I'll only say it seems highly peculiar, if he was walking a Cat into Minto, that he didn't know how to get there."

"Who was driving the bulldozer?"

"Just a local cat-skinner."

"What mining company was it?"

"That's immaterial. If you make inquiry and find out yourself, that's your business. But I'm not going to tell you."

"Why not? If things like that happen, they should be written about. It's no skin off your nose, is it?"

"Forget it," Lammers says. "When you called me, you said you wanted to talk about the situation of land and resource use in the Yukon. I never agreed that I would name names and help you be a sleuthlike reporter. What happens in the Yukon with regard to environment is a function of our bad land-use laws, and of the type of unplanned, rapacious, socioeconomic system we have. And that is what I will discuss, not what sort of jerk Smith or Jones is. Character assassination is a Yukon pastime and I won't participate in it."

We halt at the gate to Lammers's riverside property and Lammers gets off to open it. There is a small, legally worded sign on the wooden gate, warning against the discharge of firearms and citing the appropriate Yukon statutes. I wonder to myself who, besides Lammers's own guests, would ever get back in here to see it.

"You see," Lammers continues, "I think perhaps you have failed to pick up on a very basic reality of the Yukon. It is impossible up here to be critical of anything without people thinking you are bearing a grudge of some kind. The Yukon is a small enough place that someone will take it personally. If I get up at a public meeting or on a radio program and say something, for example, against building a dam, or even against dams in general, it is guaranteed that someone will say, 'Gee, Lammers must really hate Jones.' Jones, you see, is the one man in the Yukon who promotes dams. It is an associative, Pavlovian response to what I have to say, but that's the way people see it. The issues are never separated from the personalities. In fact, I rather like most of the people I argue with in public. But people here find that hard to believe. And since I'm always arguing, since I question everything, I am immediately suspect. Anyway, that's why I won't discuss personalities with you. I have to be careful. I have to live here."

"What you fear then is reprisal?"

"You said it, not I."

"Aren't you being a little paranoid?"

"Call it what you like," Lammers says shortly. "I don't give a damn. But I'm still not going to discuss individuals with you. I'm a hard-nosed son of a bitch, I know. I let people know right off where they stand. Maybe you don't like that. But I have principles, and I try not to compromise them."

We travel another three hundred yards along a narrow wood road, among snow-laden spruces, and come to a stop beside a large woodpile, near Lammers's house. We begin to unload.

I remember now the story I heard of Lammers launching a lawsuit against Occidental Minerals for staking his property, or land near his property, for mineral exploration. The lawsuit, according to the story, had an environmental basis, but was dropped after a pilot took photographs of garbage that Lammers, the environmentalist, had thrown onto the ice of the Pelly River. I mention it.

"Who the hell told you that?!"

"We're not discussing names, are we?"

Lammers almost smiles. "All right. Don't tell me. I don't care, really." He sighs. "But you see, in relating that story, which is completely false, you answer your own question about my paranoia. I am an oddball here. I would not say that I am not liked, but I am certainly not understood, and am perceived as a threat to most people's way of life. I had the gall to legally challenge a mighty resource-exploiting corporation, and the government in the process. And most Yukoners depend upon these corporations, or upon the government, for their jobs. So to them I am a threat. I make them uneasy. And the easiest thing to do about a person who makes you uneasy is to concoct stories about him, to make him into whatever you like to think he is. So I behave very carefully, because anything I do will be used against me, either maliciously or innocently. I'm sure environmentalists in the States experience the same thing. But don't forget, in the Yukon I am considered to be practically the whole environmental movement, so I must bear the brunt of it."

"What about the garbage story, then? Did you throw it in the river or not?"

"Dammit! The most frustrating part of my existence here is that I must constantly explain myself to people! Now look! Look over there. Do you see that garbage pit? Go and look at it! Our garbage goes in there. Or else I take it to the Carmacks dump when I go into town. I advise that you watch us closely while you're here! You'll see that we flatten and bury all tin cans. We bury all plastic. We burn all papers. I have *never* thrown garbage in the river!"

"Okay, okay. I believe you. But what about the lawsuit business?"

"All right. I did in fact begin a lawsuit against the mining company, and I got a lot of national publicity as a result. And I think that's all that prevented them from coming in and cutting sight lines and bulldozing the hill here behind our property. But I had to drop it when I found out how much it would cost me to pursue it. I didn't drop it because I feared some kind of blackmail photographs of garbage that I had thrown in the river, for God's sake. Now go and look at that garbage pit and draw your own conclusions from it. Unless you think that we have temporarily altered our garbage-throwing way of life for your visit."

"I'll take your word for it."

Polly, John's wife, comes out of the house and helps us unload. She is English, probably in her forties, short and dark-haired, friendly and quiet. After we unload, I look around the property. It is a tasteful and well-built place, put up by Lammers and his former wife and two sons, and is set within a natural clearing on the riverbank immediately alongside the Pelly. There are six or seven two-man guest cabins, each set within a clump of spruces to conceal them from one another. In addition to the guest cabins and Lammers's own, larger cabin, there is a cookhouse, a woodshed, workshop, and a sauna bathhouse, with a rock fireplace set into its outside wall, its damper controlled by a series of levers from inside. There are narrow footpaths among each of the buildings with occasional signs: "Please, stay on established path only." This, Polly tells me, is to protect the thirty-four species of wild flowers and plants on the property. She also tells me that no trees have been cut to make room for the buildings.

We go into Lammers's one-story cabin. Its floor is of clear, varnished boards. The furniture is homemade. There is no electricity, but propane lamps hang in the living room. Two thirds of the living room/dining room walls are lined with bookshelves. In addition to a collection of field guides to birds, rocks, and plants, the books include *Leaves of Grass, Future Shock, The Land Rover Workshop Manual, Stalking the Healthful Herbs, The Greening of America, The Whole Earth Catalog, Psychoanalysis and Existential Philosophy, The*

Second Sex. An Edmund Burke quotation is posted near Lammers's typewriter: "The only thing necessary for the triumph of evil is for good men to do nothing."

We sit down for tea at the living room table. Polly puts a Vivaldi tape on the battery-powered tape player. This is really elegant. Outside, four Canada jays hop about a bird feeder stuck alongside the house. Polly shows me snapshots of a red fox and a young grizzly taken last year in the yard. These animals, she assumes, have since been trapped or shot.

"I feel bad about that," Polly says. "Foxie was so nice. He would snooze right on the porch. And the grizzly was only a young one. He acted forlorn, poor chap, like he had just lost his mother or something, which is probably just what happened."

"How do you feel about losing these animals?" I ask John.

"Why do you ask?" he says. "Do you want to evaluate me as a nature lover and, as you see it, an environmentalist? Well, of course I feel bad about losing any animal and very much regretted losing those creatures. Now, if they were shot by a big-game hunter, I resent it, because these people are only out for sport. If the fox was trapped by our Indian neighbor downriver, I still regret it, but I don't resent this man making his living by trapping. That is an old livelihood, and I respect it, particularly among the Indian people, who are the rightful owners of this land, and whom we whites have crushed with our so-called superior society. The Indians at least knew how to live within the capacities of their environment to support them, which is more than we know, even though we are bright enough to invent snowmobiles and washing machines.

"But why did you even ask that question? That interests me. Let me point out, in case you happen to think that a nature lover and an environmentalist are the same thing, that they are not. One who is a nature lover likes trees and birds and flowers. That's fine, and I respect it. But an environmentalist, in the true sense, is concerned with all elements of the environment, including man. *Primarily* man. He doesn't just say, 'We must preserve trees or grizzly bears.' He says, 'We human beings must intereact with our surroundings in such a way as to perpetuate a high-quality existence for ourselves. Not only ourselves but those generations that follow us. And if we do this in the most prudent way we know, the welfare of trees and grizzly bears and rivers will be guaranteed, automatic. Because we will not attack our environment and gobble up our resources as quickly as we can, but will discipline our society to ration out the fixed quantity of nonrenewable resources—like petroleum—to last, and will manage our renewable resources as a farm, to keep them going.

"But we aren't doing that now. We're consuming like there was no tomorrow. And everything we consume—power, oil, metal, you name it—comes out of our environment in one way or another. Nothing's for free, you know! And the most active agents of this destruction are industry and government, controlled by inadequate laws. It is in this sphere that we can make real and meaningful changes in the management of our surroundings, and as an environmentalist, I am interested only in this approach, not simply in saving a particular grizzly or acre of land."

Lammers, long-winded and aggressive as he is, seems eminently sensible. He has apparently devoted more thought to these things than anyone I have met in the Yukon. More, perhaps, than anyone I have ever met.

"But of course, here in the Yukon, you do still have a tremendous supply of natural surroundings. . . ."

Lammers smiles. "Now you sound like a true Yukoner," he says sarcastically. "That is a refrain around here: 'But there's so much of it.' That simpleminded statement justifies every manner of abuse to our environment. All right. You happen to be right. By far the majority of the Yukon is wilderness. But let me ask you if you are aware how unique the Yukon is as a corner of the North American continent? Where else will you find such beauty and diversity of landscape? Of flora and fauna? This place is wonderful. You can get lost here. You can travel or live in real wilderness. It's a frontier. But do you know something? It's unique. Why did your publisher send you here? He could have sent you to more populated and developed places. To Ontario. To Colorado. To Alaska. But no, he sent you to the Yukon, because it is unique.

"And yet someone like you—and I thought you had some brains—says to me, 'Oh. There's so much of it.' "

"Sure. I know that. I didn't mean to . . ."

Lammers interrupts, forges ahead with his monologue. "Well, you can't just look at the Yukon alone. You have to consider what it means in the context of our total human environment, our total society. And let me tell you, there *isn't* much of it. The Yukon is a unique kind of place for human beings to experience. And the reason is because it has not been populated and developed like every place else."

Lammers becomes quiet, but just for a moment. "Unfortunately," he continues, "we Yukoners seem to feel it our God-given right to make the same mistakes you Americans made in opening your own frontier. That, the nearsighted Yukoner thinks, is 'freedom.' The freedom to proceed, as quickly as possible, to industrialize and render our country here identical to the rest of North America. To lose our identity. Well, let me tell you, that is not freedom. It is mimicry. It's anarchy, even."

I nod. "That seems to ring pretty true, from what little I've seen. There don't seem to be too many Yukoners who share your concerns."

"Not too many!? If you only knew. I don't claim to be the only concerned citizen, but I can give you some interesting numbers. A few years ago, I started the Yukon Conservation Society. I sweated blood over that thing. I financed it out of my own pocket at its onset. Do you know how many members we got? Only ninety. And over sixty of them were from outside the Yukon, mostly southern Canada and the United States. Less than thirty from the Yukon! Now that tells you something right there. And of the thirty or so Yukoners, only two or three were willing to deal with anything more controversial than motherhood issues. If you wanted to go pick up litter or build a little nature exhibit somewhere, fine, they were all together. But if you wanted to fight for something significant and basic, like pushing for legislation to change the mining laws, they all shrunk from fright. I finally resigned as president. I couldn't stand it. I can do more on my own."

"Why do you think that is? I mean, I would think the Yukon would attract quite a number of people who had feeling for the environment."

"Yes. I used to think that too. What happens here, I think, is that you get a lot of people coming in who have, or think they have, a real interest in environment . . . at least to the extent that they

In June, wildflowers burst into bloom on mountain slopes, in glaciated valleys and along the raw shoulders of the Alaska Highway (shown on previous page). The growing season is short. By September, aspen leaves have turned (opposite page, lower right).

In 1942 construction of the Alaska Highway by the U.S. military linked the Yukon with the rest of North America. In the years since, the Canadian government has pursued an ambitious road building program in the Territory, creating auto routes through previously unbroken wilderness. (At left, road signs erected by tourists stand along the highway at Watson Lake.)

Winter along the Dempster Highway, still under construction in the northern Yukon

Snow is a fact of life throughout most of the Yukon year, but accumulations in the interior portions of the Territory are relatively light due to the barrier effect of the coast ranges.

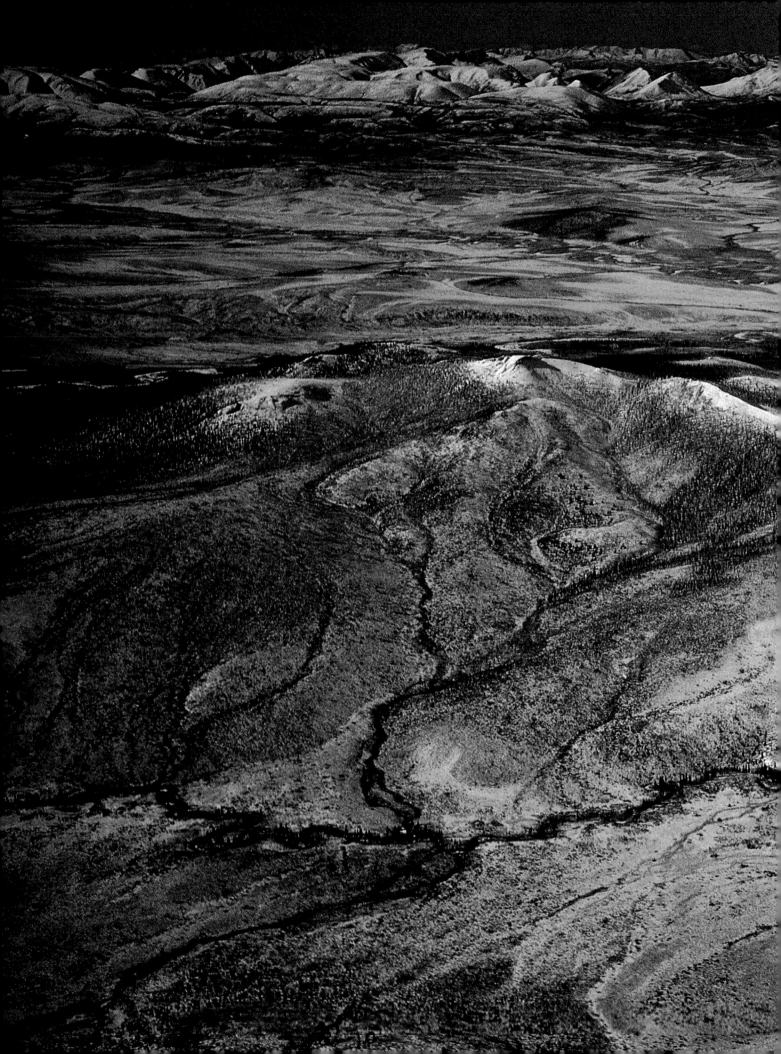

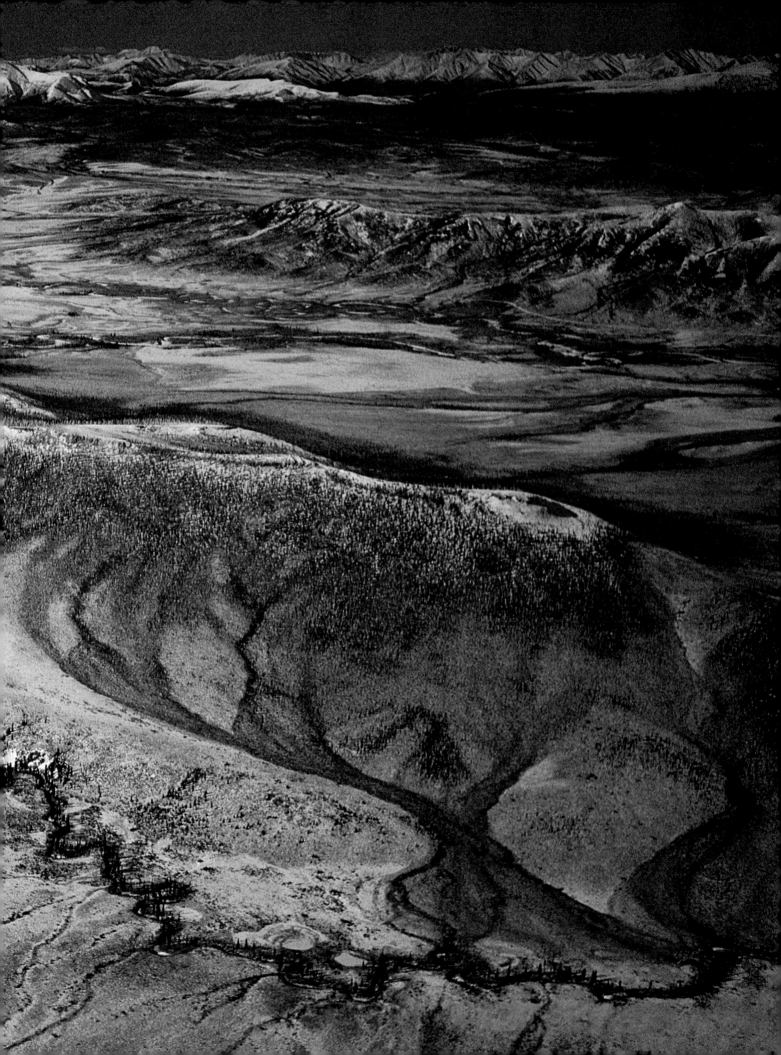

Two hundred fifty miles of mountains, plateaus and tundra (previous page) separate Dawson from the tiny Indian village of Old Crow, eighty miles north of the Arctic Circle. (Opposite page: a Halloween party in Old Crow.)

Traditional Yukon Indian crafts
have diminished since the advent
of white culture, but examples
may still be found in remote
villages such as Old Crow, and
in Whitehorse craft shops.
(At right, an embroidered
Loucheux prayer.)

...AKO·TJO...
...Z·1·CHILEH...
⋈ 110 ✠ 25 ⋈
EKWICHANCHYO·K...
...TTYI·HIANCHI·hA·N...
...Ah·NUNh·hA·EiTseH...
...AKo·EUEVIRZI·VI·UNJI·J...
...NYIWHE·KEKWAdhUL·CH...
...NYOO·KIRKHE·UNJIH·URELL...
...USUCVH·KWIIIH·PoNLIUS...

want to enjoy the outdoors. They're going to start a new life and maybe even live in the bush. But then they get here, and like everybody else, they quickly run out of money. And what kind of paying work can they get? They can work as a miner, or maybe building a road or a dam or working for an oil exploration outfit. There's not much else for people who have no specific skills. So right away, they must depend for livelihood upon those who are involved in mass development and ruination of the landscape, and they are daily in contact with people of that sort. And, understandably, they don't want to bite the hand that feeds them, at least not in public. So they ignore it. Why resist the norm? It's far easier to just have a beer and forget it."

"Do you think Yukon society is conforming, or nonconforming?"

"Good question," Lammers says. "You see, the nonconformity here is really confined to very superficial aspects of people's lives. I suspect that many people here are carrying on their private, internal rebellions. But that's it, it's private. Very few are radical or rebellious enough to work for real social change, which I think is a sad fact. The Yukon is a place where we truly have an opportunity to do something different, but we're missing the opportunity. Many people do come up here with some sort of a dream. But what happens? They are forced to get these drab, ordinary occupations, and they buy a big house they can't afford in Riverdale or Porter Creek, and then, by God, they are *really* stuck, in the same damn rut they wanted to get away from in the south, living in a suburb, commuting, associating with the same kind of people. I feel sorry for them. Their dream is ended. But in the bars you will nevertheless hear them speaking about how 'different' and 'independent' Yukoners are. But that's nonsense. Most of us are just transplanted suburbanites. Polly and I, in fact, are among the very few Yukoners who are making our living at something we could not do in the south. And we are regarded as being somewhat strange for wanting to live in the bush."

"Maybe so. I've been thinking about that myself . . . but I'm not sure that what you describe is any more true in the Yukon than elsewhere."

Lammers says emphatically, "No, of course not. But that is my point. The physical Yukon is different from elsewhere. And with planning, our society up here could easily offer human beings a life that is different. But to do that we would have to be very honest with ourselves and acknowledge that the thing that is special about the Yukon is our small population, our space, our great natural environment. And our society should steer people toward a life-style that takes advantage of our particular endowments. Now I do not contend that everyone should do as I do, be a wilderness outfitter. But as you know, there are many more uniquely Yukon opportunities than that. The government employs many people—in fisheries, forestry, historic sites, wildlife, parks. And it could employ many more. Some of the world's economies, after all, are based largely on wildlife. People will pay to see it. Okay, there is that class of opportunity. Then, some people here can earn their living by trapping, fishing, running riverboat shipping services. We have a large native population from whom we can learn, and who can learn from us: There are many, many jobs to be had in that area of helping to bridge the gap between our societies. There are opportunities for scientists, researchers, for small-time prospectors who still pan for gold. There is the bush life, building a cabin, hunting and gardening and fishing. Now you see, these are all things you can't do anyplace else. Even the guy who comes up here to live in a cabin for six months, living off money saved in the south—that is an opportunity not available elsewhere, and I feel it should be preserved, because it is something that will vanish forever if the Yukon becomes developed."

"I've heard many Yukoners say that the Yukon should not be preserved as a playground for tourists from the south."

Lammers waves his hand in annoyance. "Well, what I'm talking of is not just tourism. But you're right, the Yukon is schizophrenic. It wants the tourist dollars from the south, but it is prejudiced against the tourists themselves. But what they don't realize, for God's sake, is that the Yukon is *already* a playground for the south, an economic playground. We are digging up our landscape to accommodate the south or, at least, the outside. Our minerals leave the Yukon. We dig up our landscape to build more roads to reach the minerals, and *they* leave the Yukon. So do the profits, because the mines up here are not locally owned. Anvil Mine is owned primarily by Cyprus Mines in Los Angeles. Cassiar Asbestos is mostly owned by outfits in New York, England, and Australia. Whitehorse Copper, I think, is primarily controlled by Anglo-American, in South Africa. United Keno, I believe, is the only one that is even largely Canadian. Now this is the real harm being done to us by the outside. Because the rest of the world gets the product and the profits, even a lot of the jobs, and all we are left with, ultimately, is the hole in the ground or the road scar across the landscape."

"Okay. Sure. I see that, but . . ."

"Now keep in mind," Lammers interrupts, "that the goal is not simply to limit development. If you write this up, make sure you get it right! The goal is to safeguard the Yukon natural environment, and that environment will form the basis for a unique lifestyle and for a self-perpetuating economy that will go on and on, long after our territory's resource-exploiting industry—like mining—has run out of raw material.

"And what we need to do right now is to change some of the laws that encourage destruction of the Yukon's resources. Much of what happens here in terms of resource use is decided either in Ottawa or in the boardrooms of multinational corporations. But I believe that the resource decisions here should be made by our people. We must give our citizens a voice in the planning of what goes on, and give them all the facts, the alternatives, and an insight into what is actually happening."

I nod. "Yes. I've heard a lot of Yukoners complain about being ruled from Ottawa."

"But I'm talking about a change in planning procedure, not necessarily a change in our territorial status," Lammers says. "In fact, our territorial government seems dominated by the attitude that industrialization and development will be our salvation. They are only too happy to accommodate the corporations. Probably our local authorities have even less sophistication in planning the Yukon's future than the federal legislators, simply because our authorities are up here on the frontier and do not have the tempering influence of urban contact to remind them what the rest of the world is like. When I object to 'Ottawa,' I am not talking about legislators, but about the federal Department of Indian Affairs and Northern Development*—and

I'm sure you see the irony in that title—which essentially rules the Yukon, since we are a territory, with most of our land administered federally. The department, and specifically, the Northern Economic Development Branch† within that department, has control, or partial control, over oil exploration, road building, timber, mining, most of what goes on here. And they apparently view their function as one of a salesman. No, not even a salesman, because a salesman at least makes sure that his inventories are kept up. Rather, they are really acting only as a broker in the Yukon, selling off our product as fast as they can, without trying to ration any of it out to last for the future."

Lammers looks out the window. It is cloudy, three thirty, and almost dark. Downriver, the gray snow and sky to the south blend into one another. "I hate to interrupt a conversation," Lammers says, smiling, "especially my own. But here in the bush we have certain daily rituals to perform, one of which is chopping firewood. So let's continue our discussion out there. I want to give our visitor a little orientation tour before dark," he says to Polly. "Besides, I can see he is now clawing the table for want of a cigarette."

We all go out, spend twenty minutes chopping wood and hauling it to the house on a small homemade sled. John chops. Polly and I haul. "Don't wander off that path!" Lammers yells to me as I pull the sled.

After the wood, the Lammerses and I walk a mile up the seven-hundred-foot-wide Pelly River. The ice, having frozen, thawed, and frozen again, is jumbled pell-mell on the river surface, and we stick near shore, where it is smooth. The aspens on the riverbank, John points out, are lighter colored on their south side, almost white, oxidized by the greater exposure to sunlight from that direction. It is still and cold. There are two fresh sets of wolf tracks in the snow along shore. John observes that a sandbar in the middle of the river has, in the nine years he has been here, begun to redeposit itself close against the east bank.

"I sometimes think it would be nice," Polly says, "to spend one's whole lifetime in one spot like this, just observing the little changes, like the river altering its course. A river really is a living thing."

---

* Now called Department of Indian and Northern Affairs.

† Now called Northern Natural Resources and Environment Branch.

"Have you ever thought about moving back into Whitehorse? Or maybe into a city?"

"We have," Polly says. "We may be forced to do it, before long, out of economic necessity and convenience."

"It's a terrible decision to make," John says. "It's a wonderful place here. It's friendly. I have always felt the wilderness hospitable and warm. It's more than just the physical facts of water and trees . . . it's sort of a medium, like amniotic fluid that surrounds the child in the womb and invokes a feeling of total well-being. We feel good here. And it means something to me too to have built my home here, as carefully as I could, to fit into the wilderness."

I smile to myself at John's "amniotic fluid" and "total well-being." Everything, even his description of his feelings for the land, is worded precisely, elaborately, like a speech. For an intelligent and innately verbal person like Lammers, it seems to me that this precise speech-like quality might well be a result of many long nights spent in the seclusion of his cabin, phrasing and rephrasing every thought, every emotion.

"You don't think you'll leave, then?" I ask.

"I don't know," John says. "We can only make it here as long as we can physically cope. And that's getting harder for us every year. But I hope it will be a long time."

We turn and walk downriver, past the house, then climb the bank and loop back, recrossing the wolf tracks. We get three pails of water from the hand-dug well on the way back to the house. We stop briefly on top of the bank and listen in the gathering darkness. It is so still that we can hear the rustle of an open patch of water, a mile downriver, where the Pelly joins the Yukon.

For supper we have baked pork chops, an eggplant dish, homemade bread, and apple pie. John saws the chops from a loin stored in the cookhouse. It seems strange to me to see the meat stored frozen, simply lying on the wood table in the unheated building.

After supper, I continue my questions. "We were talking before about some of the changes in law needed in the Yukon. You mentioned that the present laws promote selling off resources as quickly as possible. . . ."

John laughs. "My God, this guy is going to pummel me with questions before my peristalsis is complete. Well, all right. But let's turn the news on while we talk. Out here we can't get any newspapers so we devour any magazines we get, and the radio broadcast." John turns the battery-powered radio to the Whitehorse CBC station.

"Remember," John says, splitting his attention between the radio and conversation, "the first whites who populated the Yukon were men who hoped to make it big in mining, and thus the early land-use laws were written by miners, for miners. Mining was given precedence over all other forms of land use." He motions out in back of the house toward the land staked by the mining company. "For example, if these jokers out here had wanted to, they could have *legally* bulldozed up this entire hillside in back of us."

"Isn't some of that your property?"

Lammers nods. "I own some of it, and I lease some of it from the crown, but that makes no difference because by Yukon law, only my house and immediate surroundings are protected from mining exploration. They control all subsurface rights. Luckily it became obvious to the company after two seasons that there were no minerals in that hill so it was not worth their while to continue, though they did a lot of line cutting and a summer of core drilling. But I want to emphasize that, by our antiquated law, they could have dug it all up, even though there were no minerals in it."

"Are you sure you're not exaggerating it a little? I can't quite believe that."

"Am I sure?" Lammers says sarcastically. "By now I know the law almost by heart."

"Would they have to compensate you for the loss?"

Lammers laughs. "There is a clause in the law that states that landowners shall be compensated for damages. But since our law was written by miners, that clause is only designed to protect one miner against another, not to protect a bush dweller like me. There is no statement in the law that a landowner or leasee must be compensated for, say, loss of the aesthetic value of his property, loss of his trapline, or of his big-game hunting territory. And the law states that such compensation is to be mediated by the mining recorder in Whitehorse. Now you tell me what *his* orientation is going to be? Will it be pro-Lammers or pro-miner? Would he see the aesthetic value of a quaking aspen grove or a patch of moss or of the solitude we enjoy here? I'm sure you realize that any bulldozing or even noise up there on the hill not only would have broken us as individuals, but would have made a joke of my efforts to accommodate guests who come here for quiet and seclusion. Probably if I had had to sue them, all I would have gotten would have been the value of any commercial-sized timber on my land, and most of the timber here is aspen, which has no commercial value anyway. You see, there is no legal precedent for paying people like me damaged by mining. The law has never been tested. That was what I hoped to do if I had had to carry through my lawsuit. But I repeat, thank God I didn't have to, because I would have had to borrow the money to do it."

"How much do you make by renting cabins and giving wilderness tours, by the way?"

"That's none of your business," Lammers says.

"Well, you give four or five river tours per summer, plus your guests here, so I'm going to guess that you take in about twenty thousand per year."

"Polly, listen to this guy," John says. "Twenty thousand! Well, I'm not going to give you that information, but I will tell you that our income is far, far less than that. And I'll tell you something else that you probably won't believe: We could do a helluva lot more business than we do each year, but we refuse it. We only take enough work to make money to live on for the coming year. And we make a determined effort not to keep setting our economic sights higher. One of your environmental groups in the States wanted me to run tours for them, with thirty people each, but I refused. We like our business, but we don't feel we can do a good job if we take on too many people. And we don't want to bring too many people on our trips because it does its own little bit of damage. The Yukon environment is a very fragile one, and two years after we have camped along a river, you can still see the impressions in the vegetation made by our tents."

Lammers grins. "All right, so much for our idealism. Now let me get back to mining. This Yukon mining law I mention is the Quartz Mining Act of 1924. There has been talk of changing that law, but I can't imagine that the changes would be substantive. Anyway, the law states that any individual over eighteen, regardless of national origin, can stake eight mining claims of fifty acres each, anyplace he wants in the Yukon, for a payment of twenty cents per acre to the federal government. He can hold those claims, regardless of whether he can demonstrate that there are any minerals in the ground, or the hope of finding minerals, or even whether he even knows anything *about* minerals! He can do anything with the land he wants. He can cut trees for sight lines, he can bulldoze, build exploratory roads, core-drill, dynamite, anything. You, a New Yorker, could legally do it! After one year, if he can demonstrate that he has spent one hundred dollars per claim, he can continue with his operation. So he rents a bulldozer, digs up access road to the claims, and they remain his, to do with as he wishes. The way the law is written, he retains his title to the extent that he ruins the land.

"The whole exploratory procedure is amazingly slipshod and speculative. What often happens is that a primary company will stake and develop the area of a find, and then a lot of other outfits rush in and stake surrounding areas in hopes that the ore body will extend. And they each build their own trails and access roads and sight lines to retain the rights to their claims. We have something like that up here at Minto. There are three or four companies in there. They have already built two access roads, forty or fifty miles through the bush, and are planning a third. And since they are competitors, whatever one company finds, or does not find, it keeps secret from the others, so they are each functioning on separate bundles of information.

"Or sometimes, phony mining companies may just want to put up a show of exploration, push in a road here and there, cut a sight line, leak out a few reports of a likely ore find, sell some stock to the gullible public, and then clear out, leaving their scars and their stockholders behind them."

"I assume that some of them lose money."

"Of course they do. But you see, there are always a few people behind the scenes who get wealthy on it, through the salaries they pay themselves while the phony company is supposedly in operation. But I can tell you that far more mining operations in the Yukon have failed than succeeded. And I do not refer just to shady exploratory operations, but to mines that have actually opened, with roads, housing, electric lines, concentrating plants, equipment, the whole infrastructure all in place. Right off the top of my head, I can think of five or six that have opened for operation and closed within a few months or a year. There's Venus Mines and Arctic Mines near Carcross—they each lasted one winter—Wellgreen Mines near Destruction Bay, Mount Nansen Mines and Discovery Mines near Carmacks. The Wellgreen Mines thing was really absurd. It was opened with great fanfare, with people telling how many jobs were being created and Commissioner Smith cutting the ribbon. And only three days later, the *Star* carried the story—Wellgreen Mines closes due to lack of ore. Lack of ore! They apparently didn't even know if there was anything worth digging for. Nevertheless, they dig, and leave their deserted plant and roads. Sure they lose money. But not as much as you might think, because we taxpayers subsidize them. During the exploration phase, the Department of Indian Affairs and Northern Development will pay a mining or petroleum company half the cost of tote roads, up to a maximum of twenty thousand dollars. They will pay half the cost of any initial access road to the mine, up to one hundred thousand. They will pay half the cost of an exploratory airport or landing strip up to twenty thousand. They give grants to approved Canadian companies of forty percent of *any* exploration costs, repayable only if commercial ore discoveries are made. Then, in the development or production phase, they will pay the mining company half the cost of any developmental access road, up to five hundred thousand. They will pay half the cost of any needed airport, up to one hundred thousand. They will pay two-thirds the cost of any permanent access road, or forty thousand per mile of road, whichever is less. Check these figures; but I'm pretty sure the amounts are precise. And to aid development, the federal government will also pay all the cost of installing power lines to mines. It's absurd. The federal government has sunk about fifty million dollars, for example, in Anvil Mine. And on top of it all, they give the mining companies a three-year tax holiday after beginning production.

"Now keep in mind that these mining companies and their supporters are always yelling 'Free enterprise!' 'Laissez-faire!' 'Let business do its private thing!' But what the hell is this mining subsidy program? It isn't free enterprise. It's welfare, on a corporate scale!

"And the net effect of all this is to encourage sloppy exploration and production ventures. It is my contention that many of the Yukon's sloppy mining projects would not even have been attempted, were it not for this government subsidy. And of course, the environment suffers needlessly in the process."

"Well, I assume that you have some ideas for terminating mining's grip on the Yukon. What are they?"

"Not for *terminating!* Dammit. Don't use that term. If you quote me, you'd better not say or even imply that Lammers wants to *terminate* mining, or I will hunt you down. You see, that's what people say about me: 'Lammers is against mining. Lammers is against this. Lammers is against that.' And Lammers is not against mining. For God's sake, don't you think I know that I use metals? Do you think I don't want even an iron pot to pee in? What I am against is the destructive, wasteful way in which ore is hunted and the speed at which they are digging it out of the ground for profit only. So don't say 'Lammers wants to terminate.' . . ."

"All right, all right. I'm not here to crucify you. I just want to hear your ideas. You do have some, right?"

I immediately feel guilty at my own sarcasm. But Lammers accepts it.

"Sure," Lammers says. "Did you think I gave you that big spiel just to conclude that I had no solution for it? My plan is very simple. It is just to change the mining laws to separate the exploration and production phases of mining, and put them under public control. The exploration phase, in my plan, is to perform an inventory of what mineral supplies we have here, to do it without needlessly damaging the landscape and without attempting to remove the mineral. So the government takes bids, from all interested mining companies, to perform mineral exploration in say, the Minto area, and it gives the contract to the lowest-priced bidder. Only one company goes in. There is no requirement to spend a dollar amount on each claim. There is no hurry because they need not worry about beating out the competition. There is no speculative staking or drilling or road building. The one company can afford the time to build the best possible access road. Or if only core drilling is needed, it may not even build a road, but land its crews by helicopter. Then it assesses the extent and richness of the ore body, say twenty million tons of two percent copper. This figure is published. It isn't kept secret. The exploration phase is complete.

"Then, if the ore is rich enough, the government takes production bids. And since everyone knows the extent and richness of the ore, nobody rushes in on a chancy production venture which leaves the area a mess and steals stockholders' money. The production job goes to the highest bidder, since the company is now essentially buying the ore from the government, from the people, who own it. Or the government may not even choose to extract the ore right now. Bids will be taken and the ore removed only when the government demonstrates to the people that the ore is needed by the nation. It may sit on it for a decade or two. There is no hurry to get that metal out of there. It isn't going anyplace. You see, that decision to dig is now in the hands of the boards of directors of these big companies, not in the hands of us who own it. And the ore is used primarily to feed you Americans. No prejudice there, but that's where most of our mineral output goes. But my plan would help to stop that. It might even save a little of our Canadian oil and mineral resource for future generations."

"I'm not equipped to judge it critically, but it does sound good to me, off the top of my head."

"Well, it's a lot better than what we have now. But I am not so naïve as to think it infallible. If society maintains its appetite for metals or oil or whatever, then all my plan would accomplish is to make the extraction of these resources more efficient and less destructive; the resources would nevertheless be quickly used up. But an indirect value of my plan is that the government must publicly demonstrate the need for the ore, and this introduces an opportunity for more public voice on the process, through public hearings and the like. This gives the public more time to reflect and to realize that the resource is theirs, which they don't now believe, and to recognize that the resource is finite in quantity. And I think people are going to start to think, and say, 'Hold it, why should we be using our metal and oil for snowmobiles, or to put two or three cars in every garage? Let's use it for essentials first.'

"And you see, this is the kind of planning and public participation we need for dealing with all sorts of resource decisions—hydro dams, roads, timber, water, oil, space, housing, population, the whole range of human interaction with the earth that supports us. This is not necessary only in the Yukon,

or in Canada, but everywhere. Ultimately, these are the most important decisions we have to make."

"Do you think it will work? Or do you think it will ever come to pass?"

Lammers sighs. "I don't know. Some days I feel it will. Some days I feel only a crisis situation will force us to a rational planned use of resources. I know what the critics say. They say it is too bureaucratic, it is too much under the thumb of government, it is socialistic, it is utopian. And they may be right. But we have no choice but to keep trying in this direction. And if it is not an elected government that sprang from the people that administers these processes, then who or what else can we rely on? Can we continue to rely upon the corporations? They are fond of saying, 'Oh, no need for restrictions, we will police ourselves.' That's like putting the fox in charge of the hen house!

"But at the same time, I am aware that the public must learn to care. I know only too well that one of the main reasons we have governmental agencies that do not solicit public opinion is because the public doesn't want to be bothered. In the Yukon, it is a territorial sport to blast the government. Not for anything in particular, but just to prove to your fellows that you disapprove of government and that you are therefore a worthy beer-drinking companion. But of course it does no good to simply rant and rave at government, at bureaucracy, at civil servants, at regulations that restrict 'freedom.' It is our own apathy and lack of insight that create a faulty government, which is then perceived as unduly heavy and restrictive. And believe me, there are many good men in government who know this too, and it disillusions them."

"And you feel, in the case of the Yukon, that this type of planning and public participation would help keep it a sort of natural and sparsely populated place?"

"Yes. If in fact it slowed the rate of industrial development, it would directly limit population growth. I'm sure you know that every time a mine or other developmental project opens up here, we get a new injection of a thousand people or so to our population. And these are artificial injections because these people wouldn't otherwise come here. But a large population here is extremely inefficient. Human populations in the Yukon can only be supported with costly imports of fuel, building materials, and food. We may someday be more self-supporting in fuel, and as big timber in the south becomes more scarce we may then use our own for construction, but we will never become supporting in food. It is just not feasible on a commercial basis. Sure, you can grow some things and grow them well, but you could do that at the North Pole too, if you built greenhouses and imported fuel.

"And I also look at many of the Yukon projects as artificial, whether they are roads or dams or mines, because there is no planned need for them at this time, except perhaps to create jobs. That's inefficient. But you see, once one of these things starts, it feeds other inefficiency. Look at the Dempster Highway. It was built as one of the 'Roads to Resources,' namely, a road to metals and petroleum. But once it's completed, it will encourage how many tourists to drive up to the arctic coast, just to say 'we were there.' But that will burn how much gasoline? And then, ten billion gallons later, someone will say, 'Gee, we need more gasoline. We better build another road to resources to find some.' It's a vicious circle!"

Lammers puts his head in his hands. "Oh Christ, I sometimes feel like giving up. It's a losing battle. I should just open up a snowmobile resort and forget the whole fight. At least then I would be accepted." He laughs. "Forgive me. I've been in the Yukon too long. I spend my whole life talking about these things and all I get in return is 'Lammers is a nut.'"

It is late. Lammers's thinking sounds right to me. Right, and maybe even profound. But I am exhausted, just from listening.

During our long discussion, Polly curls up on the couch and goes to sleep.

"Look at that," John says. "She can sleep anywhere, any time. And it's a good thing she can. It must drive her crazy to live with me and listen to this kind of conversation all the time."

I get up and go out to my cabin. John walks out with me. The sky is clear. From over the hill behind the house, pale green streaks of the aurora borealis extend out over us, wavering, leaping from left to right. The action is so dramatic that it seems strange to me that no sound accompanies it. John tells me that there is supposed to be a meteor shower tonight. We watch a few minutes and see two or three meteors falling, in the west. Short, bright balls of light, streaking for the black silhouette of the

spruce-covered cliff across the river. The slight sound of the mukluks packing the dry snow seems very loud.

It is 9:00 A.M. and still pitch-dark when I awake. It is 24° below, according to the outside thermometer, but my cabin fire has kept going most of the night, and it is probably about 30° inside.

The propane light shines through the window of Lammers's house. I hear some noise in the workshop and go over there. John is replacing a split ax handle. When he finishes, we go in the house and eat rolls and bacon. Polly tells me that eggs are sufficiently bulky and freezable so that they seldom try to bring them in. The Land Rover is usually loaded, on a winter trip back from Whitehorse, and if they got stuck on the twenty-five-mile road into the house, the eggs plus anything else with liquid in it—canned vegetables, juice, milk, soda, dressings, anything—would freeze and burst.

At ten it is light. We take another walk, going downriver toward the confluence of the Pelly and Yukon rivers. It is a clear day, and when the sun eases over the line of hills to the southeast, its beams sparkle through the big crystals of frost on the aspen and spruce limbs. Across the river, small white patches of snow make a regular geometric pattern against the black rock of the palisade cliff. Today, I cannot hear the sound of open water downriver. A slight change in the wind, perhaps.

We do not reach the confluence. We get as far as a slough, with dark, open water gleaming between the sheets of snow-covered ice along its banks. The slough cuts across the angle made by the confluence, connecting the two rivers. The slough reverses, John says, flowing from Pelly to Yukon or vice versa, depending upon which is higher. In spring during breakup, the Pelly crests first and water flows into the Yukon. Two weeks later, with the Yukon's cresting, it reverses. Right now, it is flowing from Yukon to Pelly. We clear some snow from a log and sit down. I light a cigarette.

John looks at the cigarette, pretends to be sickened by its smell, staggers around in the snow, coughing dramatically. "Twenty-four hours he's been here and he still hasn't learned not to pollute the air," he says to Polly. "Well, thank God, in another twenty-four he'll be gone. No, wait. A better idea would be to keep him here till he runs out of cigarettes. That's it. Hope, I refuse to take you back to the road tomorrow. You're here for the winter. He'll go mad!" he says to Polly. "He'll never get his book written."

"But maybe he'll write bad things about us when he gets out," Polly says dryly.

"I'd hate to go with you on one of your river tours. Do you let the smokers smoke?"

"We make the smokers take the downwind raft," Polly says.

"And we make 'em swim the last two miles every day," John says, "to get rid of that damn smell before we stop to cook supper."

We walk back, going up on the bank. We see a ruffed grouse and follow the fresh track of a loping wolf, with the little streaks in front of each paw print where the big animal dragged its feet in the snow.

"Just how do you feel about the environmental impact of your own business?" I ask. "One of your Whitehorse critics pointed out to me that even Lammers causes pollution with his vehicles and motorboat engines."

John stops walking. "This guy has the capacity to ruin my day with a single sentence," he says to Polly. Then to me: "Tell me you're just saying that to bait me, please. Tell me you see the stupidity in that statement. If not, you're going to swim back, under the ice."

But without waiting for my response, John forges ahead.

"First, your informant obviously does not even understand the environmental problem, because he emphasizes the pollution my engine causes, not the fact that I am using up a nonrenewable resource. He does not even understand that this pollution we hear about is only a side effect of consumption, which is the primary problem. Second, does he really believe that anybody can live, much less make a living, without consuming something? He could've just as well said, 'Well, Lammers eats, doesn't he? So he's part of the problem.' And he would be right. Just by living, we consume and therefore we pollute. The point is, the perfect citizen of this planet doesn't engage in needless consumption. But he doesn't commit suicide, to spare the world the burden of supporting him. He has a right to live, and to earn a modest living. If he is a commuter, he tries to ride a train or in a car pool to save fuel, but he doesn't stay home from work. And if he is a river tour operator, like me, he tries to stick to a small boat engine. But if an engine is necessary, he doesn't quit his business.

"And for your information, we usually use only small outboard motors, either six or nine horse-power. On a ten-day tour, we bring only enough gasoline to run a motor for six hours, and we usually finish the trip with half of that left, because we drift and paddle downriver, and use a motor only for making safe landings in the river current.

"It really doesn't take much to wind you up, does it?" I say to Lammers.

"No," he says, "it doesn't." Somehow, though, I feel that he has not even heard me. He talks on.

"Now, if your friend were really on the ball, he would have pointed out not the minimal pollution of Lammers's boat motor, but the fact that most of my clients come from southern Canada or the United States, and probably burn many gallons of fossil fuel coming up here to go on vacation. And *that* I do have guilt pangs about. I am also very aware of the fact that when I meet my people in Whitehorse, we all stay in a hotel one night, and as you know, all sewage in Whitehorse empties directly, untreated, into the Yukon River. So yes, my business *does* have an impact.

"I could give several responses to this. I could ask why our territory doesn't treat its sewage. I could ask why our society uses cars and planes to travel rather than trains. I could ask why our society has so decimated its wilderness that these clients of mine need to come all the way up here to find it. But as far as my own responsibility is concerned, the only response I have is that we really try to give these people an intense, in-depth experience. We don't just give them a sight-seeing tour as we would if we were really commercial and didn't care what they got from the trip. Whenever the opportunity arises, we talk to them as we have been talking to you. We challenge everything. We talk about how many cars they own, and if they need them. We show that we destroy ourselves when we destroy nature. If they show a concern for what is happening, we ask what changes they are prepared to make in their own lives—and in society—in order to improve things. We ask if they now promote those alternatives, and if they are willing to stand up and fight for them. And if they give us some lame answer like 'Oh well, we pick up litter,' we damn well let them know how lame it is, and why. I don't want to imply that we lecture constantly. Most of the day we don't say a word. We just look. But at meal times, and at night, the discussions naturally turn to man and environment. And hopefully, this sort of exposure, together with the example we try to set, will help to change their awareness."

We reach the house and go in, thumping the dry snow off our boots.

"Do you think you're accomplishing what you hope to?" I ask.

Lammers pauses. "I don't know. I ask myself that question all the time. . . . And I can't honestly give you an answer. We certainly get lots of letters from our guests, telling us what a good time they had. And some of them—I like to think it's an unusually large number—even hint that it was an exceptional experience. That it changed their lives. I like to believe that, but I never really know. I don't know if what we try to give them here, packed into a week or two, will translate into behavior, once they're back home. For some, I suspect that might really be true. For others, well, maybe they think of me just as my Yukon neighbors do: Lammers is

against things. Lammers is inconsistent because he drives a truck. Lammers means well, but he's a little off.

"Oh hell, I don't know. Is it worth it? It's a difficult life, always to be mistrusted and to feel you're never getting through. Lately I feel that maybe some of us are starting to wake up, through painful experience. Like the Alaskans with that damn pipeline they wanted so badly. But most of us would rather not rock the boat. And when some guy like me comes along, who gives it a real jolt, he is immediately defined as an oddball. I'm only human and let me tell you, it's no fun to go into the Whitehorse post office and think that people are saying, 'Oh, there's that crazy bird watcher.' "

"Well, it must at least give you some consolation to feel that you are right in what you say."

Lammers looks out the window. "I don't know," he says. "It's not much good being right if you're all alone."

OLD CROW

HEADS DOWN, Larry Burgis and I walk along the snow-covered road through the Indian village of Old Crow, past the sixty or so log cabins perched on the west bank of the Porcupine River. A strong wind sweeps down the road and drifts the two feet of dry snow up to the eaves of the cabins on our left. It is 1:45 P.M. Across the frozen hundred-yard width of the Porcupine, the flat, snow-and-spruce-covered land stretches away endlessly to a thin layer of red-gray cloud resting on top of the southeastern horizon. The December sun is behind there somewhere, sunk out of sight, and its indirect light gives the snow around us the lonesome pale blue color of early evening. To our left, the Virgin Mary perches above the entryway of the small Roman Catholic church, with a foot of snow piled on her head. Ahead, two parka-clad Indian men struggle with a stalled snowmobile, lugging it out of the road and in through the front door of their cabin. It is 20° below zero and, with the twenty-mile-per-hour wind, this is equivalent to a temperature of 50° below. My cheeks are numb, and I rub them with the wool patches sewn on the back of my mittens. My left ear hurts. In getting off the plane, an hour and a half ago, I was foolish enough to stand for five minutes without a hat, while our packs were being unloaded, and now it is paining.

It is a little scary. Not only the cold, but the fact that we know no one in this little Indian settlement of 200 people, except the white school principal, Tom Steel, whom I have met only once. Foolishly, we have made no preparations for our visit, and Steel has just told us that the only two places for Old Crow visitors to stay are the co-op store (a heated room and meals for twenty-five dollars per person per day, which we cannot afford) and a small camp trailer with wood stove and gas plate, for nine dollars per person per day. The trailer has no cut firewood, and only a miniature backpacker's saw to cut it with. We have agreed to rent the trailer, but only out of desperation. We are now 80 miles above the Arctic Circle, 150 miles south of the Arctic Ocean, and 250 miles north of Dawson, the next town to the south. There is no way to shop around for more ideal quarters. There are no roads in here and only one weekly plane, which has just taken off. Old Crow is one of the most remote Indian villages in North America.

"I wonder if we made a mistake in coming here?" My face is stiff with the wind and cold, and the words come out clumsily.

Larry reminds me that there is a special freight flight in tomorrow to accommodate the Christmas mail; if we get really desperate, we might be able to persuade the pilot to take us out. This thought consoles us.

We came up here to see the town, to see how the Old Crow people live. The Old Crow people, who speak a language called Loucheux, are part of a larger Indian group—the Kutchin—who inhabit parts of the Yukon, the Northwest Territories, and Alaska. Traditionally, these people have led a semi-nomadic life, residing in small towns, but traveling widely by dog team to trap fur-bearers, trading these furs with the white merchants who boated to the Indian settlements in summer. The people netted fish, hunted caribou, moose and smaller animals. The life, in some ways, resembled that of the Eskimos farther north along the Arctic coast.

Within the past decade or two, the amount of white contact with the Old Crow people has increased considerably. Still, not many white men, not even many white Yukoners, have visited Old Crow. Among the people I have asked about it, the place is generally regarded as the one community

where the Indian life-style is still close to the traditional one. In conversation, this comes through in different ways: that the Old Crow people are "unspoiled"; that they still live off the land; that the women still make mukluks, and the men kill caribou; that they are happy; that the whole town comes down to meet the weekly plane. There is prejudice and paternalism in many of the comments I have received, I know. But my interpretation of them, as a group, is simply that Old Crow is a community that, because of its remoteness, is able to coexist with white culture without being dominated by it. Perhaps it is even one of those few places that —come the revolution, or the depression, or the bottom of the oil barrel—would still be able to survive, as a hunting and fishing community. This thought appeals to Larry and to me.

We continue walking north through the mile-long town. Paul von Baich and Bob Frisch have given me the names of three or four people to visit, and we are now headed to Fred Throndiuk's cabin, about three quarters of a mile from the airstrip, at the north end of town. It is getting dark now, and there are a few lights on inside the cabins.

It suddenly occurs to me that these are electric

lights, and I am reminded that while Old Crow is the most isolated, most Indian town in the territory, white society has nevertheless made its inroads. In addition to its five-thousand-foot airstrip, Old Crow has an oil-driven power plant, streetlights, telephones, a new school and teachers' residences, and a few other large government buildings. The town also has many new Indian homes, large, two-to-four-room cabins, recently built to replace the older smaller cabins. The Indian people built the new homes, but the federal Department of Indian and Northern Affairs supplied materials and paid Old Crow people an hourly wage to build them. Even the people's current homes, then, sprang from the white culture.

Fred Throndiuk's home is just beyond the two-story co-op store, and we find him sawing wood beside the cabin. Fred is a short, strong-looking Indian, probably about forty-five years old, wearing a big old olive-green parka, blue corduroy pants, and moose hide mukluks. We introduce ourselves as friends of Bob Frisch and Paul von Baich, and he peers at us curiously, tilting his head to see out from under the hood of his parka. Then he begins to nod, slowly, and grins. "Bob Frisch? You know Bob Frisch?"

"Yes."

"I send him .303. He tell you about that?"

"I'm not sure. He just said he knew you."

"Paul," he says. "He take pictures before. I remember." He moves his hand near his face, to indicate Paul's beard. "You know Paul?"

"Yes. I just saw him two days ago, in Ottawa. He gave me a pair of snowshoes to give to your brother. He says to say hello to you."

Fred now nods vigorously and breaks into a smile that nearly hides his dark eyes. "Paul," he says. "He take pictures of us. He tell me there is another white man coming. From New York City?" Without waiting for an answer, he giggles, puts down his saw, invites us in for tea. "Paul stay in Tom Steel's trailer. But we tell him to stay here. You have place to stay? You stay with me?"

With Fred's invitation, our perspective on staying in Old Crow quickly changes, and we accept, with only a polite pause. This is a break, a chance to spend a week with one of the native families, and deliverance from the unheated house trailer.

After having tea with Fred and his wife, Lillian, we go back down the road to get our gear from the

house trailer. It occurs to me now that Larry and I must make a strange and somewhat pathetic-looking pair to the Throndiuks. We are white, first of all, and the only other white men in this town of two hundred are the Anglican priest, the storekeeper, the mountie, the nurse, the schoolteachers and their families, all faces Fred is used to. We wear more or less typical Yukon winter garb, but Larry's several layers of sweaters give him the look—and almost the dimensions—of a forty-five-gallon oil drum. I wear a grossly oversized pair of my cousin's Korean War boots and his red wool hunter's pants; the suspenders holding up the pants have already broken and I resemble a baggy version of Charlie Chaplin. My face is bright red from the cold, and Larry's blond beard and moustache are tinged with frost crystals.

It is three-fifteen and almost dark by the time we retrieve our gear. My ear hurts again, from the mile-and-a-half walk down and back. We stop by the small two-aisled co-op store for a few minutes and buy some groceries for ourselves and the Throndiuks. The prices make me remember that everything here in town must come in by plane, at a freight cost of 35¢ per pound. Eggs are $1.93 per dozen. Butter is $1.93 per pound. Condensed milk is 67¢ per can. Potatoes are 72¢ per pound. A box of thirty small oranges (from Japan) costs $10.20. The stale white bread is $1.07 per loaf, without even pretending to be enriched. There is no liquid milk, we hear, because of its freezability. There is soda pop, however, several flavors of it.

When we return to the cabin, Fred is sitting to the left of the door, skinning a marten caught in his trapline. The marten is dark brown and, except for its broader, shorter head, looks very much like a big mink. There is another marten on the drying rack over Fred's head and a stiff, dead, and grinning cross fox lying on the floor. The knife Fred uses is old and dull, but he does a good clean job on the marten, better than I could do with a razor blade. He makes a neat slit along the underside of the tail and quickly pulls out the tail vertebra and flesh without breaking the delicate hide. He splits the pelt down the inside of each hind leg and breaks the paws loose from the carcass, then, grabbing the hind legs in one hand, the hide in the other, strips the pelt from the body, inside out, down to the front paws and head. He pulls the hide down the front legs and cuts off the paws, leaving only the toes inside the pelt, then very carefully works the hide loose from the head, cutting carefully around the ears, eyes, nose, and mouth. The whole process takes no more than five minutes. He leaves the pelt inside out and thrusts into it a handmade wooden stretcher about four inches wide, and twenty-four inches long, tapering to a rounded point at the fore end. He pulls the hide tight and tacks its rear edge, feet, and tail to the wooden stretcher.

Fred smiles when he is done and stands the stretcher head up in the corner to dry. "I get forty dollars for this one," he says. He drops the marten carcass in a cloth sack and jabs the frozen cross fox with his toe. "Too stiff," he says. He lays the fox's body back up on the rack over his head and then starts on the second marten. This one is slightly smaller than the other and its fur is a light, golden color.

As he works on the second marten, our conversation picks up where it left off earlier, a conversation that is designed, I think, to establish some common ground between us.

"Bob Frisch walk from the Dempster to Old Crow," Fred says. "Without gun! Hundred fifty mile. He say, 'No bear gonna eat me, I don't taste good.'" Fred giggles, remembering. "But no good

to walk without gun, so I send him .303 if he's gonna walk up here again."

"Bob is really a tough man in the bush," I say.

"You know Hans?"

"Algotsson, you mean? Yes. I stayed with Bob and Hans in their cabin this summer."

"I know lots of white man, but I forget their name," Fred says as he strips the hide down the body of the marten. "You know Bill?"

"Oh. Bill Schroder, you mean?"

Fred nods. "Bill stay in Bob's cabin too. You know him?"

"Yes. He and I were there at the same time." I had forgotten Bill. I am surprised to hear that he got here. He is a Swede who came to make a film on the Yukon for European TV, and I now realize that the orange T-shirt Fred wears was given to him by Bill. It has the name of a Swedish film company printed on it. I am reminded now that the Old Crow people are visited each year—or invaded, depending upon your point of view—by several people like myself: filmmakers, writers, anthropologists, medical researchers, and others who wish to document some aspect of their remote existence. And of course, each one of us makes that existence a little less remote.

"You know him?" Dick points to one of several photos pinned above the table.

"No. I don't know him."

"I know lots of white man," Fred grins. "Most they come in summer. But they don't like black flies. They're tick. I have to shoot at them with shotgun they're so tick." I start to laugh. "Sometimes I wound one," he says laughing. "You come at the right time. No bugs. But bad wind this winter. You stay with me one week, I see what kind of man you are."

"What will we do, Fred?" Larry asks.

"Fish. Get wood. Maybe trap."

"How many traps do you have set?" I ask.

"Not many," Fred says. "A few where I cut wood."

"Not many. You mean you used to have more?"

"Sure," Fred says.

"How many?"

"Oh, maybe hundred. Maybe two hundred."

"And where did you have them set?"

Fred gestures toward the south and east. "Out there," he says. "Far. Far away."

"And now you trap nearer town?"

Fred nods. "Two miles," he says.

"Do most people in town trap now?"

"No. Not so many. A few."

"How about fishing? Do a lot of people still fish?"

"I fish," Fred says, grinning. "Some people fish. But not so many as before."

Larry is bothered by this information. "Why, Fred?" Larry says. "Why don't you trap much now?"

"Other work now," Fred says.

"And what work is that?" I ask.

"We cut wood for school now," Fred says. "I work for Resources too."

By "Resources," I believe Fred means a consulting firm, Renewable Resources, doing preliminary wildlife study work for one or more of the oil companies that have an eye on the north.

"How long have you been doing that? How long is it since you trapped a lot?"

Fred thinks. "Maybe a few years," he says. He seems reluctant to further discuss the topic.

"But why, Fred?" Larry asks. "Wasn't it nicer when you were trapping full time?"

Fred does not respond. He slips the second marten on the stretcher and lays it up on the rack.

"What does a marten eat?" I ask.

Fred looks up and grins. "Oh, mouse. Rabbit. Once in a while a hot cake."

We all laugh.

The door now bursts open and cold air rolls in along the floor, condensing immediately into a cloud as it hits the hot air of the cabin. Behind the cloud is Chris—Fred's youngest son—a cute seven-year-old with a purple jacket and his long jet-black hair tucked under a red ski cap. A few seconds behind him are Albert, nine, Harold, eleven, home from school, and Diana, their teenage sister. The kids stop suddenly as they see Larry and me. Diana comes in only briefly and then retreats back outside. The boys are less shy and they come over to where we sit. Larry and I shake hands with them all. Only Chris is bold enough to speak.

"You come from United States," he says to me. His two front teeth are missing and he lisps.

"That's right. Who told you that?"

"School," he says. Word travels fast.

Fred grins and pulls down Chris's cap over his eyes. "I call him little white man," he says to me. "He ask a lot of questions." Chris pulls up his hat and stomps off in mock indignation.

"Who wants an orange?" Larry says. He offers the boys some we got at the co-op.

The boys come over shyly. "Yes," Harold says, and holds out his hand.

"Yes what?" his mother says.

"Yes please," Harold says. Larry hands him one.

The kids run outside to play, in the dark.

Fred pours dog food into a five-gallon can that already contains kitchen scraps, adds some hot water from the tea kettle on the wood stove, and goes out to feed his team, a hundred yards behind the house. Larry goes with him. I stay inside and make another pot of tea—for the Canadians—and a pot of coffee for me.

For the first time, I take a careful look at Fred's government-sponsored cabin. It is a strange, sometimes comic, often disfunctional combination of Indian traditional and contemporary white suburban. The place has three rooms—the large 15 × 20 front room or kitchen and two 10 × 15 bedrooms. The cabin's outside walls are built of locally cut logs, but all its inside walls are covered with imitation wood paneling. Other Yukon cabins I have been in have wood floors and log ceilings. Fred's cabin has white vinyl tiles on the floor and a ceiling made of white squares of Celotex. The white vinyl tiles have begun to wear and chip at the edges, and the absorbent Celotex ceiling, which cannot be readily washed, is already blackened by woodsmoke from the flat-topped cookstove and the forty-five-gallon-drum heating stove in the middle of the front room. Fred has built a long drying rack, made of two peeled, twenty-foot spruce poles, running diagonally across the ceiling of the front room and reaching from the front door into one of the bedrooms. On the rack are socks, jackets, two steel traps, and the grinning carcass of the fox. Near one window, a three-pound chunk of caribou fat, for cooking, is nailed to the imitation wood paneling with a twelve-penny nail.

To the right of the door there is a large pile of wood, stacked neatly against one end of a fifteen-cubic-foot freezer. In a conversation at the co-op, I have heard that freezers and some other large appliances have come to Old Crow recently, via the various assistance programs run by the federal government. But now that I think of it, I realize that a freezer probably has a very limited usefulness in a place where the temperature averages below zero most of the time. Fred's freezer, in fact, is unplugged, and has a half-dozen frozen salmon, brought in to thaw from the outside cache, stacked on top of it.

To the left of the door, against the wall, there are new plywood dish cabinets, and below them is a white Formica counter with a stainless-steel sink set into it, with more plywood cabinets beneath the counter. But the house has no running water and no septic tank. The sink drains into a five-gallon oil can below, within the cabinets, which Fred periodically empties. The cabin has electricity, a wall phone, a wringer washer, a toaster, and three or four unshaded light bulbs. But it does not have a refrigerator, so that things can be kept cool without freezing.

In general, the place has a look of disorientation, but it is clear that this comes chiefly from the government-sponsored attempt to emulate the interior of a white man's modern home in a more urban part of the continent. In other Yukon cabins, with less space and far fewer conveniences than this one, it has never occurred to me that the lack of running water or the presence of woodsmoke were signs of poverty. But a stainless-steel sink without running water, or a white Celotex ceiling blackened by woodsmoke, or an electrified household without a refrigerator—these somehow advertise poverty. And a house done in interior paneling and white floor tiles means that dead foxes, caribou fat, maybe even woodstoves are out of place. If not now, then in the near future. The direction is there. The Old Crow people have only to visit one of the few modern white residences in town—with carpeting, electric stoves, baseboard heating—to know how a home "should" look.

When Fred and Larry return from feeding the dogs, Fred picks up two plastic garbage-pail-sized containers near the door, and says he is going to get water. I hurry to get on my parka and go with him. I realize that I do not know where water comes from in this household. Many Old Crow people with snowmobiles haul large barrels down to the river, near the south end of town, where there is a red pump house with an enclosed, gasoline-driven water pump set out on the ice. But Fred is a long way from there, and has no snowmobile to haul the big drums.

He uses snow. We go outside, into a patch of six-foot alders fifty yards beyond the dogs, and scoop the light, dry snow into the plastic containers, using a tin water pail to scoop and a metal dinner plate to work the snow down and compact it within the large containers. The snow is so light and dry that you could not make a snowball with it if your life depended on it. Fred giggles as Larry and I overzealously lug the big containers back to the cabin, stumbling over the drifts and sinking in up to our knees. On the way, I spot the outdoor toilet, about fifty yards behind Fred's cabin, apparently located to service his place as well as two or three other homes nearby. I'm glad to find out where it is. But strangely, there seem to be no tracks leading to it. I walk over and open its door: There is no toilet paper, and there is a three-inch layer of fresh snow on the seat. This is something I'll have to find out.

The wind is still strong, and it is snowing hard. My cheeks are just beginning to feel numb again as we get back to the house. I wonder if it is possible to walk more than a mile in this country, if you do not have a face mask, without really damaging yourself.

We eat at five o'clock. Fred cooks, on the flat-topped stove. We have some of the bread and canned beans Larry and I got at the co-op and some big fried chunks of fresh salmon that Fred caught in his winter net on the river. The food is good. There are only three chairs and one backless wooden bench in the house, not enough for everybody to eat at once, so Larry and I are given the guests' honor of eating first. Then the boys eat. Then Fred and Lillian. Diana does not appear. Apparently, out of shyness, she has gone to a friend's house.

The phone rings after supper. It is Mary, the Throndiuks' fourteen-year-old daughter, calling from Whitehorse, where she is attending high school. Since Old Crow's school only goes through eighth grade, all Old Crow children in higher grades are removed from their parents and sent to Whitehorse, where they live in dormitories or with families while finishing high school. Apparently, the school attendance law was laxly enforced until recently, but within the past ten years or so, all Old Crow children have had to go to Whitehorse. The Throndiuks have two daughters there, Mary and Betty. Mary has been there only since September. She is lonesome.

"She call almost every day, at first," Lillian says after she hangs up the phone. "But now I think she like it better."

"I would think it would be tough on a girl raised in Old Crow to be taken away from her family," Larry says.

Lillian nods. "It's not a nice place, they say. Unless they stay with a family. I like that. But if they stay in the other place, it's not nice. Gosh, I worry about that Mary."

"It seems to me it would be better for the kids if they had a high school here," I say.

Lillian nods again. "They get in trouble with drink down there," she says. "Betty and another girl get into trouble. Someone give them drink." She shakes her head. "But I guess that's okay now."

"We used to drink pretty bad," Fred says. "Now no more. We drink one, that's all. On my birthday we don't have any drink. We cook a big pot of moose meat. And soup. And toast. People come in all day and we give them some. But no drink. Not even home brew." He ruffles Albert's hair. "I love my kids too much," he says.

"There's no liquor store in Old Crow, is there?"

Fred is briefly angry. "No!" he says. "No good here. Nobody want one. If we have liquor store, everybody drunk all the time. No good! We don't want our kids to see us drunk. We say no. We vote twice." He raises his hand.

"You voted? Who wanted one?"

"Government," Fred says.

"The government wanted one?"

Fred does not seem so sure now. He simply nods quietly. I find out later that the government has not—at least not in recent years—advocated any Old Crow liquor store. What happened, apparently, is that some Old Crow resident—perhaps one whom the people tend to identify as being a spokesman for the white or government interests—mentioned the idea at a town meeting. It was never brought to formal vote, since people overwhelmingly opposed the thought, and the idea was dropped.

Fred is apparently a little embarrassed at his sudden show of temper, and he turns on the small transistor radio that hangs on the wall above the table. He looks at us and smiles. "Maybe we hear United States," he says.

We do hear the United States. The only station we can get is one near Fairbanks, three hundred miles to the southwest. The radio squawks and Fred fiddles with the dial. ". . . My dear friends, I believe, I *know*, that God is still in business. Some say He is taking it easy, sitting back, taking the weekend off. But we have ourselves to blame for this. We don't have to worry about the infidel, the atheist, the communist, because he'll tell you right out what he is. But we have ourselves, our *selves*, to blame. Now, why do I say that? . . ." We listen to this for a while, then the news and the weather: it is −18° in Fairbanks, −8° in Fort Yukon, +14° in Whitehorse, +42° in Seattle.

It is uncomfortably hot in the unventilated cabin now, especially in our wool underwear. Larry, Fred, and I go out for a walk. As we step outside, it occurs to me that the human body, up here, is regularly subjected to temperature changes of 130 degrees. I tie my hood securely and cinch the fastener at the throat. It has stopped snowing briefly, and we can see a few stars. They look closer than I have ever seen them. I remark on this, and Fred looks up. "Twinkle, twinkle, little star," he says. "How you wonder where I am." He looks at me and giggles.

Fred and Larry walk one way, I walk another. Larry wants to be introduced to the mother of an Indian girl he has dated in Whitehorse, and Fred goes with him. I walk on down a half mile to the nursing station where I have noticed a thermometer. On the way, I see other people driving their snowmobiles into their cabins for the night, so they will start in the morning. The thermometer reads 26° below. I stay out only thirty minutes. Fred is home when I return, and Larry returns shortly after. We have more tea. Lillian and Diana are already in one of the two bedrooms, sewing. Diana stays in the back of that room, out of sight. Harold, Albert, and Chris are playing on the floor of the cabin. The kids have cut a sugar doughnut box into toy snowmobiles and are racing them around the wood stove, prrrpping and zzzzpping. Chris's prrp has a little lisp in it. He crawls rapidly around the floor and pretends to accidentally run his paper snowmobile into my foot. He looks up at me and I smile. He breaks into a big grin and zooms off around the stove.

"Little white man," Fred says grinning.

I wonder if, five or six years ago, before snowmobiles reached the village, Old Crow kids pushed around toy dog sleds and yelled mush, or whatever it is they yell. Probably not. A silent, nonmotorized dog sled simply does not have the lure of a snarling, fast-moving machine.

"You never use a snowmobile?" I ask Fred.

"Oh no," he says, gesturing in annoyance. "They break. When it's cold they don't start. You can't get parts in the co-op. The dogs are good. I don't need one." He smiles. "*He* need it," he says, pointing to Chris. Chris putts around the stove again and runs his snowmobile nonchalantly up my leg.

It is nine o'clock. Fred turns on the radio again.

171

". . . We hear today that we have been abandoned. But friends, God loves you. He loves all of us. And He has given to us. To you, and to me. Man has constantly been able to improve the material conditions of his life, and so I say . . ."

Fred turns off the radio. "What time you go to bed?" he says to Larry and me.

The perfect guests. "Oh, anytime you do," we say. I suddenly realize, though, that we may be putting somebody out of his bed and we mention this to Fred and volunteer to sleep on the floor.

"No," Fred says. "No trouble." He takes us into the nearest bedroom and shows us. Fred and Harold will sleep here, on the double bed. Larry and I each have a cot in the same room, and someone has already spread out caribou hides on them. Lillian, Diana, Albert, and Chris will sleep in the other bedroom.

Fred puts a spruce log in each of the two stoves, and the rest of us get in bed. Larry and I have sleeping bags. Fred and Harold have blankets. Fred turns out the light. He takes off his mukluks but leaves on his corduroy pants, his Swedish T-shirt, and his blue wool cap, and lies on top of the covers instead of getting under them. He lights a cigarette and uses a sardine can alongside the bed for an ashtray. The partition between our room and the other bedroom is poorly fit to the ceiling, and we can see light over it. We also hear Chris, or Albert, I cannot tell which, reciting a bedtime prayer.

"Tomorrow maybe we check net," Fred announces to the darkness.

"Good, that sounds nice."

"Maybe we find a fish come up from United States," Fred says. I can see his grin in the dark. Then he bursts into a streak of curses. An ash has dropped from his cigarette and has burned a hole in the blanket. He pounds it out.

I am exhausted from two or three days of plane and bus travel. The wind howls outside, rhythmically banging a door on a nearby outbuilding. I can see snow falling. I am glad to be here, in this isolated Indian village north of the Arctic Circle. I have some trouble in going to sleep, though, because of the glare of a streetlight that comes in through my window.

I half wake in the morning when I hear Fred jump out of bed and start the fire, and then pad back to have a smoke while the cabin heats. It is cold in the cabin. Not freezing, but probably in the forties. I am grateful we are not in the little camp trailer where, due to its small size and our inability to bank a fire properly, the temperature would probably be the same as outdoors. From bed, I can hear the radio tuned to its only station. Someone is leaving us with the reminder that "the man who lives it up will also have to live it down," and wishing us "a good day in Christ."

The cabin warms up within ten minutes. Fred cooks breakfast, and Larry and I lie in our bags as the kids eat and get out to school, in the dark. It is 9:00 A.M. The wind bangs the outbuilding door.

When the kids leave, we have breakfast with Fred. He has noticed my preference for coffee over tea, and has fixed a pot for me. Lillian is not up. She has something wrong with her leg. Maybe arthritis, Fred speculates. He seems worried and asks me if I know what kind of a pill she should take for it.

Larry asks if we will check the nets before noon.

Fred shakes his head. "No," he says. "Too cold. Bad wind this winter. I don't fool around. You could freeze your hand."

This is a disappointment. I wonder if Fred is worried about his guests' capacity to walk to the net, a mile and a quarter up the Porcupine River, without turning into icicles.

"Maybe we can check them in the afternoon," Larry says.

Fred looks skeptical. "Never know," he says. "We wait for the wind." He leaves the table and begins to saw a stretcher for the cross fox pelt out of a one-inch plank.

There is nothing to do. Larry and I wash the dishes, then go out for a walk. A walk here, though, is unlike a walk anywhere else. By the time we have reached the RCMP barracks, a quarter mile down through town, I see why Fred was not in a hurry to check the net. It is only 19° below, but the wind sears our faces whenever we turn to the north. In five minutes, I again have the numbness in my cheeks and have to rub them. At ten-fifteen it is still pitch-dark. I wonder now why the Indian and Eskimo people never migrated farther south. It just seems to me that they would have been better off in San Diego. I wonder how Fred, or any of the other Old Crow people, can take it. I would go nuts, I think, with these four-and-a-half-hour days and with the necessity of having to take so much account of the weather. Of course, I do not have 10,000 years of arctic ancestry behind me, as Fred does.

At ten-thirty, the light begins to show to the east,

across the Porcupine River. Not the sun, just the light. To the west of town, we see Crow Mountain, two to three miles away. It is a strange sight. The country here in the northern Yukon is not as mountainous as farther south. It is more rolling. But with no other peaks in sight, the white bulk of Crow Mountain, a rounded, treeless promontory of maybe three or four thousand feet, seems more massive than it is. It towers above the relatively flat land surrounding it, and shuts off any view to the west. And in the diminished winter light, its pale silhouette blends with the sky around it. Your eye, unless it looks carefully, does not see the outline.

Caribou appear on Crow Mountain each fall, parts of the Porcupine herd, the 400,000 animals that migrate south and east into the Northwest Territories each autumn and back into northern Yukon and northern Alaska to have their calves each spring, as they have done for thousands of years. Usually several thousand caribou sweep down the slopes of Crow Mountain each October, wandering through town or within a few miles of it, finally swimming the Porcupine River and continuing their journey to the east. But this year, people tell us, the animals did not come. Just a few stragglers. And only a few people, who hunted hard up and down the Porcupine, were able to kill their winter's meat.

Fred was one of the few. He shot ten caribou, and he shows me the hides of four or five of them remaining in his outdoor cache, an 8x10 tin-roofed building beside the cabin. The rest were given away to people who got none.

"Why do you suppose they didn't come this year?" I ask Fred.

Fred shakes his head and grunts. "Maybe the pipe," he says. "They dig in Alaska. Caribou no cross it." He looks at me, and it seems that he looks at me as someone who should know more about it than he does. "You know?" he says.

"No. I don't know either. I thought that they were experimenting with some kind of ramp things to help the caribou get used to crossing the pipeline."

Fred shakes his head. "They don't like it," he says. "They come and walk back. Come and walk back. Maybe they go someplace else." He shakes his head again with a puzzled look on his face. "Maybe caribou don't come anymore," he says fatalistically.

I suspect, in fact, that the pipeline is not the cause of the animals' disappearance, at least not yet. More likely, it was simply one of the caribous' tem-porary changes in migration route. But from Fred's point of view I can see that it might well be believable that we white men had overnight made a herd of 400,000 animals go away. It would be no more dramatic than many of the changes white magic has already imposed upon Fred's life.

Fred reaches up to a shelf above the table and pulls down a topographical map of northern Alaska and Yukon, from just south of Old Crow up to the Arctic Ocean. I do not quite understand Fred's explanation of who gave him the map. It was a white man, but it is not clear whether it was one of the many oil exploration people who came through Old Crow or someone from a governmental agency. On the map there are two heavy black lines, drawn in ink, sweeping from the Brooks Range oil and gas fields in northern Alaska, through the northern Yukon and over to the Mackenzie River, in the Northwest Territories, where additional large oil and gas discoveries have just been made in the Mackenzie River delta. It seems that it is the intention of one international petroleum conglomerate —if Canadians and Americans are on sufficiently good terms—to join the Alaskan and Canadian gas supplies and to deliver them to southern Canada and the lower forty-eight states with a single pipeline running south along the Mackenzie River, through Alberta, and into the American Midwest. The Canadian oil would go along the same route, in another pipeline. (The Alaskan oil, of course, is already slated to flow south in the Alaskan pipeline now under construction.) The ink lines on Fred's map represent the two possible routes of a gas pipeline from Alaska to the Mackenzie delta area, through the Yukon.

"This one," Fred says, pointing to the lower line, "go through Old Crow. We don't want that. Caribou never come then. Other one go on coast, up there."

"Would that one cross the migratory route of the caribou?" I ask. Fred looks as if he doesn't understand; I rephrase it. "Would that one hurt the caribou?"

He shakes his head. "Don't know. I go up there before in plane with Resources. Maybe lotta caribou have calf up there. Don't know. We vote on it here. We say we don't want both."

"Old Crow people don't want either pipeline?" Larry says.

"Sure," Fred says.

I later check this and find that a Canadian university gave all Old Crow adults—about eighty of them—a questionnaire, in regard to a cross-Yukon pipeline. The result was almost unanimously "strongly object" to the pipeline through Old Crow, and about two-thirds opposed any pipeline what-soever. But I can't imagine that the Canadian and United States governments, and their oil companies, would be deterred by an opinion poll of 80 people.

"Didn't they do some exploration drilling up on Crow Flats?" Larry asks. Crow Flats is the Old Crow muskrat trapping ground, between fifty and one hundred miles north of town. The people go up there each spring. One or more oil exploration outfits drilled in the area, built a winter road in to Old Crow and on up to the flats in 1969, and found oil. I have recently been told that the volume of oil there is small, but that the oil people may keep drilling, now and then, as a tax write-off.

"Sure," Fred says, nodding his head seriously. "No good. They spill oil or something up there two, tree year ago. I see it when I go up. All on top of water. They want Crow Flat. But we don't let them. That oil no good for rats. When they come back I gonna 'splain that to them."

"Are they going to come back?"

"Sure, maybe," Fred says.

"If they do, do you think you could stop them from drilling if you told them it's bad for the musk-rats?"

Fred gives me a puzzled look. "Sure," he says. "Maybe. The rats don't like that oil. I gonna tell them that."

The weather stays bad for the rest of the day, and we do not go out to the nets. The wind keeps up, and the temperature drops to almost 30° below. We stay close to the cabin and cut firewood, gather snow for water, feed the dogs, and drink endless cups of tea and coffee.

In early afternoon, Larry goes to meet the freight flight, down at the airstrip, to pick up the frozen hind quarter of moose that he had flown up from Dawson to give our hosts.

The freight flight also brings toilet paper; the co-op has run out, which is probably why I did not find any in the outdoor toilet yesterday. Late in the evening—or what is now beginning to seem to us to be late in the evening: eight-thirty—I brave the elements to walk out back to use the toilet. There are still no tracks leading to it. Apparently people use pots, or the indoor toilets in the school or RCMP station, during winter.

The outhouse door, unfortunately, cannot be latched from the inside; the wind wildly whips it open and shut as I sit there. The noise is loud enough that I expect people to come running out of their cabins. I also expect to be found frozen, ingloriously, in the morning. But no one comes out, and I survive. I remember somebody telling me once that American pioneers, in winter, often did not move their bowels for a month or more. I can now see the wisdom in that. Or if not the wisdom, the set of natural and sociological conditions that could bring about such discipline.

In the morning, it is 46° below. We can tell the difference the minute we go out into the ten o'clock blackness. The cold air stays cold for a while after you breathe it in. The snow makes a different sound under your feet. And, as with most very cold days, there is no wind. The smoke of the Old Crow chimneys rises straight up, even drifting a little to the north, instead of streaming off to the south as during the last two days. It is quiet, and dry. There are only a few clouds on the horizon. Again, though, the sun remains beneath the horizon, all day.

We go up to the net after lunch. Fred takes a burlap sack, an ax, and a pair of plastic-coated gloves. We walk the shortest route, through a 150-yard patch of alders behind the cabin and onto the airstrip, then north along the strip to a bulldozer road that extends a mile or so from the strip almost to the Porcupine River. The ground is level all the way. I realize now that the town is located within a big oxbow bend in the river, and that the airstrip cuts across the inside of this bend, enclosing Old Crow between it and the river. I realize too that this 5,000-foot airstrip is larger than the needs of Old Crow dictate. It occurs to me that the government built it not with the Old Crow people in mind, but in anticipation of an increased volume of air traffic through here; once the Mackenzie delta oil fields get in operation, Old Crow would be a stopping point and the strip would have to handle bigger planes than the ones that now use it.

Despite the temperature, it is far more comfortable today than when the wind was blowing. Fred walks quickly, almost at a jog, along the hard-packed snow of the trail. He and Larry wear mukluks but I have on my big insulated boots, and in five minutes I am sweating from the added effort of moving them along. We do not talk. Before we reach the river, our eyelashes and eyebrows are white from the moisture we breathe out.

The river ice is not smooth, but is rough and uneven, looking like a lake frozen suddenly in big waves, from the alternate freezing and thawing in November. The last 150 yards of our walk are through the two feet of unpacked snow on the ice, and Larry and I are snorting and puffing when we reach the two upright poles, sixty feet apart, that mark the ends of the gill net. Only five feet of the poles are showing, but they extend down through the ice another ten feet and rest on the river bottom. A few other people have nets nearby. One of Fred's net poles is marked with a red, plastic buoy. A tin pail and an ice chisel tied to a six-foot pole lie on the ice alongside this pole.

Fred does not pause. He quickly clears the snow at the base of the pole and begins to chop a hole, eighteen inches across, with the ax. I expect there to be two feet of ice, but there are only six inches; flowing water below, insulating snow above, and Fred's periodic opening of the hole have kept the ice shell thin.

Dark water appears in the white bottom of the chopped hole, and Fred switches to the long ice chisel to avoid splashing water on his body. He scoops the slush out with the pail. I now realize —and it seems strange to me—that water in this temperature is dangerous. A bootful would freeze your foot.

With one hole open, Fred runs to the opposite end of the net and opens another, then hauls the fifteen-foot net pole up out of the river, lays it on the ice, and pays out the long rope fastened between this pole and the net. The rope will enable him to retrieve the net from under the ice when we are done. The skim of cold water on the pole freezes immediately as he pulls it up through the hole. He runs back to our end of the net and begins to haul the pole out of the water. I start to help him, but Fred knocks my hand away. He looks at me briefly, scowls, shakes his head. "Can't get wet hand," he says. Fred pulls up the pole, I now notice, by holding it under his arm, never grasping its wet surface with his mitten. With the poles out, he gets down on his knees over the hole, changes into his plastic-coated gloves, and begins to haul the net up out of the hole. The sixty-foot-long net is four to five feet wide and has a four- or five-inch mesh. Its upper edge is kept afloat, against the underside of the ice, with wooden two-by-four buoys; its lower edge is weighted with rocks tied to it with seven-foot cords. Fred pulls up a length of the net at a time, letting it slide back into the water if it has no fish instead of piling it alongside him on the ice, where it would freeze.

It seems impossible to me that any creature could survive under this ice, that there is moving life down there. I feel—though I know better—that the temperature under there must be the same as up here. It isn't, though. There is a difference of at least seventy degrees.

The first fish caught in the fragile gill net is a whitefish, an eighteen-inch-long, slim silvery fish, already dead, with a cold, staring eye. Fred quickly loosens its gills from the fine strands of the net and tosses it out on the snow behind him. The fish is coated with a thin skim of ice before I get it in the sack. Next are two big, hooknose dog salmon, probably seven pounds apiece, both tired and sluggish from their time in the net, maybe two days or more. They flop feebly. The white snow freezes to their wet, red sides as they land on the ice. Then another whitefish, recently snagged and still thrashing. Then a fat, chunky grayling, the biggest I have ever seen, about three pounds. Then another big salmon and a small arctic sucker, a bottom feeder, with an ugly white fibrous mouth extending like a long moustache beyond the sides of its head.

Fred's hands work quickly and the fish come flopping and flying at me. The thrashing whitefish lands to one side, flops madly for ten seconds, lifting its own body up off the ice with the thrusts of its tail. Then the bitter cold slows its motion. The tail flops slower, slower, and finally stops in a half arc. It takes no more than eight minutes to inspect the entire net, and by that time the body of the four-pound whitefish is stiff.

Something about the operation frightens me a little. I think it's the quickness. There is no stopping for a cigarette, or to look at the country or even to admire the beauty of the big red salmon, as there would be in the recreational fishing I am used to. There is little time to consider whether to keep a certain fish or not; once the animals are out on the ice for a minute or so, they are dead. And this consideration, this debate, is not even relevant, because there is no question of throwing anything back. Every fish is kept, to eat. And something about Fred's movements says that there is no room for error. Feeding yourself is not fun; it's a serious business. I know that if Fred's rope came loose and the net were lost, it would not be a matter of life and death. Not these days. But it would be something more than the minor inconvenience it would be for anyone fishing just for sport.

Fred jumps up, slides the net pole back into the water and gets it upright, and dumps the last few feet of the net back into the river. One of the rock weights plops in the water and throws up a spray. Fred moves his head quickly to the side. The water misses his face, loops over his shoulder, lands on the back of his parka, and freezes. He runs to the other end, retrieves the net, and again gets it aligned perpendicular to the flow of the river by hauling up the long rope fastened between the net and the pole. He slides the pole back in, straightens it, changes to his mittens without touching the surface of his plastic-coated gloves to his bare hands, and we are done. We have nine fish, probably weighing a total of forty pounds. I pick up the sack. The surfaces of the soft, fat bodies of the fish are stiff and slide icily against one another as I throw it over my shoulder. I find now that I am cold, from the sweating I did earlier.

Fred does not slow down until we are off the ice and back on the packed snow trail. He runs, picking out a trail around and over the drifts where the passing of other fishermen has packed the snow and it will support our weight. The packed snow, for me, is barely detectable from the fluffy snow alongside it. I stray slightly—a foot or so—from the center of the narrow width of packed snow, and sink in up to my thigh. Snow goes in the top of my boot and melts. Fred runs in short, choppy little steps from the top of one drift to the top of the next, never halting. He too breaks through the snow once or twice, but his forward momentum keeps him from sinking in deeply.

When we hit the packed road, Fred slows down, glances back at the river, and grins. He looks like an ancient Oriental sage, with his white lashes and brows. "Bush life good," he says smiling. "You got your fish. You got your wood. You got your meat. You got your water. All free."

But Larry and I are puffing hard enough that we cannot answer immediately except to nod, and Fred goes on. For some reason, he is talkative.

"Before, we live in bush all the time. Whole family go out sometime. For moose, for rat, for fish, for trap. I go with two men sometime for trap. Just come back here for Christmas, New Year's. I go to Whitestone River, to Ogilvie, hundred mile, all over." He moves his hands in a mounding gesture and grins. "Sometime sixty below. But I don't care.

We make little snow house, pull snow over door. One candle keep it warm. Sometime I go to Dawson to sell fur. One time I have hundred fifteen marten. We get fifty dollar for one. We travel all over. Good time."

"When was that, Fred?"

"Before. Maybe. . . . fifteen years."

"Families still go up to trap together at Crow Flats, don't they?" Larry asks.

"We go up a little while," Fred says. "But kids got to go to school now. Before, we go up April, May, June."

"Before, then, most of your money came from trapping, right?" I ask.

"Sure. Before, *all* money from trapping. But we don't need much money then. Now, money don't last."

"What did you spend your money on in those days?"

"We buy gun, pants, ax, sugar, trap, sometimes drink," Fred laughs.

"And now you don't catch nearly as many animals as before, right?"

"I just get a few marten and rabbit and fox. Sometime lynx. You want to see lots of people trapping, you should come around 1940. Now we have other job. Everybody cut wood for school. I get twenty-seven dollars a cord. Sometime I work for Resources. I fly with them and they pay me."

"Is there as much game around as there used to be?" Larry asks. "I mean, is there as much fur and moose and fish as there used to be?"

"Not as much," Fred says.

"I know a lot of people in Dawson who trap," Larry goes on, "and they say there's just as much as before."

Fred grunts.

"Where were you born anyway, Fred?" I ask. "Old Crow?"

Fred grins. "Eagle, Alaska," he says. "I'm 'merican. We come here with my father in 1926."

This surprises me. "You must have been just a baby, right?"

"No. A boy." Can Fred be that old?

"Any white men around then? When did planes and things start to come in to Old Crow?"

"Always a few white man," Fred says. "Priest. Police. First plane, I think, in 1937. But not much after that for a while."

"Well, when did you start getting regular commercial flights in here?"

"Don't know," Fred says. "Maybe fifteen years. They come slow. Maybe one, two in summer. Then one a month. From Alaska. They don't have airstrip then. They land sometime eight mile . . ." He points upriver. "They land on sand, on ice." He grins. "We go meet them with dog. Everybody go. Whole town. Now they got airstrip a few years. Every week plane come. You know. We like them. But 'spensive." He shakes his head.

"You had a freight boat coming in here before, didn't you?"

"Sure," Fred says. "Boat always come two, tree time in summer. We buy from him. We like him too. Don't cost too much. But he don't come no more this year."

"Why not?"

Fred hunches up his shoulders. "Don't know," he says. "You know?"

"No. I don't know."

Fred smiles. "We even have truck come in here one time. Great big truck. You know that?"

"Trucks? When? How the hell did trucks get in here?"

Fred smiles. "Winter road," he says. "Few years ago. Truck come right in over ice."

I had known about the oil companies' winter roads to Old Crow, built from the Dempster Highway. I have even seen the roads, leading across the Dempster. But having never seen one in use, it had not occurred to me that a standard commercial vehicle could travel them.

"My God, a truck in Old Crow. Well, what do you think about that road, Fred? I mean, do you think they might bank it someday and make a summer road out of it?"

My tone of voice, I'm sure, almost gives away my feelings about the idea of an all-weather road into Old Crow, and Larry's comment is even more unsubtle:

"Fred, I don't think a road into Old Crow would be a good thing, do you?"

Fred nods his head slowly. "Maybe be a good ting," he says. "Plane 'spensive. We get tings cheaper that way."

"But Fred," Larry says, "if you had a summer road in here, you'd have thousands of tourists and cars and you'd probably get in a liquor store and a lot more government buildings. The game would go away. The caribou might not cross the road. You said you were worried about oil up at Crow Flats. Well, if you had a summer road in here, you'd have people

drilling everywhere. They'd come in here and tell you you could get jobs, but the money you could earn would be gone in no time. Prices would go up. Your town would be full of these drunk guys all the time. And your land would be gone. You wouldn't have . . ."

I finally slow down and let the edge of Fred's hood cover his line of sight to us, and then jab Larry in the ribs. Cool it. I want to hear what Fred has to say on this, without prompting.

But Fred does not seem to have much to say. He looks a little puzzled, very pensive, as if he has never thought of this before. I change the topic:

"I wonder what you ate before there were many planes and things in here? Did you have eggs and butter and stuff like that?"

"No," Fred says. "Life all different. No egg. No milk. Not much drink. No bread. No ice cream. No chain saw. No Skiddoo. All different."

I can't resist asking the question. "And what life do you think was better—before or now?"

Fred is serious. He looks over his shoulder. "Oh," he says, "that one."

Back home, Fred cleans two of the salmon and gives the fat grayling to Isaac Njitlin, who comes in for tea. The rest of the fish he stores in the cache outside. He has a big pile of them out there, stacked frozen, like firewood. "This is my bank," Fred says, grinning.

He also has some raw, dried strips of moose meat that he brings in and slices into thin pieces. With tea, he offers us some of this, to be eaten along with the raw caribou fat hanging on the wall. I like the dried moose meat, and I know it has been frozen long enough to kill anything bad in it. But I remember that Caribou is notorious for its parasites, and I do not eat any of the fat. Fred laughs at this. Actually it looks good, and I'm sure it would lend some lubrication to the dry moose meat. And Fred and Isaac have been eating it for decades, and they seem healthy enough. I recall, fifteen years ago, before I knew better, drinking fresh moose blood as it spurted out of a slit in the animal's neck. I lived. I wonder if one cannot become, after all, too civilized.

For supper we eat moose and salmon and onions, potatoes and bread. The food tastes wonderful after having been out fishing for the afternoon, even the white, stale, unenriched bread. After supper, Lillian shows me a new pill the government nurse has given her for arthritis and asks if it is a good one. I don't know what it is, but she is no longer limping, so

I guess that it must be good. We have some ice cream for dessert, and Lillian remarks that they can only get ice cream in winter; not in summer when it is hot. Of course. I never thought of that. In summer, it would melt on the plane from Dawson.

Fred grins as he eats his: "I eat all this white man's food," he says. "I gonna die soon."

After supper, Larry goes out. Fred works on the broken chain of his chain saw. The co-op has no parts for the saw, and Fred tries, unsuccessfully, to splice a link from another saw's chain into his own. He finally gives up and tosses the chain angrily into a corner.

"I cut four cord a day with that ting," he says later. "Little while ago it break and I tink I gonna go back to my Swede saw. But it's hard. I work one day and my arm hurt. I get used to that chain saw."

I go out for a walk and try to put together some of the things Fred has told me about the changes that have occurred in his life-style. Due to our inability to communicate precisely, I am fuzzy on the times when certain changes occurred—changes in Fred's diet and in his means of livelihood, when planes began to come in regularly, when cutting wood for the school and collecting government assistance began to appear more attractive than trapping. But as I think of it, probably the timing of single changes is unimportant. What is more important is that all events in Old Crow's recent history have worked in the same direction, toward a rapid dismantling of the community's traditional culture.

And these events fit together so intricately that they all seem to be part of a plan to deny these people their self-sufficiency and to render them completely dependent upon the white man and upon his view of how the planet should function. The simple existence of the Old Crow school, for example, means that Indian men can earn good money cutting wood to heat the big school building and the white teachers' residences. It also means, in conjunction with the government's financial assistance programs and other white jobs, that Indian men are now persuaded to forsake their long traplines, far from town, which once provided their primary livelihood. Now, men like Fred maintain only token traplines, near the village.

Compulsory school attendance means that Old Crow children and their families cannot travel very long together in the bush and the children are thus not exposed to many of the bush skills of their parents. It means too that some Old Crow children will

be leaving Old Crow for Whitehorse, 500 miles south, returning to their hometown only two or three times during the school year.

To facilitate wood-hauling for the school and for their homes, many village men have bought snowmobiles. But snowmobiles take gasoline, and gasoline is expensive ($1.50 per gallon at the co-op) when flown in by airplane. So are chain-saw blades, ice cream, snowmobile skis, grain-based dog food, soda pop, sugar doughnuts, electric toasters, and every other white creation that the Old Crow people have come to depend on or want. And so, completing the cycle, people like Fred are now looking more and more toward the money income jobs—cutting wood for the school, working for oil exploration outfits or government agencies—that will give them the cash they need to purchase these many items newly introduced by the white culture. They are also beginning to give favorable consideration to the notion of an all-weather road into Old Crow, which would reduce the freight charges and thus the prices they pay for these items. And if that road were built, it would have precisely the final, killing impact upon Old Crow culture that Larry mentioned earlier.

Of course, this sort of an analysis of a crumbling culture need not start with a school. The school, in fact, is probably among the better white introductions into Old Crow. But it could start with an airport or an oil find or a snowmobile; they all end at the same place.

We are presumably hoping that anything we introduce into this remote native culture will enable its people to free themselves of that culture and some day make it in ours. But even assuming that this happens successfully, we are still left with the very unsettling question: Is ours really any better, or just more powerful?

I get angry thinking of these things. I walk over to Jacob Cado's house, where I know some home brew has been whipped up, and have a drink. I don't like home brew—a yeasty-tasting mixture of sugar, malt, and water—but it does the job. Michael Snow is there, and three or four other men. Larry appears later; the town is small, and it doesn't take many inquiries to know where people are congregated.

At Jacob's I find out that Daniel Throndiuk, Fred's nephew, has made a snowmobile trip out to see his father, Roy, twenty miles out of town up the Porcupine River. Roy, as far as I know, is one of only two men in town who still stay out in the bush to trap. I wanted to visit him, and I have spread the word around town, and at first I am a little annoyed that no one invited me to go. But Jacob tells me that Daniel's snowmobile got into overflow—water that remains unfrozen because of the insulating snow above—and that the passenger, Tom Frank, stepped in it as he leaped to safe ice, and froze his foot. "He scream all night," says an old man who attended Tom. "The boot freeze on his foot." The nurse will look at him tomorrow. Had I gone, that could have been me.

I also learn that tonight, as Jacob returned from downriver with his last load of wood, his snowmobile swerved on the icy road through town and its toboggan slid and hit Toby Snow, Michael's wife, and knocked her unconscious. Toby remained unconscious for a while, and was then flown by charter plane to the hospital at Inuvik.

Larry and I stay and have three or four or more drinks of the home brew and then walk back to Fred's. On the way back, I perform an experiment. I remember from Jack London's story "To Build a Fire" that the man spat and that his spittle froze before reaching the ground, telling him that it was much colder than 50° below. It is now only 45° below, but I can extrapolate. When I spit on the ground, it does not freeze for about eight seconds.

The stuff starts out at 98.6°, after all. I do three replications, bending down and watching with the flashlight. I conclude that London was stretching the truth.

"Jack, what the hell are you doing?" Larry asks as I spit and peer.

"Scientific experiment," I tell him.

"I think you're a little drunk," he says.

The next day is clear again and a little warmer. We are almost out of firewood, so in the afternoon Fred and I go after some. Most people in town seem to get their wood at a wood camp eight miles downriver, using snowmobiles. But people with dogs typically get their wood nearer by. Fred goes two miles north of town, on the east bank of the Crow River, north of where it joins the Porcupine. I am looking forward to going out with the dogs, although I am a little skeptical about whether I can keep up with them. Instead of wearing my big boots and heavy wool pants, I put on a pair of borrowed mukluks and my blue jeans and leave the tops of the jeans outside the moose hide mukluks so no snow will get in, as it did yesterday. I am getting accustomed to the cold, as long as there is no wind, and I feel that the lighter clothing will be enough.

Fred carries his wooden toboggan out back and we hitch up the dogs. Fred's five dogs, like most Yukon sled dogs, are relatively small and slim, about sixty pounds apiece, and do not look as if they could work very hard. Three of them look like pure Siberians, complete with the eerie, white-pupiled eyes; the other two seem to have a little shepherd mixed in. They are friendly and like to be petted.

The harness consists simply of five padded collars and chest bands, spaced far enough apart for the dogs to work in line, with two leather side straps running from the collars and bands to the front of the toboggan. There are no reins, as I somehow imagined there would be. The dogs are controlled only with the driver's voice or, more typically, are not controlled at all. There is a ten-foot yellow plastic hold rope that drags behind the toboggan, like the one on a small sailboat or canoe, in case the driver has to hold back the team.

As Fred hitches the team, he notices that the second dog has chewed a strap almost in two. He repairs it temporarily, with a piece of rope he takes from his pocket, and at the same time gives the dog a sharp kick in the ribs. The dog goes down on the snow and cowers, which only seems to increase Fred's anger.

"Cross-eye son of a bitch! Goddamn fuckin' fuckin'!"

He kicks the dog again and tells me to go on ahead of him, since the dogs can travel faster than I. He tells me to follow the same route as yesterday, but to turn on a small trail leading off to the left before reaching the Porcupine River.

I start jogging. I run through the alders, onto the airstrip, and along it to its end before I slow down. It feels good to have on lighter clothes. I can feel the pebbles on the airstrip through the mukluks, and am careful not to run across any stony spots. But the mukluks are nice and light, and I do not sweat in them as I did in the heavy rubber boots—or else it evaporates out through the tanned moose hide. Under the mukluks I wear two pairs of wool socks and a felt inner liner. I find the trail and turn left. It is packed, from other teams and a snowmobile or two, and is easy going. It feels good to be running along at 40° below, up the bank of the Crow River, with spruce trees on both sides.

I glance back over my shoulder. Fred is catching up with me rapidly, standing balanced on the toboggan as it skids back and forth on the trail. The dogs see me and start to run close to me to be petted. Fred curses and yells for them to stop. "Hyut! Hyut!"

The dogs do stop, but only after tangling them-selves together in their attempt to catch me. Fred leaps off the toboggan, belts the lead dog in the head, then the second one, as he untangles the team, tossing one dog over another as if untying a big, cumbersome knot. "Stupid fuckin' fuckin'," he says quietly. I feel sorry for the dogs.

"I go ahead," he says to me, tossing me the hold rope tied to the back of the sled. "Give me head start."

He jogs off on the ice, going along the left bank of the river. The dogs watch him anxiously. They start to pull slightly, but I wrap the rope around my shoulder and step off the packed trail into the deep snow and lean back on them. We wait.

A quarter mile ahead, Fred tires and slows his pace. He pauses to look back over his shoulder and the dogs see this and start to pull. Again I hold them by leaning back on the rope. It is a close tug-of-war though, and I call out, as closely as I can imitate Fred's "stop" command:

"Hyut!"

Apparently, though, "hyut!" does not only mean stop; it means stop, start, do whatever it is you're not doing. The dogs surge ahead, really putting their strength into it this time, and I am pulled out of the snow and dragged across the ice on my belly. Ahead, Fred is waving me back, signaling me to slow down. But how the hell can I slow down?

Somehow I get my legs under me, and again dig my heels in. There is no deep snow here, though. I am puffing and blowing. I roar at the dogs. "Now stop! Stay! I'll break your goddamn heads!" As I yell, the dogs take off again. I wonder, as I am dragged along the second time, whether Fred has trained the dogs in English or in Loucheux.

For a moment, I wonder whether it would be better to simply let them drag me, slowing them enough this way that they will not catch up with Fred. But they seem to be catching up anyway. Who would have thought that these five slim little dogs could pull so much?

Once more, I bounce upright without releasing the rope, dig in my heels, and yell. The dogs never even think of stopping. I am no match for them this time and I am jerked forward. But I am close to the sled and fall on it. I lie there for a minute, then stand up and ride erect, as Fred did. It's hard to maintain your balance, though, and I am first on one leg, than on the other, almost falling off, doing a little drunken dance, trying to avoid stepping on the saw which is tied on the toboggan, as we career across the ice. I feel like a first-time skier on a slope too steep and narrow for his ability, flying along with no idea whatsoever how to stop. We catch Fred and zip by him. He gives me a quizzical look. The dogs apparently know just where they are going, and they turn and go across the river, heading for a point on the steep, twenty-foot spruce-covered opposite bank. The sled hits something, and I am jerked down to my knees and continue to ride this way.

This is easy. I wonder now why Fred didn't just put the two of us on the sled originally. To make it easier on the dogs, I guess. Though, from their strength, I don't think it would slow them much. In fact, I think each one of them could use a fifty-pound weight tied around its throat.

At the bank, I leap off again. But there is no need for it; the dogs are stuck in the deep snow on the slope. Fred finally catches up and signals me to come on ahead to help break trail for them. I would rather break their skulls, though I am starting to cool down. We struggle up the bank and head into the spruces. The trees are thick and snow-covered, and there is a thigh-deep accumulation of snow on the ground. My heart pounds madly with the effort. Fred stops about a hundred yards in, and gets an ax and a pair of old, beaten snowshoes that he has hung in a tree above the trail. Once he gets the snowshoes on, the snow gets packed down better and it is easier walking behind him; I sink in to my knees instead of to my thighs.

We go a quarter mile and stop. Fred points to a dead, standing spruce with a ten-inch-thick trunk, near our trail, and smiles. "Good tree," he says. "Dry." He seems truly happy to find it. He taps its trunk with the ax. "Not rotten."

We stop. The dogs sit down. Fred begins to chop.

What white man, I wonder, would smile at a tree, especially a dead tree, and call it "good." It occurs to me, though, that Fred's perception of a forest—or a river or a moose—is entirely different from my own. His is practical. Mine is aesthetic. In fact, it now dawns on me that I have never heard any Indian person exclaim over the beauty or looks or smell of a landscape the way I might. Fred, despite the many ways in which he has become civilized, is

still dependent upon the bush for his well-being, and this is what shapes his outlook. He necessarily prefers big fish; I prefer colorful ones. He prefers moose with big bodies; I prefer moose with big antlers. He needs dry, dead trees to heat his home; I prefer living, pitchy trees because they look and smell nice.

Fred finds three or four large dead trees and cuts them, notching them first on the fell side and then cutting through from the opposite side with the Swede saw. Then he trims them with the ax.

A dog sled has no reverse on it, and Fred leads the dogs around in a twenty-foot loop and heads them back before loading on the trees. I help load the trees, three on the bottom, two on the second layer, and a cluster of thin ones on top. The dogs have about a three-hundred-pound load.

We start back. Fred walks ahead, leaves his ax and snowshoes, helps the team pull the load around corners, over snags and trunks. I push from the rear.

We stop briefly to examine the snares and traps Fred has set for fox, rabbit, and marten. They are right next to the trail, but I did not notice them coming in. Fred points them out. He has a dozen, #1½ steel traps set back inside little eight-inch-wide stick pens, with a piece of fish inside the pen to lure in the carnivores. I notice that the traps are set casually, barely concealed, compared to the ones I have seen set in upper New York State, where animals are more wary of human beings. There is nothing in the steel traps.

The wire snares are set in places where the animals pass naturally—under logs, between close-spaced trees, within depressions where a fox or a rabbit might travel in their search for food. In some cases, Fred has placed a stick in the snow to help force the animal unknowingly into the path of the snare. The snare consists only of a loop of fine, tough wire with a slip loop in it big enough to accommodate an animal's head, and is fastened to a nearby log or standing tree. The animal begins to pass through the space, sticks its head through the wire loop, becomes cinched, then either remains quiet and freezes or fights and chokes itself.

The fox snares are empty. One small snare has a big white snowshoe rabbit in it. The dead body lies frozen and flat-looking against the snow. Fred quickly removes the rabbit, opens the snare again to its four-inch width, and we go on. He gives the stiff rabbit to me and I stick it inside my parka.

The dogs have trouble with the load at the bank leading down to the river, and Fred and I pull on the sled and then step aside, once we start it in motion. There are no stiff side shafts on a dog harness to keep the load from running into the team, and the dogs run wildly to escape being hit by the three hundred pounds of logs sliding behind them down the twenty-foot bank. The team disappears down over the bank and reappears a third of the way across the river. Fred and I run after them.

On the flat the animals pull hard on the load of wood, their heads down, moving it easily across the ice though sometimes slipping on the smooth surface. When a dog falls, he scrambles to get upright and going again; the others do not stop to wait for him. It seems good to see an animal working, physically exerting, instead of padding around a cramped apartment, being sweatered to go out and pee. Fred's rear dog limps, and continues to limp, throughout the two miles back to town, not using his right-rear foot. That leg, apparently, was caught and hurt under the load of wood.

Fred and I jog alongside the sled, but it is slower, and easier, now that the dogs have the load to pull. When we get back, we unhitch the dogs and unload the wood. Fred hangs the snowshoe rabbit by the neck to the light cord in the kitchen, to thaw out.

We eat the rabbit for supper, along with some moose and some caribou soup.

After supper, I sit down to catch up on my notes. Diana is not visible, as usual, but the boys have completely lost their shyness by this time and crowd around me to see what I am writing, while running their toy snowmobiles up my leg, around my coffee cup, over my head. My beard is starting to grow in a little, and Chris is fascinated by it.

"Holy, holee," he says, "look at this fur, Harold. It feel like porkypine. Holee!"

"What are you writing?" Albert asks.

"About you guys," I say.

"What? What about us?" Chris lisps. "What you write?"

"Well, just what you say and do. About our snowfight. About the kind of tapes you see on that television set in school. Things like that. What programs did you say you saw, again?"

The boys scramble to tell me.

"*Ironside!*" Chris says. "We see *Ironside* and *Get Smart* and *Beachcombers!*"

"And *Cannon*—a big fat guy—and *Black Beauty* and *Sesame Street!*" Harold and Albert yell.

"Oh yeah," Chris says. "You know Cookie Mon-

ster? He's so hungry he gives him that plate and he eats that plate. And Big Bird tell Ernie to answer the phone and he says he can't find it and he tell him to look in the pail, so—"

"Wait. Hold it a minute! You guys are talking too fast, I can't get it all down."

"You get down *Beachcomber?*" Harold says.

"Yeah, what else?"

"*Sesame Street! Black Beauty! Wild Bill Hickok!*" Chris yells out.

"*Wild Bill Hickok?* Tell me about that one."

"See!" Chris outyells Albert and Harold. "Wild Bill Hickok he's up on the rock and one Indian comes and he shoots him with one gun. Then two Indians come and he shoots them with *two* guns."

"Then the girl—" Albert starts to say.

Chris interrupts. "The girl, two girl, they're in house together and they look out and see all Indians and she tell other girl to get on horse and go get soldiers!"

"And then what happened?"

"And lots of Indians get killed," Albert says.

"They're in water," Chris says excitedly, "and soldiers get up beside river and shoot! *Powrr! Pnrrr! Peeeng!* Like that! And all fall down and drown." Chris himself keels over, to demonstrate.

"Did you guys like that movie?"

"Yes!" they agree unanimously.

"Except scary parts," Chris says.

"What were the scary parts?"

"Where that girl in house and look out and see all Indians," he says.

The boys now ask me what New York City is like. I give them a superficial description, trying not to make it sound like either a land of wonders or a sink of filth and iniquity. The direction of the discussion changes and the boys and Fred, who comes over to join us, interview me. I talk about subways and waiting lines and apartment buildings, the variety of job opportunities, crime, elevators, parks, political attitudes, civil rights movements. The boys, since they have seen television tapes in school, are familiar with many of the things I talk about, at least in the abstract. But they are still wide-eyed to hear about these things from a person who has actually seen Big Bird and who lives in an apartment building that is eight cabins wide and fifteen tall and contains twice as many people as Old Crow.

Fred listens attentively to my talk of crime and general urban-industrial violence, nods, and then tells me that he has begun to notice something parallel to this within Old Crow in the past five or six years—events generally involving petty theft or drunken incidents with snowmobiles.

He smiles incredulously when I tell him that we have 25,000 policemen in New York City and that this is not enough to maintain law and order; Old Crow has only the one mountie whose law-enforcing capacities are rarely tested. Fred giggles and shows me a real-looking toy revolver with which he began a mock stickup, in the local mountie's presence, on April Fools' Day. "I have fun with that police," he grins.

The boys now draw me some pictures and Christmas cards to take home to my parents and friends. They are extremely artistic and draw both realistically and impressionistically, making cabins, spruce trees, dog sleds, ballet dancers, swimming caribou, bicycles, Santa Clauses, automobiles, and, most frequently, snowmobiles. Fred gets a piece of paper and he draws too. His picture is of a man on snowshoes, rifle in hand, chasing a moose.

He finally urges the boys off to bed. They go reluctantly. Chris keeps coming back into the kitchen with new schemes to permit him to stay up

another fifteen minutes. Fred finally yells at him, then laughs once Chris is back in the bedroom. "Little white man," Fred says, grinning.

After the boys are in bed, I find myself speculating on what they might be doing in ten, fifteen, or twenty years. Some of Old Crow's young people remain in town and work at the same sorts of jobs that Fred now has. Some leave, more or less permanently, to take work outside. Some alternate between the two. No young people, as far as I know, have chosen to revive the full time hunting, fishing, and trapping occupations of their fathers.

I ask Fred if he would like the boys to remain in Old Crow.

"What they want is okay. I love my kids." He gestures toward the outside. "It's okay," he says.

"Do you think they'll be living here in ten years?"

Fred shakes his head. "Don't know," he says. "Things change pretty quick."

We drink our coffee and tea. "You know," Fred says seriously, "those boys don't speak no Loucheux. Before, they don't like them to talk it in

school. Now they teach it a little, but not so good. They just know English."

The days seem to flow into one another. Or rather, the nights do, since the days are only five hours long. Larry and I are well known in town by now. The Old Crow people are extremely friendly and invite us constantly for tea, for supper, for home brew. We notice that few people in town, besides Fred, have much caribou or moose or fish. They eat turkey and spareribs and other meats flown in and sold at the necessarily high co-op prices. We also notice that many of the people in town—especially the young people—do have electric stoves, stereos, and other appliances and conveniences, far more of these things that Fred has. We find out that only one or two women have any moose hide for making mukluks.

We also go to all the town's social events—a dance at the log cabin community hall, a TV tape showing of *War and Peace* and Ultra Ban in the school, and Anglican church on Sunday. Different parts of you, I suppose, notice different things at these town gatherings. The aesthetic or spiritual or romantic part notices that it is somehow nicer, warmer, more human, to attend *any* social event in Old Crow—it could even be an X-ray clinic—than to attend similar events outside: The stove is cozier; the people are closer; God is nearer by. The sociologist part notices that the Old Crow population is somewhat lopsided, heavily weighted by children and middle-aged to older adults. The political part notices that social gatherings in Old Crow often revolve around white leadership, in one way or another. The town does have a chief and band council, and these are the important positions in community decision-making, but the day-to-day life of the Old Crow people is dependent upon skills or authority held by whites—the schoolteachers and principal, the nurse, the Anglican priest, the storekeeper, the mountie.

Fortunately, most of the town's white leaders are sensitive to the community, are friendly, social, and straight with the Old Crow people, and do not seem to be trying to actively encourage the Indian people's dependence upon them or upon white society in general. Father Jean-Marie Mouchet, for example, the itinerant Old Crow Catholic priest, is well known for his rigorous and successful efforts to teach the Old Crow youngsters cross-country skiing and to otherwise foster their physical skills to enable them to maintain, and take pride in, their physical

relationship with the land that has sustained them. (Mouchet, by the way, has no parishioners; the Anglican missionaries apparently got to the Old Crow and other Kutchin people before the Roman Catholics did.) But while most of the current group of white Old Crow leaders are in tune with the community, it would probably be very easy to get in a group who were not, or who simply did the government job for which they were hired, and no more.

The weather is bad—cold and windy—during most of our stay, and we wait for clearing spells before we go out to fish, cut wood, or look at the traps. Most of our time is spent in the cabin, talking, drawing pictures, drinking enormous amounts of tea and coffee. I begin to get anxious for the plane, and the sunshine.

It clears again on the day we leave. The town comes down to the airstrip with its dog sleds and snowmobiles and its blue co-op tractor to get the freight, and we all help to unload and reload the plane. As we work, people wish us well and seem genuinely sorry to see us go—Father Bill Powers, Tom Steel, Jacob Cado, Michael Snow, the storekeeper Sam Karadine, Fred's brother Roy, who has finally been able to snowshoe into town for Christmas over the thin river ice that his son's snowmobile went through three days ago. It strikes me strangely that Roy, who has a crippled leg and arm from a childhood injury, is one of only two Old Crow men who continue to live in the bush and maintain long traplines. A tough man.

Chris cries when we leave. Fred and Jacob Cado give me letters and packages to mail when I get back to Ottawa, so their friends in eastern Canada will get them before Christmas.

Fred takes me aside: "Jack, I want you send me someting for Chris."

"Sure. What is it?"

Fred moves his hand near his head. "How you call it?"

"Tonic? Hat? Comb?" I say.

"No," Dick says. "Black."

"Black? Hair color? Is that what you want?"

Dick nods, grins a wide grin. "Hair color. Yes. Black. His hair look too brown. Too much like a white man. Want him to look more Indian."

We laugh, get on, and are away. The plane rises up above the cold white land, passes through a layer of gray clouds, and Old Crow is gone. Above the clouds, it is bright and clear, and we have more sunlight than I have seen in a week.